A MILE OF MAKE-BELIEVE

A History of the Eaton's Santa Claus Parade

Examining the history of the Santa Claus parade in Canada, *A Mile of Make-Believe* focuses on the Eaton's sponsored parades in Toronto, Montreal, and Winnipeg as well as the shorter-lived parades in Calgary and Edmonton. It also discusses the proliferation of parades outside the large metropolitan centres organized by civic groups, service clubs, and chambers of commerce.

Studying the pioneering effort of the Eaton's department store Steve Penfold argues that the parade ultimately represented a paradoxical form of cultural power: it allowed Eaton's to press its image onto public life while also reflecting the decline of the once powerful retailer. Penfold's analysis reveals the "corporate fantastic" – a visual and narrative mix of meticulous organization and whimsical style – and its influence on parade traditions. His considerable analytical skills have produced a work that is simultaneously a cultural history, history of business, and commentary on consumerism.

STEVE PENFOLD is an associate professor in the Department of History at the University of Toronto. He is the author of *The Donut: A Canadian History*.

T0338788

A Mile of Make-Believe

A HISTORY OF THE
EATON'S
SANTA CLAUS
PARADE

STEVE PENFOLD

UNIVERSITY OF TORONTO PRESS
Toronto Buffalo London

© University of Toronto Press 2016
Toronto Buffalo London
www.utppublishing.com

ISBN 978-1-4426-3096-3 (cloth)
ISBN 978-1-4426-2924-0 (paper)

Library and Archives Canada Cataloguing in Publication

Penfold, Steven, 1966–, author
A mile of make-believe : a history of the Eaton's Santa Claus parade / Steve Penfold.

Includes bibliographical references and index.
ISBN 978-1-4426-3096-3 (cloth)   ISBN 978-1-4426-2924-0 (paper)

1. T. Eaton Co – History.   2. Santa Claus.   3. Department stores – Canada – History.
4. Parades – Canada – History.   5. Christmas – Canada – History.
6. Consumption (Economics) – Canada – History.   7. Canada – Social life and customs.
I. Title.   II. Title: Eaton's Santa Claus parade.

GT4013.A2P45 2016   394.26630971   C2016-903481-X

This book has been published with the help of a grant from the Federation
for the Humanities and Social Sciences, through the Awards to Publications Program,
using funds provided by the Social Sciences and Humanities
Research Council of Canada.

University of Toronto Press acknowledges the financial assistance to its publishing
program of the Canada Council for the Arts and the Ontario Arts Council,
an agency of the Government of Ontario.

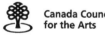

Canada Council   Conseil des Arts
for the Arts   du Canada

ONTARIO ARTS COUNCIL
CONSEIL DES ARTS DE L'ONT
an Ontario government agency
un organisme du gouvernement de l'(

Funded by the   Financé par le
Government   gouvernement
of Canada   du Canada | Canadä

"Sans aucun doute, la parade annuelle organisée par le magasin Eaton était une concrétisation des plus fabuleux rêves d'enfance … Partout dans la parade il y avait des danses, de l'animation, de la vie, de la joie, et du bonheur."

La Presse, 24 November 1930, 17

"He came riding in at the tail end of a Mile of Make Believe and close to 700,000 strong, the kids – and those who could be kids again for this one morning – came flocking to bid him hello. With him came good cheer, fellowship, and the sure knowledge that it's great to be alive."

Jack Karr, *Toronto Daily Star*, 17 November 1951, 1

Contents

Illustrations and Maps

Maps

Acknowledgments

The final release of a book is less exciting than you imagine. A book starts with glorious possibility, but by the time you hold it in your hand, you've seen many drafts, redrafts, conference papers, notes for talks, chapters given to reading groups, revisions and re-revisions, copy-edits, and proofs. At some point, you really just want it to be over. By the time it is actually published, you have generally moved on to something else. It doesn't help that this book took a particularly long time to finish. When I started it, my second daughter wasn't born; now, the girl does shtick.

Long projects produce many debts. My Canadianist colleagues at U of T are a great bunch: long-timers (Heidi Bohaker, Ian Radforth, and Franca Iacovetta); more recent arrivals (Paula Hastings and Brian Gettler); and fellow residents of the Hallway of Souls (Sean Mills and Laurie Bertram). A few of them read parts of the book, but mainly this is just a list of great colleagues, something more important than university buzzwords about Excellence. I could add many non-Canadianist colleagues to that list: Alison Smith, Carol Chin, and many others. I owe particular thanks to Dan Bender and Sean Mills for interventions at key moments – Dan near the beginning and Sean near the end. Dan suggested that a bad draft of a paper might make the basis of a book (so, really, this whole thing is his fault), while Sean delivered several highly unsubtle reminders that forced me to finish, read the entire manuscript chapter by chapter, and warned me off some blunders about Quebec. Even better, Sean made me several coffees on his fancy machine while we had fruitful discussions about both history and life. Dale Barbour did some helpful research in Winnipeg and Toronto and suffered through a complete reading of the manuscript. Simon Vickers provided quick translation help at the end. Nadine Oliver made the maps. Finally, Jarrett Rudy saved me a trip to Ottawa by snapping some photos of key documents in the Canadian Broadcasting Corporation collection at the National Archives (repayment to be made in beverages).

Several audiences provided helpful feedback. Parts of the book were presented at the Annual Meeting of the Canadian Historical Association, the Department of History at the University of Manitoba, the Department of History at the University of Alberta, the Tri Campus Graduate Program (Guelph, Waterloo, Wilfrid Laurier), Historical Studies at the University of Toronto at Mississauga, and Historical and Cultural Studies at the University of Toronto at Scarborough. Many of these audiences raised questions that I never managed to answer, which is surely a sign that excellent issues were being raised. For invitations and hospitality, I owe particular thanks to James Muir and Adele Perry.

Ever since I left a meeting at an inopportune time and ended up being the departmental Grad Dude, I have acquired many debts in the History office. Thanks to Carol Chin, Elysha Daya, Jennifer Evans, Adrienne Hood, Elisa Lee, Christine Leonardo, Therese McGuirk, Anna Mozharova, Vicki Norton, Alison Smith, and Nick Terpstra. Davina Joseph, my colleague on the other side of the Grad Office, deserves special thanks for enduring three years of my disorganized style with good humour.

At U of T Press, Len Husband was his usual patient and supportive self, Frances Mundy moved the book along the pipeline, and James Leahy did a thorough copy edit. The anonymous referees provided thorough and helpful feedback that strengthened the book. Rob Vipond offered helpful suggestions on Santa Claus and religion.

The families who inhabit scholarly Acknowledgments always seem so helpful, but mine mostly got in the way. Daughters have a way of destroying your authorial focus – distracting you, interrupting you, asking you to play, or getting hungry at all the wrong times. You sit at your desk trying to write and they wander in to offer a cuddle, to tell you a joke, to get a ride to a swim meet, or to announce some vomitous incident. None of these things, I am sure, is as vitally important as an academic book on Santa Claus. So thanks a ton, Ruby and Mira, for all of that. Diane Swartz, meanwhile, showed a suspicious independence of mind, undertaking multiple professional and academic pursuits in blissful ignorance of my much greater needs.

That last paragraph was (mostly) sarcasm, but this is not: thank you to the staff at Kinko's for not calling the police that time long ago. You probably don't know who you are.

A MILE OF MAKE-BELIEVE

A History of the Eaton's Santa Claus Parade

Introduction

Alfreda's Lament

Toronto was hot in August 1982, but Alfreda Hall was upset about Christmas. Eaton's, the city's iconic department store, had just announced that it would no longer organize its annual Santa Claus parade. "Is this another insidious encroachment on our Canadian and Christian heritage?" Hall wondered in a letter to the editor of the *Globe and Mail*. "Who will come to Santa's help? For the sake of our dear children and our delight in seeing them enjoy the world of fantasy ... the parade must be preserved – for Toronto's tradition, too."[1] In an immediate sense, Hall's lament was understandable. For much of the twentieth century, the Eaton's Santa Claus parade was the most popular moment in Toronto's festival calendar. Initiated in 1905 as a relatively simple public event, the parade was recast into a new form of Christmas spectacle in the decades after the First World War, becoming the now-familiar mix of clowns, fairies, floats, bands, and (of course) jolly old St Nick. Throughout this process of cultural invention, the parade was a key part – indeed, *the* key part – of the company's public relations strategy, the most dramatic of many efforts to insinuate what we would now call "the Eaton's brand" into local community life. By any standard, as Hall made clear, this project was successful. The year before the Eaton's announcement, tens of thousands of delighted spectators had lined the downtown route. The company itself, though falling on increasingly hard times, remained a "national institution," and the Eaton family was firmly ensconced in Toronto's business and philanthropic elite. The parade form that the company had helped to pioneer was ubiquitous, attracting wide imitation by civic organizations, Chambers of Commerce, fraternal societies, and entrepreneurs across Main Street North America.

Hall's letter is analytically rich beyond the bare facts of popularity and longevity. Indeed, her letter provides several clues to the overall appeal of the parade, which, in her mind, was a fusion of secular, spiritual, fantastic, and familial traditions. Childhood, religion, heritage, civic identity, and national life were all at stake in its survival. A spectacle of fun and fantasy, it brought delight to children, who in turn brought happiness to adults. It took a commercial approach to Christmas, and contained few religious symbols, but for Hall it retained spiritual, even Christian, meaning. As a piece of heritage or tradition, it was by 1982 a multi-generational experience, changing in style at times but providing a sort of continuity through decades of social and cultural change. It was a key part of Toronto's popular culture: the Eaton's Santa was widely considered to be the "real" one, and his march through the streets marked the beginning of the city's Christmas season. And while that live performance had deep local resonance, its appeal was much wider. For many years, Eaton's had mounted parades in other cities – in Winnipeg and Montreal for several decades and in Calgary and Edmonton for somewhat shorter times. By 1982, only the Toronto version survived, but while thousands of spectators lined the city's sidewalks to enjoy the Eaton's parade each year, many more huddled in living rooms across the country to watch the event on television, creating a national broadcast spectacle of considerable power and appeal. Hall's lament made it clear that the parade had transcended its corporate origins, resonating beyond its local performance and in many spheres of Canadian life.

This book traces the history of the Eaton's Santa Claus parades from their origins in 1905 to their final disappearance in 1982. Like Hall, I am interested in the many levels of the Eaton's parades, from their production as corporate spectacles to their broader import as a Christmas tradition. Yet my concerns are somewhat different than Hall's, not to lament the parades but to understand their character, power, and appeal. The Eaton's parades were created and produced by a single corporate institution, but they synthesized and expressed wider forms of culture and became an important piece of Canadian social and cultural history. They emerged from the kinds of commercial structures and institutional networks that shaped Canada's consumer society and public life in the twentieth century. They stand, moreover, at the intersection of several topics of historical and scholarly interest. The spectacle continued and updated a long history of parading in central streets, it was a new expression of Christmas culture, and it was a product of the most powerful institutions of twentieth-century consumer capitalism.

"Under the guise of service"

The Eaton's parades built on a long tradition of occupying public space to communicate a message. For more than two centuries, North Americans (rich and poor, elite and ordinary, religious and secular) have organized parades, processions, and public performances for a wide range of purposes, from celebration through commemoration to protest. In recent decades, historians have viewed these events as opportunities to glimpse deep structures of thought and belief, viewing parades as texts or documents whose structure, content, and organization could be "read" to reveal clues to the always imperfect and incomplete processes of identity formation and meaning creation. "The parade offers a well-rounded documentation of past culture," Mary Ryan wrote in a classic essay. "It conjured up an emotional power and aesthetic expressiveness that the simple literary formulation of ideas or values lacked … [It] can posit answers to basic questions of concern to social and cultural historians. It reveals, in a particularly powerful, publicly sanctioned way, how contemporaries construed, displayed, and saw the social order."[2] These studies have revealed much of analytic interest: we now understand the importance of parades to invented traditions, social identity, the public sphere, urban space, and several other issues. We also understand the way parades became a sort of language, a form of communication with well-understood vocabularies and syntax, the former referring to the visual, aural, symbolic, and narrative elements that make up the procession (each helping to communicate some aspect of the message) and the latter to the organizational politics (the rules for bringing the vocabulary together to form longer chains of meaning).[3] We have a particularly rich understanding of what Brooks McNamara called "the great age of public celebrations," a long nineteenth century stretching back to the American Revolution and forward to the First World War.[4] Throughout this period, vibrant parading cultures were sustained by their place in relatively compact urban geographies, by changing populations and economies, by intense battles over democratic politics, and by conflicting norms of public behaviour.[5]

The story of the Eaton's Santa Claus parade reinforces, extends, and revises these themes. Like many other groups and institutions, Eaton's used public space to communicate a message. At its most basic, then, Santa's astonishing popularity reflects vibrant parading traditions outside the long nineteenth century. Yet the Eaton's parades emerged from a different moment in the history of public presentation. As a corporate spectacle that experienced its golden years in the middle decades of the twentieth century, the Eaton's Santa Claus was one example of a powerful new form of commercial speech and holiday culture – the Christmas pageant – that proliferated across North America in the years after the First World War. In the United States, iconic and influential department stores – Gimbel's of Philadelphia, Macy's of New York, and Hudson's of Detroit – initiated Christmas pageants in the interwar years.[6] Soon, the familiar mix of clowns, fairies, floats, and bands was taken up by multiple groups in cities and towns across North America. If these forms of invented tradition extended and updated a long-standing processional culture, they did so in distinctive ways. Christmas pageants embraced new visual and narrative vocabularies, becoming fantastic spectacles that fused many contemporary forms of popular culture. Within this process of cultural invention, department stores were distinctive players, forging a new kind of parade by extending their corporate agendas into public space. The Eaton's parade offers an opportunity not to glimpse the totality of the social order, but to analyse one powerful slice of public life, a holiday spectacle that played out at multiple scales, from sidewalk and city to nation and continent.

The Santa Claus parades also fit into a longer trajectory of public holidays. They stand as one moment in the making of Christmas iconography, reflecting the increasing centrality of one image of Santa in emerging forms of Christmas celebration but also contributing to the making of other seasonal icons. Department stores solidified a long-standing process of reinvention and revision in Santa's visual character and emotional meaning. Santa Claus emerged from a synthesis of many images, and as late as the mid-nineteenth century, his personality remained plural, from whimsical through mischievous to bawdy. Over the Victorian period, however, Santa iconography increasingly settled on its modern form: chubby, bearded, genial, and jolly. By the twentieth century, department stores reinforced that trend in many ways. Their parade promotions narrated Santa's trip south from North Pole to city streets, playing on his elfish northern image. They built wondrous Toylands and Santa Palaces to stimulate childhood imaginations, featuring live Santas in the heart of their stores. Today, such displays have become commonplace, even trashy and mundane, at least to adult eyes. But when they emerged at the end of the nineteenth century and developed in the early twentieth, they represented a pioneering expression of the new aesthetic impulses of twentieth-century consumer culture. They also captured and extended the image of Santa as a jolly and generous saint dispensing joy and wonder to eager children.[7]

The Santa Claus parades took these processes out of the stores and into the streets, one part of a reformulation of the seasonal public sphere. Christmas had long been commercial, but by the twentieth century it was becoming more aggressively public. Business groups sponsored public decorations, civic officials set up Christmas trees at city and town halls, and electricity companies held domestic lighting contests to encourage holiday power use. Even churches got into the act, making peace with the sensual side of Christmas by mounting evergreen boughs, lighted crèches on front lawns, and other more overtly religious displays at holiday time.[8] In this sense, Eaton's was one of many institutions that marked Christmas in public. But it would be wrong to imagine the Santa Claus parade was simply one part of a multidirectional Christmas pluralism. The Eaton's parades were stunningly powerful, asserting their hegemony over the seasonal calendar and holiday practices to an unmatched degree. They were also stunningly singular, an extension of one company's Christmas spectacle into public space and public consciousness. Ultimately, many groups were involved in the dissemination of the Santa Claus parade idea, but the origins of the form lay in the promotional and commercial motivations of department stores.

The parades, then, also represented a particular moment in the cultural history of capitalism. As a spectacle forged in the decades after the First World War and tied to the seasonal high point of the commercial calendar, the Eaton's parade was as much an expression of the North American consumer revolution as of Christmas traditions and parading cultures. At the time they invented the modern form of Santa Claus parades, department stores were dominant retail institutions, standing at the vanguard of commercial culture, and Eaton's was in many ways simply one local expression of that broader set of developments. Department stores emerged slowly and incrementally from the expansion and diversification of several dry goods entrepreneurs in the mid- to late nineteenth century, and by the time Christmas pageants came on the scene, they had become "symbolic of the very essence of the consumer revolution."[9] Key figures like Rowland Macy in New York and John Wannamaker in Philadelphia built the form by innovating and borrowing modern practices like heavy advertising, cash-only sales, high turnover of low-priced goods, multiple lines of products, and guarantees of customer satisfaction. Macy began with a one-price policy in 1858 and expanded beyond dry goods in 1860. By 1877, his twenty-four departments sold everything from furniture to flowers.

John Wanamaker set up a men's clothing store in Philadelphia in 1861, expanded into dry goods and women's clothing in the 1870s, and finally moved to an enormous downtown store in 1910. He even opened an opulent branch for affluent customers in New York, aiming for the so-called "carriage trade."[10] Eaton's also began in dry goods before branching out, first in St Mary's, Ontario, then in a small store at 178 Yonge Street in Toronto (founded 1869), and then in a large (and, it seemed, constantly growing) physical plant at Yonge and Queen after 1883.[11]

As they emerged as the leading retail institutions in the decades before the First World War, the largest department stores represented pioneering assemblages of old and new economic, organizational, and cultural practices. Department stores were huge, much larger than even the most sophisticated dry goods stores in the mid-Victorian period. Eaton's grew from 50,000 square feet in 1886 (already large for its time) to 326,000 in 1897 and an astonishing one million by 1919, a time when the average Canadian store was about 3,000 square feet. When Eaton's arrived in Winnipeg in 1905, its five-storey branch towered over Portage Avenue, but the structure had been built to accommodate even more upward expansion. Nor were such figures unusual for the largest department store companies at the time. In 1902, Marshall Field's in Chicago opened a new twelve-storey store with more than a million feet of selling space, while Macy's in New York was of similar size at the time. Owners filled these huge stores with a stunning variety of products: fabrics, carpets, furniture, hardware, cooking appliances, musical instruments, toys, and many other lines, all systematically organized into different departments. Department stores had massive revenues to match their physical plants and range of products. "The modern department store is a wonderful business mechanism," Paul Nystrom declared in 1919. "[It] actually stimulates new demand, by showing to customers things about which they might not otherwise know anything." Indeed, already by 1907, Sears-Robuck earned $50 million a year, Macy's $16.8 million, and Eaton's $22.5 million, but over time revenues grew. By 1930, the three largest Canadian department stores (Eaton's, Simpson's, and Hudson's Bay) made up 15 per cent of all retail sales in the country. Nearly one out of every six shopping dollars, in other words, flowed through the cash registers of the largest Canadian department stores.[12] The biggest North American companies, moreover, ran operations that were geographically extensive and socially expansive. A few opened branch stores in other cities – Macy's, Simpson's, and especially Eaton's (the latter was in almost a dozen cities by 1930) – and most Canadian firms spread further using mail order catalogues.[13]

Size, scale, and variety required more advanced organization. Department stores were among the most efficient businesses for their time, one part of the organizational revolution that saw more systematic control of distribution and marketing, commodities, and workers.[14] Even before the First World War, the largest stores had more than one hundred different departments, a scale that both required and facilitated more intense surveillance of sales, products, and labour. Departmentalization allowed for a wide variety of products with strict inventory and accounting control. Timothy Eaton originally gave his department managers considerable autonomy, so that the store was almost like a cluster of different shops with distinct staffs. Under his successors, buyer and manager autonomy continued, but the central office also asserted itself in more systematic ways, both in terms of financial operations and store layout. By the 1910s, a formal Space Committee in Toronto considered the arrangement of goods to stimulate impulse buying. Eaton's also engaged in mass purchasing and ran an extensive network of buying offices. The company also expanded into manufacturing and delivery. In Toronto, underground tunnels connected store, warehouse, and offices. In all these spheres, Eaton's forged labour policies that combined rigid control and codification with modern forms of paternalism and authority.[15]

Department stores were also social and cultural institutions, pushing consumption beyond buying and selling to new forms of service and spectacle. By opening far-flung buying offices – by 1920, Eaton's had offices in London, Paris, New York, Yokohama, and Kobe – they became, in many ways, local interpreters of international trends, delivering Paris fashions and exotic furnishings to provincial customers through stores in cities like Toronto and Winnipeg and through catalogues to many more places.[16] Many also opened soda fountains, lunchrooms, restaurants, theatres, and libraries and provided public phones, clean washrooms, and even child care, usually to attract women, their key customers. "Special conveniences [are] offered to all shoppers whether they buy or not," Paul Nystrom wrote in 1919. "Under the guise of service, the modern department store has come to be a sort of club house and amusement place for women."[17] Many of the largest department store owners also became committed to monumental design and spectacular selling, using cathedral-like lobbies, installing grand statues, and manipulating light, colour, and glass to excite the

Table I.1 Revenues, selected US and Canadian department stores, 1919/1920

Sears Roebuck (US)	$235,000,000
Eaton's (Canada)	$123,590,000
Macy's (US)	$35,802,808
Simpson's (Canada)	$33,444,765
Hudson's Bay Company (Canada)	$14,865,000

US company revenues in American dollars. Canadian in Canadian dollars.
Source: Donica Belisle, *Retail Nation*, p. 36.

imagination of consumers. John Wanamaker was particularly energetic in this regard. His store in New York opened to a Grand Court that contained the world's largest organ, not to mention a 2,500-pound bronze eagle, and led customers to museum-like rooms called the Egytian Hall and Byzantine Chamber. Many other department stores undertook similar projects. Simpson's buildings, in particular, were considered architectural classics. Street-level windows – sites of rather haphazard and cluttered display for most stores in the Victorian period – became opportunities for department stores to catch the eye of passers-by with sophisticated and artistic mini-spectacles. Torontonians eagerly anticipated the opening of Eaton's Christmas windows in particular, which were considered the height of Christmas wonder and artistic display. By the early twentieth century, all of these techniques were being professionalized into formal display departments, which eventually took control of the Santa Claus parades.[18] For all these reasons, department stores were widely considered (and, indeed, sold themselves as) icons of modernity. They had not taken over urban retail by any means, but when boosters, observers, and critics thought of modern selling, they pointed to department stores.[19]

In fact, all of these organizational, marketing, and social approaches grew from emulation as much as innovation. Department store officials kept a close eye on each other and on developments in other retail sectors. Eaton's may have been "a unique institution of extraordinary magnitude," but its early catalogues frankly admitted that the company was "doing for Toronto" what Wanamaker had done for Philadelphia, Macy for New York, and Marshall Field's for Chicago.[20] Frank Beecroft, an early manager of Eaton's mail order department, modernized his section by copying procedures from Montgomery Ward.[21] This process of borrowing was widespread among early department store owners and managers. "I have read everything that I could see in print about your opening," John Wannamaker wrote to H. Gordon Selfridge of Marshall Field's in 1902, "and confess that I feel more interest in what you are doing than in any other business except our own. I hope to make a visit to see with my own eyes."[22] In Toronto, Eaton's and Simpson's were also hyper-conscious of each other, though publicly they claimed to follow their own path.[23]

Over time, the department store idea spread extensively across North America and around the world. By the Great Depression, versions could be found in the biggest cities of western Europe, Latin America, Australia, New Zealand, Asia, and even (in state-run form) in the Soviet Union. In the largest cities – places like London, New York, Boston, and Detroit – shoppers could choose between several department stores. In the United States, the form spread well beyond the biggest cities, appearing on the main streets of mid-sized regional centres and even some larger towns: places like Buffalo, Rochester, and Milwaukee, where they emphasized their cutting-edge modernity and their connections to local consumers and civic identity. Some of these operations grew to be quite large, extending markets to a wide local range. Sibley's in Rochester claimed to be the "largest department store in New York outside Manhattan." By 1918, it was spread over fourteen acres of selling space. Eight years later, it added six more floors to its downtown store, now occupying a whole city block. Nonetheless, as a more provincial version of metropolitan commerce, the company made great efforts to emphasize its attachment to the local community.[24]

The story was similar in Canada. Eaton's spread to Winnipeg in 1905 and to many other cities after 1920, including Halifax, Moncton, Montreal, Edmonton, and Calgary. In the largest cities, the company had many competitors. Department stores lined up along Montreal's Sainte Catherine Street after 1890: in the anglophone west end, Morgan's, Ogilvy's, and Gibson's; in the francophone east, Dupuis Frères, which borrowed the basic ingredients of international department store development – turnover, economy, mail order, and spectacle – and refracted it through nationalist ideas like family, language, and faith.[25] In Toronto, Eaton's and its key competitor Simpson's crowded the corner of Queen and Yonge by the 1880s. In Winnipeg and Edmonton, the Hudson Bay Company established a presence alongside Eaton's as a significant player in the local retail scene. In Vancouver, both Woodward's and Spencer's plied downtown markets. But even many smaller cities had a department store by the 1930s. They were not as large as the metropolitan majors, but they nonetheless towered over their local competitors. Even comparatively tiny Charlottetown had Holman's, which gained catalogue sales across the Maritimes. Such smaller operations hardly adopted every strategy of the major stores, but they were modern enough to be recognizable to boosters and critics alike.[26]

Over time, department stores faced many threats, but they had remarkable staying power well into the twentieth century. In the interwar years, they faced challenges from five and dimes, shifts in spending habits, retail decentralization, and small-business critics, but the combination of these developments produced only relative decline. Even during the Great Depression, when construction and renovation slowed or came to a halt, market share declined, and staffs were reduced, department store sales in Canada still increased by 7 per cent, a modest figure but a gain nonetheless. After the Second World War, when department stores had ceased to be symbols of the most progressive retail practices, they remained (to use the words of one *Maclean's* report) "the Big Stores," with almost $1 billion of sales in Canada alone. The postwar years saw new forms of suburban commerce that provided alternatives to big downtown department stores, but companies slowly adapted and by the 1960s came to anchor shopping malls like Yorkdale in Toronto (which had *both* a Simpson's and an Eaton's), Polo Park in Winnipeg, and Park Royal in West Vancouver. Department stores also formed a central part of downtown re-developments in the following decade. Throughout this process, to be sure, the fortunes of specific companies waxed and waned, but the department store idea didn't face a fundamental, structural crisis until the 1970s, a theme taken up in more detail in chapter 5.[27]

As should be clear by now, Eaton's stood in the mainstream of department store developments, but it also dominated its markets to an almost unmatched degree. While big American stores loomed large in local markets and sometimes expanded beyond them, Eaton's forged a national retail space. Early in its history, it published massive numbers of its iconic catalogue, set up a coast-to-coast mail order service, and opened a branch store in Winnipeg (1905). In the 1920s, it opened outlets in Montreal, Halifax, and Moncton, and other cities. By the end of the decade, the company's sales totalled 58 per cent of all department store revenues in Canada and an astonishing 7 per cent of all retail sales. Other department store leaders recognized its importance, as when Macy's officials travelled to Toronto in 1924 to borrow the Santa Claus parade idea. As with other department stores, Eaton's growth slowed during the Depression, but after the Second World War, it accelerated again, as the company moved into suburban shopping centres and opened more branch stores. In 1955, when it faced the threat of the newly merged Simpsons-Sears, Eaton's estimated revenues were still more than double those of its competitors. By 1962, the company operated 72 stores and 345 catalogue sales offices and distributed seventeen million catalogues.[28] The company remained privately owned but became geographically ubiquitous. As one ad proclaimed in 1956, "No one is far from Eaton's."[29]

Eaton's size and scale were absolutely central to the success of its Christmas parades. The company expended stunning resources on the events: by the 1950s, the parade ate up more than half the company's public relations spending; by the time of its cancellation in 1982, the budget was a half-million dollars. The company's geographically extensive operations provided the incentive, but also the infrastructure, to run a parade in several cities by 1929 and to expand their reach through television in the postwar years. The parades were clearly important public relations moments for the company. Indeed, in each city, a parade was mounted at almost the first opportunity: Winnipeg opened and mounted its first parade in 1905; Montreal opened in 1925 and held a parade that same year; Calgary and Edmonton both opened and mounted their first parade in 1929. In all of these cities, the company's sophisticated organizational resources, particularly its modern display and public relations departments, were marshalled to mount the parade. By the 1950s, the biggest Eaton's parades were year-round operations with a permanent staff of artists, carpenters, painters, and seamstresses, supplemented with temporary staff in the few weeks leading up to the event. The Santa Claus parade, then, was at once a colourful procession, a popular Christmas spectacle, and an expression of corporate power.

An Archive of Good Cheer

A Mile of Make-Believe explores the history of the Eaton's parades over five chapters. The first three focus on the making of the Eaton's parade and its growing influence on popular culture across Canada. Chapter 1 examines the invention and development of the Eaton's parades from

Table I.2. Approximate budgets for Eaton's Santa Claus
parade, 1938–1982

Year	Budget	In 2016 dollars
1938	$10,000	$164,000
1956	$62,000	$562,000
1971	$130,000	$811,000
1981	$500,000	$1,333,000

The figure from 1956 is a "projected budget." The figure from 1971 does not include
broadcast costs.
2016 dollar equivalents calculated with Bank of Canada Inflation Calculator.
Sources: TEF, F229-51, BF, "Santa Claus Parade – Fall 1938," file 124: Santa Claus
Parade, 1937–1941; Sales and Expense Office to Brockie, 17 January 1956, file:
Santa Claus Parade, 1957, part I; TEF, SCP, Box 1, Minutes and Arrangements, 1971,
"Santa Claus Parade Expenses to Date," 6 December 1971; *Globe and Mail*,
10 August 1982, 5.

1905 to 1982. In these years, Eaton's helped to create a new form of
spectacle – the Santa Claus parade – by blending several familiar narrative, aesthetic, and organizational strategies. I call this style "the
corporate fantastic," a term meant to capture the blend of meticulous
organization, company control, wondrous characters, and sophisticated popular art that characterized these pioneering Christmas pageants.
It was fantastic in the narrative and aesthetic sense. The parade drew
on strategies common to department store interior display but also to
most popular forms of commercial spectacle (from circuses and amusement parks to movies and later television) to produce a spectacle of
colour, wonder, and fantasy. At the same time, the spectacle was corporate at three interrelated levels. First, in the most basic organizational
sense, the parades were the products of the company's local display
staffs, though planning and production engaged employees in several
departments, from advertising through construction. Second, the Eaton's
parade makers inhabited a pan-national corporate structure, which had
spread from Toronto to Winnipeg by the time the parades were initiated in 1905 and to many other cities after 1920. In each city, the local
display department took the lead in producing the spectacles, and
through Eaton's national corporate structure they communicated and
collaborated in making their local events. Third, this pan-national

corporate structure connected the Eaton's parade makers to other key commercial institutions and to like-minded experts across North America. In this sense, while Eaton's represented an early version of this emerging parade style, the corporate fantastic was a metropolitan form of popular culture, taking shape within a growing continental network of parade makers, mainly tied to department store display departments in major cities. As such, the Eaton's parades represented local versions of a continent-wide form of commercial expression.

Chapter 2, "Santa in Public," follows the Eaton's parades into the lively local public spheres of Canadian cities. Any parade, as a public event, seeks to build a crowd and to communicate a message. Santa Claus parades extended the company's display vision – already well developed in the stores themselves – into downtown streets and pressed Eaton's own promotional agenda onto the wider public. Yet entering the streets raised different – and less controllable – dynamics than in-store spectacles. Santa's parade promoted Eaton's, but it also entered a public sphere with its own codes and practices. The parade and its enormous crowds needed to be accommodated in the bustling downtowns of twentieth-century cities, a process that was certainly not easy or entirely seamless. In the end, however, the intrusions were largely accepted, partly owing to the distinctive nature of the Eaton's crowd, dominated by cute and joyful children, nostalgic adults, and a feeling of festive good cheer. Canadians even began to speak of the parades as the real beginning of the Christmas season. Indeed, in Eaton's hands, the corporate fantastic had a powerful public effect, calling together large if well-behaved crowds, disrupting the normal uses of public space, and pressing the company's promotional agenda onto the very shape of the season.

Chapter 3, "The Mediated Santa," probes another element of Santa's public sphere, the company's efforts to reach out beyond local audiences through various forms of mass media. Broadcasting represented the most powerful expression of the metropolitan dynamics of the parades – metropolitan in the sense that an important city can project power and influence well beyond its own borders[30] – and loosely paralleled the company's own mapping of a national retail space. By the interwar years, the company was experimenting with ways to reach out beyond local performance: distributing films, using radio broadcasts, and finally moving the spectacle onto television in the 1950s. In some ways, the power of the mediated Santa increased over time, as the company replaced local events with a national broadcast of the Toronto parade, which by 1969 reached households from Newfoundland to British Columbia. None of these processes was without difficulty. It was a challenge to translate a street performance to speaker and screen, to control meanings in far-flung media markets, and to negotiate with other powerful commercial and cultural institutions. Still, my discussion stresses the metropolitan nature of the mediated Santa as another expression of Eaton's power, which allowed it to play at multiple scales at once.

Chapter 4, "The Civic Fantastic," moves beyond metropolitan centres in a different way, examining the proliferation of Santa Claus parades across North America in the middle decades of the twentieth century. In this period, when the corporate fantastic was at the height of its influence, thousands of smaller communities mounted their own Christmas pageants. The artistic approach of these civic celebrations was often consciously copied from the department store version, but the organizational politics were quite different, refracted through many forms of civic organization and identity. Service clubs, voluntary groups, and local chambers of commerce were particularly active in this process of proliferation, sponsoring and organizing parades in an astonishing range of communities across North America. But as they mounted their local parades, organizers eagerly embraced many forms of mass culture, even while interpreting them through local priorities and organizational forms. In one sense, this process inverts our usual understanding of consumer culture, where some authentic local phenomenon is co-opted by corporate processes. Community Santa Claus parades represented a form of reverse co-optation, where a metropolitan cultural form took new life outside its corporate origins. I call these parades "the civic fantastic" to express the potent mix of popular art, whimsical style, community spirit, and civic cooperation at the heart of this process.

Chapter 5, "Casualty of the Times," traces the cancellation of the Toronto parade, the last remaining Eaton's event in the country. In 1982, with Canada in the midst of a deep recession, the company announced it would no longer organize the parade. Critics of the decision often saw larger trends at work, so the announcement became another chance to link corporate decisions to broader narratives of social and cultural change. In the end, alternative business elites took control of the Toronto parade, making it (on the surface at least) an expression of one kind of Toronto civic politics, refracted through new forms of corporate philanthropy and promotion. Nonetheless, the end of the Eaton's parades introduces a sort of ironic twist to the story. The original power of the spectacles flowed from their corporate and singular character – as a creature of Eaton's, the Santa Claus parade could mobilize the different registers of power that lay behind the company. In the end, however, the corporate fantastic turned out to be a brittle form of hegemony, too reliant on a single institution. At the same time, the very fragility of the civic fantastic – its dependence on the initiative and labour of many non-professional volunteers, who could by turns become exhausted or overwhelmed by the project – was a source of resilience, as new community groups stepped forward to continue or revive the tradition.

None of these points could be examined without the rich archive available on the parade, itself a product of the spectacle's popularity and of the Eaton's iconic image. Historians need evidence, and my discussion builds on three main sets of sources. First, I tapped the extensive Eaton's Collection at the Archives of Ontario, surely one of the finest examples of archival acquisition in Canadian history (something to be celebrated at a time of reduced funding for public archives). The collection is rich on many facets of the company's history and with some exceptions open to public and scholarly examination.[31] Many of the files contain excellent detail on the making of the Santa Claus parades (most notably, the papers of long-time Toronto parade producer, Jack Brockie). Other files, including records of key public relations officials, minutes of various merchandising meetings, corporate newsletters, correspondence between stores, interviews with company officials, films of the parades, and the files of the Santa Claus parade itself, were also useful. Second, I consulted a wide range of newspapers, which often provided extensive coverage of the parade and its organizational background. For civic parades, I also relied heavily on an extensive survey of local newspapers.[32] Finally, I tapped other archival collections, largely to fill in secondary gaps on specific issues. The CBC Collection at the National Archives, for example, contains a small amount of material on the Santa Claus parade, while various city council records fill in details about congestion, traffic, and noise. Scattered records of service organizations provide some details on efforts to create the civic version of the spectacle for local consumption.

As with any study, these sources contain both possibilities and perils, shaping both what we can know and what we can't know about the parades. The Eaton's Collection is much richer on the Toronto parade than on those of other cities and is deepest on the period from the late 1930s to the mid-1970s. We get only periodic glimpses behind the scenes of the early parades or those in other cities. Readers will notice that story of parades outside Toronto is much more (though not totally) reliant on press coverage. From another perspective, not surprisingly, the Eaton's collection provides us with much more detail on the thinking of parade makers than on popular reactions to their efforts. Even then, since much of the planning was oral (meetings, chats over drawings, impromptu consultations at the construction site), we often get a haphazard peek at planning and organization. Nor can we be sure whether any material was destroyed for the sake of corporate image. That said, the Eaton's records are not simply boosterish; they were created as working files, saved by parade makers with an intense interest in the successes and failures of their spectacle, so records of complaints and problems were often saved and taken seriously.

Newspaper accounts have their own strengths and limitations. To put it politely, neither the corporate nor the civic version of the Santa Claus parade attracted especially rigorous journalism. In small towns, local newspapers were key community boosters and were often intimately involved with planning and organizing the civic fantastic, so they had relatively little incentive to offer critical assessments on a regular basis. In the case of the larger Eaton's parades, celebratory journalism was probably tied both to the nature of the parade and to Eaton's public image. On the one hand, the parade was a popular form of childhood wonder and Christmas universalism. To criticize it, Scrooge-like, was to court vigorous backlash. On the other hand, the parade was produced by an iconic, well-regarded, and (not incidentally) powerful company, and Eaton's mobilized its considerable corporate and professional resources to court positive media coverage. Company employees prepared parade scripts, background material, and biographical profiles of major figures; they facilitated interviews with key parade producers; they arranged pre-parade previews and access to production facilities. By the 1950s, printed press kits grew to enormous proportions, more than an inch thick, so descriptively rich and precise in detail that journalists could probably have covered the parade without attending it at all. On occasion, in fact, newspaper stories drew heavily on this material, and the result was sometimes boosterish accounts that barely modified the company's potted descriptions. When all this media relations work failed, moreover, the company could throw its weight around. Mark Starowicz claimed that he was fired by the *Montreal Gazette* after writing a less than positive account of the city's 1967 parade, a somewhat bizarre presentation that included psychedelic colours and probably deserved a sarcastic reading.[33] It is not clear how often this kind of pressure occurred – and it didn't seem necessary very often, given the largely positive coverage year after year – but it could have loomed in the background at key moments.

Still, the print media remain an absolutely essential source for both corporate and civic parades. Mainstream journalism did acquire a bit more bite by the late 1960s, and before then reports can be usefully read against the grain: reports of crowd sizes and traffic challenges, for example, which seemed intended to highlight the popularity of the event, also spoke to the frustrations and disruptions of parade day. Some more specialized articles – in trade magazines and the business press particularly – often provide unromantic details on production and organization. At the same time, because civic parades required cooperation between many groups, debates and conflicts were often open and public, allowing us some glimpses of problems, criticisms, and tensions.

In the end, this book is about corporate power and, in a more complicated way, its limitations. While I argue that the spectacle was never the whole story, the Eaton's Santa Claus parades nonetheless represented, in their time, astonishing examples of the influence of one company's seasonal and promotional priorities. This argument is not intended to debunk happy parade experiences, emotional connections to Eaton's iconography, or nostalgic Christmas memories. Obviously, many people like Christmas, and the Eaton's parades were often a large part of that positive feeling. The parades became a key part of seasonal traditions that gave people pleasure, joy, and fond memories. I have no doubt that Alfreda Hall, faced with the extinction of the Eaton's parade, felt a genuine sense of loss – by this, I mean she literally *felt* it. Her lament, like those of so many other Canadians, came from the gut and the heart rather than the mind. That sense of joy in watching the parade, and that sense of loss in confronting its end, came in many flashes of deep emotion and feeling. The thousands of words in journalistic accounts, letters to the editor, popular books, and personal memories – all organized neatly into archival files and newspaper fonts – probably translate those emotions rather imperfectly. To simply dismiss such accounts would be boring and cheap. Any decent history of the parade needs to recognize the authenticity and emotion of Alfreda's lament.

But historians want to explain things and to understand their context, and while joy and delight were surely part of the success of the Eaton's parades, such emotions can come in many forms and attach themselves to many events. We do need to account for how and why this particular holiday tradition became so popular, powerful, and iconic, for the particular ways its disappearance was mourned and lamented, and for the ways its contributions to seasonal joy and familial emotion were authorized and reinforced by broader social and cultural developments. This question leads us to the history of culture, Christmas, family, and childhood, but it also takes us back to Eaton's corporate power. In assessing the popularity of the parade, and the joy it produced, there is no sense denying the important role of Eaton's as a business with considerable economic, organizational, and cultural resources. It was a powerful department store at a time when the form was the dominant expression of North American consumer capitalism. Its display staff had a sophisticated understanding of spectacle. It could promote the event heavily in newspapers and on radio and television. Its advertising department understood how to communicate with mass media outlets. It could fly its personnel to New York and Philadelphia to check out the latest in parade-making technologies. It could mount parades in several cities and ensure that the largest were broadcast widely. It had the institutional continuity and stability to make its parade a tradition rather than a fragile or short-term affair. These assets and advantages hardly guaranteed hegemony in the jostling to create and shape Christmas or consumer culture, but they did make the company much more powerful than most other groups and institutions engaged in similar projects. This point is not the end of analysis, however, and should not be confused with a one-dimensional critique of commercialism. My argument is a more precise one about the possibilities and limits of corporate power and about the ability of one company to integrate itself into diverse social practices.

As with any parade, however, the most intriguing matters begin in the street.

1

The Corporate Fantastic

At first, the parade was a sound, because spectators always heard it before they saw it. The noise began quietly and remotely and grew in intensity, stirring impatient children and increasing their sense of anticipation. Crowds pressed forward, straining to see. Soon, figures appeared in the distance down Jasper Avenue. The first glimpse was of something large, colourful, and probably moving. "Heralded by a fanfare of music in the distance and a sight of giant balloons floating in the air," the *Edmonton Journal* reported in 1946, "the parade evoked excitement before it actually arrived." As the parade passed, specific characters came into view. The large, colourful float at the front turned out to be Mother Goose, "riding a beautiful pink goose with blue ribbons for reins." She led the parade almost every year, and was followed by a stunning but bewildering array: animals, clowns, dragons, characters from nursery rhymes and fairy tales, interspersed with bands, and – a special treat – fifty "Sarcee Indians" from a nearby reservation, dressed in "feather headdresses and moccasins." The "interest grew to a fever pitch" as Santa finally approached, shouting his greeting with scripted regularity along the route. After about half an hour, it was over, as Santa arrived at Eaton's to mark the official opening of Toyland.[1] Children were excited, adults satisfied, but perhaps there was a man in a suit taking notes – he must work for Eaton's – who seemed very tired and just a bit grumpy. There was a lot to worry about: he had been up all night, perhaps Santa had shown up late, the parade could have gone over time, or it could be that, as the parade dispersed, his day still wasn't done – he was fretting about getting floats and costumes back into storage.

Eaton's had been running Santa Claus parades for many years and in many cities before the old saint delighted Edmonton children in 1946. The tradition lasted longest in Toronto (1905–82), for several decades in Winnipeg (1905–66) and Montreal (1925–68), and for shorter periods in Calgary (sporadically from 1929 to 1953) and Edmonton (sporadically from 1929 to '39 and again from 1946 to 1957). From humble beginnings in Toronto and Winnipeg, the parades grew to enormous proportions in all these cities, with the largest stretching to over a mile of fantastic and wondrous presentations, all drawn from traditional and modern forms of children's culture. Eaton's did not invent the Santa Claus parade – there were a few scattered versions in other North American cities before 1905 – but it was an important player in their redefinition into a sophisticated form of commercial art and popular culture. I call these parades "the corporate fantastic" to highlight two key themes: their corporate organization and their fantastic aesthetic form. To build the parades, Eaton's marshalled its impressive resources to produce a sophisticated form of commercial culture, to export it across Canada to reflect the company's national retail structure, and to link the parade makers to like-minded cultural producers across North America. As in Edmonton, Eaton's parades played on wonder and fantasy, building a basic script from standard forms of commercial and popular culture: fairy tales, Orientalism, slapstick humour, childhood wonder, and visual strategies borrowed from circuses and amusement parks. Indeed, while the parades were large and popular, they were not stunningly novel in artistic or theatrical terms. Eaton's combined existing forms of culture into a pioneering mix of fantasy and wonder, and did so with almost relentless continuity across space and time. Indeed, in each city and across the years, the Eaton's parades showed remarkable aesthetic and stylistic consistency, despite the occasional shift in strategy and various local wrinkles. These two elements of the parade – the corporate and the fantastic – defined and shaped the company's Santa Claus parades within the broader meaning of the Christmas season.

"A whole cavalcade of queer, dear people"

For all their storied history, the Eaton's parades began in inauspicious fashion. On 3 December 1905, Santa arrived by train at Union Station in Toronto and travelled in a wagon through the central streets to Eaton's downtown store; that same day, he arrived in Winnipeg in similar style, travelling from the Canadian Pacific Railway station to the company branch at Portage and Hargrave. These journeys were anything but spectacular, mainly extending the company's indoor Christmas displays, which at various points before 1905 had featured Toyland menageries and live Santas. Nor were such journeys completely novel. In 1888, Chipper and Block Department Store of Peoria, Illinois, sent Santa on a tour through the city's streets, while the Hayden Brothers department store in Omaha also ran several parades before 1905, which became quite large and impressive by the mid-1890s: "With prancing teams, with band of brownies, with spirit stirring strains of melody, with mounted couriers, with cavalcade of faithful followers … came the king of all fairies, the crowned monarch of the nursery, the beloved of all men, the immortal Santa Claus." The Omaha parade was impressive, filled with floats displaying products from the store's many departments. "It was not a cheap array of empty boxes or bulky wares, but an artistic, rich and elaborate showing of merchandise," the local paper declared. "The decorations were not cheap and gaudy, for the glare and glitter of tinsel gave way to the gleam and glint and the sheen and shimmer of real and solid worth."[2] It is not clear how much Eaton's knew about these early parades by 1905, but the similarity in form is striking.

While neither novel nor sophisticated as a spectacle, the Eaton's parades proved popular in both Toronto and Winnipeg. Crowds of delighted children and parents arrived to greet the old saint and, over the next decade, the company experimented with new characters and different routes, though the parade remained basic compared to later years.[3] The first parades had Santa arrive at the train station and travel through downtown to Eaton's. By 1910, Santa began from some outlying point – in Winnipeg, for example, from the streetcar suburb, St James, and one year in Toronto from Aurora, a small community about 20 kilometres north – and then followed a reasonably straight line to the company's store, usually down Yonge Street in Toronto and Portage in Winnipeg. Some early parades in both cities featured a tie-in theatrical event later in the day – at Massey Hall in Toronto and the Walker Theatre in Winnipeg. Here, the spectacle became more impressive and fantastic. In 1915, the Walker Theatre was transformed into "fantasyland" with the stage done up as "a cave of wondrous beauty, where multi-colored spars of rock, crystal clear, formed a fitting background for monster sea shells, which when opened exposed to view dainty fairies of hellpin beauty." The show that year presented a fairy-tale story centred on Princess Curly Locks, weaving in such standard characters as Old

Mother Goose, Simple Simon, Jack and Jill, and others, supplemented by gnomes, fairies, policemen, a child imitating Charlie Chaplin, and, at the end, a dramatic appearance by Santa Claus on stage in a chariot to lead the whole crew in patriotic songs.[4] By the interwar years, however, the standard practice in both Toronto and Winnipeg was to finish at the local Eaton's branch, with Santa climbing a ladder to a second-floor window, where he entered the store to take up residence in Toyland.[5]

The modern form of the parade began to emerge around the First World War. Simple floats became more complicated; rudimentary designs became more artistic; Santa's small retinue began to grow larger. In 1916, seven floats, each representing a well-known nursery rhyme or fairy tale, joined Santa in the Toronto parade. That same year, Winnipeg's parade featured eight "huge" floats, including a jazz band, a giant mushroom, a duck with bobbing head, and three mice chasing cheese. By the end of the war, the basic narrative structure had congealed around what Eaton's called "a whole cavalcade of queer dear people from the story books, nursery rhymes and picture pages" and journalists dubbed "all sorts of funny characters that live in Fableland." Santa was the anchor, but Mother Goose also appeared every year, while Cinderella, Humpty Dumpty, Jack and the Beanstalk, Bo Peep, and The Old Woman Who Lived in a Shoe were mainstays of the post-1920 decades. Over time, the company integrated characters from mass culture, ranging from specific icons from comic strips, radio shows, movies, and then television (e.g., Amos and Andy, Mickey Mouse, the Lone Ranger, Yogi Bear, the Flintstones) to more generic cowboys, Indians, and Mounties.[6] Eaton's also invented its own characters. In 1935, Ducky Dandy and his Ducklings, characters that were apparently developed by Eaton's designers, joined Santa in Winnipeg. More famous and influential was Punkinhead, a bear character developed by Eaton's in the late 1940s to compete with Rudolph the Red Nosed Reindeer. Punkinhead appeared in all the cities and was often featured prominently in promotional efforts as well.[7] Santa, Mother Goose, and Punkinhead were joined by an assortment of fairies, elves, and animals – often featured in terms of comedic inversion and whimsical juxtaposition, like the bears dressed in suits like "ladies and gentlemen" in 1936 or on skates in 1949. Clowns filled the gaps, as in Winnipeg's 1921 parade, which featured "gentlemen clowns and lady clowns [and] bunnies shaking friendly paws with the spectators." Throughout this process of addition, subtraction, and revision, however, "traditional"

Mother Goose, Toronto, 1930.
City of Toronto Archives, Fonds 1266, Globe and Mail Collection, item 22531.

storybook characters remained the core of the spectacle and formed the basic structure of the parade well into the 1970s.[8]

When the company expanded the parade idea to Montreal, Calgary, and Edmonton in the interwar years, local organizers simply adopted this narrative approach. In 1925, at Montreal's first parade, Santa arrived "heralded by music, and with his retinue of fairy folk, toys and all familiar associates of playtime," from animals on horseback through zany clowns to Mother Goose rhymes. Santa himself sat on "a gigantic balloon-spouting whale, borne along on huge ice-burgs, with polar bears and Eskimos for companions," the latter with the clever names Jiv-Ien-O-Si and Jev-Eu-Ia-Lé. Four years later, Calgary's first parade was startlingly similar, featuring musketeers on horseback, a

Ad for Eaton's parade, Winnipeg, 1919.
Winnipeg Evening Tribune, 14 November 1919.

nine-member clown band executing "antics of every description," a "woozle-fish" measuring 85 feet in length with rolling eyes and a wagging head, Ali Baba and his forty thieves, a turkey "about twice the size of the world's largest eagle," and Santa Claus with a big bag of toys. Edmonton's parade that same year also featured "all the joys of the Land of Make Believe," from huge walking sticks of peppermint candy, clowns and circus floats, and nursery rhyme characters like Humpty Dumpty.[9] Thus, all the Eaton's parades took "make believe" as their narrative base.

This narrative strategy was somewhat novel, at least in parades. Unlike the great parading traditions that dominated the nineteenth century – the Glorious Twelfth, St Patrick's Day, trades processions, coronation celebrations, and city anniversaries – the Santa Claus parades made no serious reference to civic, national, fraternal, ethnic, or

Ad for Eaton's parade, Winnipeg, 1926.
Winnipeg Free Press, 19 November 1926, 8.

religious identity. The parade was filled with people: children recruited from local schools sat on floats; teenagers pulled mini-displays or
danced along the route; teachers dressed up to act as marshals; Eaton's
employees skipped along as clowns and fairies. Identities were generally obscured, however: participants wore masks, make-up, or costumes;
even children, easily recognized by their size and much appreciated for
their cuteness, were dressed up and reduced to the generic adorable. In
a way, masking and dressing up sent its own message. In this parade,
identity was less important than theatre. Spectators would look in vain
for the typical members of Victorian and Edwardian era processional
culture: the parade had no unions, no fraternal orders, no Orangemen,
and no civic officials. Indeed, in the parade, there were few substantive
references to the outside world at all: the company occasionally added
touches of the moment, like national or historic symbols during significant anniversaries and celebrations of cultural diversity in the 1950s.
Such references, however, were few in number, romantic or folkloric in
thrust, and ruthlessly subjugated to the aesthetic agenda of the parade
makers.[10]

Masking and costuming were hardly unprecedented in parades, but
they had rarely been so central. In the Victorian period, raucous parades

Storybook Land, Montreal, 1937.
BANQ, P48,S1,P1635, Photographer: Conrad Poirier.

of Calithumpians and Ragamuffins embraced costuming, masking, and performing. Largely young men, these groups took to the streets at night or at significant moments to make noise, adopt grotesque style, clown around, and lampoon their social superiors.[11] For their part, circuses normally heralded their arrival in town with a raucous parade, featuring (in one quite typical case) "music, banners, knights, ladies, and cages of wild animals," though this practice was becoming less common by the 1920s.[12] Historical pageants featured elaborate and theatrical floats to depict earnest messages about history, civic identity, or local pride, serving as mainstays of special events like Quebec City's Tercentenary in 1908 or Canada's Diamond Jubilee in 1927.[13] But before the Santa Claus parade rose to hegemony, the most common form of annual street parade was the respectable march, in which participants walked in ordered formation, donning fine clothes, adopting a military bearing, and carrying earnest symbols and fancy regalia. In Toronto, this form was typical of the most popular annual events like the Orangemen's Glorious 12th, the Irish Catholic St Patrick's Day, and the craft union Labour Day, but most cities in North America would have witnessed a similar mix. In such events, parade vocabularies

Time for Stories, Toronto, 1957.
York University Libraries, Clara Thomas Archives & Special Collections,
Toronto Telegram fonds, ASC34677

flowed from the cultural politics of identity and respectability, as participants announced their status as ethnic subjects, honourable men, skilled workers, democratic citizens, or some combination of all these at once. A few participants might serve explicitly symbolic roles (e.g. Britannia, liberty, progress), and floats might make up one part (on Labour Day, floats often featured workers practising their craft), but in the Santa Claus parade, everyone was a character, everyone was acting, everything was theatre.[14]

An Eaton's parade was more than its characters; it was an assault on the eyes and ears. The parades were loud, often announcing their arrival

A Mile of Make-Believe

Mary Had a Little Lamb, Edmonton, 1947.
City of Edmonton Archives, EA-275-1337.

with approaching sounds. In Calgary, the standard bearer's car with a Union Jack led the first parade accompanied by two pages on horseback sounding their bugles at each intersection, while Edmonton's 1937 effort included "an ear-splitting, rackety bang band of musicians who played brisk march tunes on washboards and tin pans."[15] Brass bands were the loudest of all, blaring out Christmas carols and proliferating as time went on (Montreal had three or four in the 1920s and more than half a dozen by the 1950s). There was always one near the front – in 1938, the band of the Black Watch led the Montreal parade, blaring out *Jingle Bells*[16] – and the rest were carefully spaced so that music was consistent along the route. Many costumes had bells attached for "added jingle," and most characters carried noisemakers of various sorts. "It's tradition ... that every parader carries something to blow, to jingle, whistle or wave. No one goes along empty handed," the company declared.[17] For a modern parade in the emerging age of electronic amplification, the sounds of bells, bands, whistles, and horns were quite traditionally acoustic, with Santa's microphone and loudspeaker (which by the late 1930s "made his voice audible for hundreds of yards" and both overcame and contributed to the cacophonous effect of the parade) as the only concession to modern technology.[18] The effect was a dramatic wall of festival sound. "How shall we describe it?" one Eaton's newsletter mused in 1951. "There was music – band music to set the hearts in tune with marching feet – gay lilting laughing music."[19]

The look of the parade was equally striking. Eaton's combined motion, light, colour, inversion, juxtaposition, and distortion of scale into a thrilling display. Clowns spun around on gymnastic bars, mechanical dolls waved, heads bobbed up and down, mouths opened and closed, ferris wheels and mini-trains spun and whirled. Edmonton's 1953 parade featured life-sized elephants and a "whirling carousel."[20] The parades were held in daytime, so much of the sparkle came from using mirrors, glitter, and "metallic papers" to reflect or amplify natural light, though after the Second World War some electric lights added sparkle to floats.[21] Colour heightened this sparkling visual effect. "It was an extremely brilliant pageant that used all the colours on the futurists' palette," the *Toronto Daily Star* enthused in 1926. Three decades later, the company made "Christmas Colour-Rama" the overall theme, bragging of "pretty gentle flowery colours," "bright exciting crackling colours," and "sparking, gold and silver ones."[22] On floats, colours were carefully coordinated: in some cases, they were matched to the theme of the float (for the Fairy Queen, parade makers aimed for a dream-like and beautiful effect; for King Arthur, they tried to evoke grandeur and ruggedness; for Jack and the Beanstalk, an outdoor country atmosphere); in others, wild colours might add a whimsical quality to an otherwise plain character (a cow, festooned with pink and purple polka dots, jumping over the moon). Colour needed to catch the eye of adults and children, so Eaton's designers chose paints to "glitter" and fabrics to "shimmer."[23]

Eaton's also created spectacle by distorting size and scale. Parade entries included "clowns of gigantic proportion" (Toronto, 1928), giants "as high as trees" (Montreal, 1928), "la plus grande canne en bonbon au monde" (Montreal, 1930), fifteen-foot ducklings (Winnipeg, 1924), and an 85-foot lizard-like "woozle-fish" (Calgary, 1929). "Did you ever see such huge sticks of peppermint candy?" one description from Edmonton wondered. "If they were 'really-truly-true' they'd keep an army of girls and boys in sweets for many a day."[24] Big displays made for easier viewing, but also for dramatic effect. In 1929, Santa rode in Montreal and Toronto astride a giant arctic fish, which though confusing by any standard of Christmas symbolism, fit nicely into the spectacle of bigness. "It was the biggest, shiniest, scaliest, prettiest, fish that ever came here," the *Toronto Star* reported.[25] The spectacle of size continued after the war. In

1952, the Toronto parade contained a fifty-foot wriggling caterpillar and a fifty-foot alligator (both operated by more than a dozen boys). Like these displays, the spectacle of bigness distorted length more often than height, since the parade confronted the practical issue of overhead trolley wires, but distorting scale could also mean shrinking things down, or playing on the juxtaposition of big and small: "There were funny little people with big heads, and even funnier big people with little heads," the *Montreal Gazette* reported in 1942.[26]

The company was also fond of depicting the unusual and exotic, especially images of racial and ethnic difference for a variety of narrative and aesthetic purposes. A few presentations integrated floats of local ethnic groups, an increasingly common style in all mainstream parades after the mid-1920s, reflecting both the assertiveness of immigrant communities and the folksy but tame multiculturalism being slowly embraced by many urban elites. In one Toronto example, children of "all nations" (which, in this case, meant English, French, German, Italian, and Irish, a limited range compared to the local population) marched in a body wearing "quaint costumes."[27] These sorts of presentations were rare, however, compared to exotic and comedic racial imagery. In 1923, the Toronto parade included an "Oriental float with Arab attendants" and a "Chinese band on pagoda float"; thirteen years later, nine "nubian slaves, each taller than the one ahead, with big golden faces and red lips, leered at everybody" on the sidewalks. In 1921, the Winnipeg parade featured brown-skinned men from Africa, while the 1935 version contained the incongruous image of "black cannibals with their frightening grins in their hula hula skirts."[28] In postwar Edmonton, "coolies" danced with toy soldiers and peasant girls amid the floats.[29] Comedic blackface and straightforward racism were common: advertisements for the 1928 Toronto parade bragged of "Ten little nigger boys sitting happily on top of a crocodile," while Amos 'n' Andy minstrelled their way through Montreal in 1930, down the Toronto route in 1931, and along Winnipeg's streets in 1951. "Two burnt-cork coons drove by in what must be the world's worst car," the *Gazette* reported.[30] The parades in all their versions also contained numerous examples of what Philip Deloria calls "playing Indian" – white people in indigenous garb or the use of indigenous symbols for theatrical effect.[31] In 1925, two Eskimos assisted Montreal's Santa; a decade later, "a beautiful savage" could be found "at the head of a group of Indians."[32] Hiawatha and Minnehaha appeared on a Winnipeg float, surrounded by "three braves doing a war dance" in front of a teepee.[33]

The racial exotic: "Arabian" figures with spears in Montreal, 1937.
BANQ, P48,S1,P1635, Photographer: Conrad Poirier.

Such racial images both reflected and reinforced the Canadian racial imagination. Orientalism, blackface, playing Indian, and the racial exotic were standard forms of popular culture in Canada at the time, reflecting the common-sense whiteness of cultural producers and most Euro-Canadians. Indeed, such exotic and highly stereotypical images were staples of circuses, amusement parks, advertising, theatre, movies, and many more sites. The seamlessness of their integration into Eaton's parades makes their absolute familiarity clear. "There were enormous quacking ducks, out-sized Zulus, and a score of other fairy-tale characters not to mention a highly-realistic and somewhat terrifying dragon," the *Calgary Herald* commented in 1935. Ducks, dragons, Zulus: all part of a seamlessly integrated and fantastic presentation. And it goes without saying that racial images were hardly invitations for real people to appear; rather they were spectacles, common sense in inspiration if fantastic, exotic, and comedic in effect. Indeed, parade makers often didn't bother to distinguish between the various racial stereotypes they deployed, assembling a range of images into a generic exotic. In 1930, Winnipeg's parade provided an almost complete tour through the stable of exotic images from near and far: camels from

Ten Little Indians, Edmonton, 1950.
City of Edmonton Archives, EA-600-6232c.

Egypt, elephants from India, Chinese and Japanese figures with huge lanterns, Eskimos with igloos, and "Red Indians of the prairies." Three years later in Toronto, the exotic spanned the globe in a bizarre pastiche of inaccurate geography. Floats represented each of the four winds: the Kingdom of the North Wind (penguins, an airship, Eskimos), the South Wind (sunflower girls, sombrero-topped Mexicans, a huge butterfly), the East Wind (Zulus, elephants, bears, lions, monkeys), and the West Wind (cowboys, Indians, totem poles).[34] Such presentations powerfully articulated the Occidental geographic imagination and the Canadian racial gaze, where difference provided exotic, comedic, and fantastic images for mainstream amusement.[35]

All of it, of course, built up to Santa, who fused all of the elements of the parade vocabulary – character, colour, costume, size, and sound – into a single presentation. "The parade as a whole must be thought of as a production in which each section builds to a grand climax – in this case, Santa Claus waving and booming out 'Hel-lo my dears' to the children that line the route," noted Toronto parade organizer Jack Brockie.[36] Santa's float changed in the early years – from a simple wagon, to an enormous arctic fish, to a "great Indian canoe" pulled by silver dolphins, before settling onto a more traditional sleigh skimming across rooftops – but every year, its design, size, and effect attracted considerable attention. "Right down through two aisles of what looked like millions of kids came a big affair on wheels," a typical report noted in 1933. "It must have been 50 or 60 feet long. And up there on top was the King of Christmas. His Royal Merriness Santa Claus, with his sleigh and all his toys." Two years later, Calgary's Santa float had him "riding high on top of the roof of a gaily-painted house over which the reindeer … pranced and beside him was a pack bulging with toys."[37] Reporters also delighted in detailing Santa's own appearance, especially his body, size, and colour. In 1925, he was as "large as life and 'shaking all over like a bowl full of jelly'"; the following year, he wore a "crimson velvet tunic that matched his frost-touched cheeks … his matchless snowy-hair and flowing beard serving as a silver frame for the benign kindly face beloved by thousands." Other reporters were attracted to his magic voice: "as it rolls and booms, the voice of this Santa soothes and excites. Try that sometime; try soothing and exciting at the same time." In the final moment of the parade, Santa arrived at Eaton's and ascended a ladder into the store.[38] Wherever and however he arrived, Santa's centrality in the fantasy and magic of the parade was crystal clear. "Because the Santa Claus that our children saw on

Santa Claus, Toronto, 1930.
City of Toronto Archives, Fonds 1266, Globe and Mail Collection, item 22538.

Saturday morning was not the personification of a myth," declared one *La Presse* reporter in 1947. "It was the realization of their most cherished dreams."[39]

"Too much for little heads to remember"

None of this was unique or particularly surprising. Journalists often pointed to the unique longevity of the Eaton's parade, but such historic boosterism seems less relevant than the way the procession fit into an emerging, continent-wide culture of commercial expression. Indeed, as the parade took modern form in the decades after the First World War, several other department stores began to mount their own annual

Christmas pageants. In 1920, J.L. Hudson's of Detroit set up its own parade. Macy's of New York and Wannamaker's of Philadelphia followed in 1924, with Bamberger's of New Jersey and many others initiating their own spectacles in subsequent years. Department stores in smaller cities followed suit: Sibley's in Rochester, Spencer's in Vancouver, Robinson's in Hamilton, Wurzburg's in Grand Rapids, and many others across North America. These Christmas pageants – which, south of the border, gravitated towards the American Thanksgiving weekend – were institutionally and aesthetically similar, organized by department stores that deployed the same basic characters and styles.[40] "First there was music, music heard only when Santa is at hand, then there came clowns and a host of fairyland characters," the *Hamilton Spectator* reported after the Robinson's parade in 1950, which included Rudolph, Cinderella, Noah's Ark, Mother Goose, Prince Charming, and a Monkey Band.[41] Three decades before, the first Hudson's parade had featured seven bands, ten storybook floats including Mother Goose, and several marchers with oversized papier mâché heads. Macy's first parade adopted a similar strategy, with children's characters, floats of Robinson Crusoe and Little Red Riding Hood, and various costumed and whimsical marchers. In 1927, the company introduced oversized animal balloons, measuring more than two storeys tall, an element that soon became emblematic of the Macy's pageant; at the time, however, the balloons simply represented a particular take on the spectacle of size common to all the department store parades.[42]

Two factors – one broad and cultural, the other more precise and institutional – explain the similarity of department store Christmas parades. It was partly the result of everyone dipping into the same set of cultural influences, creating a spectacle by blending a variety of aesthetic trends and reworking familiar forms of performance and display. In many ways, department stores borrowed from the circus, one of the most popular forms of public entertainment in this period. Large railway circuses like Barnum and Bailey's and Ringling Brothers traversed North America, while several smaller operations plied regional and local markets. On occasion, Eaton's made this influence explicit, promising "a whole circus of animals and clowns and bands and wagons" in Toronto while "carrying out a circus theme" in Winnipeg, where "many of the floats were animal cages, in which were curious 'critters' which delighted children with their funny antics."[43] But the similarity would have been obvious without such explicit references. Department store parades and circuses shared boisterous, colourful, and exotic performances, built around animal menageries and whimsical storylines. Indeed, virtually any newspaper report of a circus could have been covering a Santa Claus parade: "First came the elephants – a dozen of them, big and little," the *Globe* enthused about one circus in 1923,

> and the camels, with two humps, just like the story-book, only they didn't 'hump' themselves away. They just stayed and watched the long line of queer people that filed through the tent. The Zulus, with their tin cans, came first, and then the Zouaves, with their funny-coloured pantaloons, and a whole host of others. There were a lot of pretty Arab ladies on prancing white horses, and they had African slaves, and then there were a lot of Egyptian girls on black horses and a lady who sang, sitting on the biggest elephant of all, with ostrich feathers like a big canopy.[44]

Circuses, moreover, normally announced their arrival in a city with a grand street parade: "All of the animal cages are open, and the ponderous elephants and clumsy camels, the four bands with their continual fanfare, the scores of funning clowns, the Wild West contingent, the piercing shrieks of the two calliopes – all these lend animation to the briskly moving procession."[45] This practice was in decline by the 1920s, at just the moment the corporate fantastic was on the rise. Yet to an even greater extent than the larger circus operations, busy stripping away the disreputable elements by the turn of the century, Eaton's and other department stores took the style in sophisticated and artistic directions, turning this form of popular theatre towards more respectable and stable commercial ends. Eaton's parade contained no whiff of danger, no disreputable carny folk, no travelling companies – just the performance of an iconic local department store.[46]

   Christmas pageants also resonated with the visual style of amusement parks and midways, where fairgoers confronted a boisterous atmosphere, frenetic motion, colourful design, and the distortion of scale. Places like Luna Park at Coney Island in New York set the international standard and became widely copied across North America. In Toronto, three large amusement parks operated at various points in the first quarter of the twentieth century: at Hanlan's Point from the 1880s, Scarborough Beach after 1907, and Sunnyside Beach after 1922; in Manitoba, Winnipeg Beach became a popular midway destination for urban residents. Not only did the invention of department store Christmas parades coincide with an upsurge in amusement park development across North America, but some parks had turned to parade-like pageants to attract attention, the most famous version (again) at Coney Island, where after 1903 the annual Mardi Gras carnival included a raucous procession with colourful floats and oversized costumes.[47]

Department stores also created their spectacles by adapting contemporary styles of commercial display. Strategies of presentation in the parade – colour, motion, scale, juxtaposition, and abundance – merely extended standard Victorian and Edwardian methods of presenting commodities. These strategies were familiar to North Americans from industrial and commercial exhibitions, advertising, merchants' windows, and department stores themselves. Across North America, department store windows were the cutting edge of display, hosting elaborate presentations that became small but powerful forms of commercial theatre. Each year, urban residents eagerly anticipated Christmas windows in particular, with their miniature trains and ferris wheels, elaborate town scenes, and portrayals of Santa's workshop. In Toronto, Eaton's and cross-street rival Simpson's were the key agents in bringing this new commercial aesthetic to local consumers, undertaking an annual rivalry that pushed the windows to new heights of appeal. By the 1920s, across North America, these basic strategies were being professionalized and regularized into the dominant display aesthetic of the period, with specialists often taking the lead in designing or overseeing Christmas pageants. At Macy's, for example, pioneering commercial artist and puppeteer Tony Sarg designed the first oversized animal balloons. At Eaton's, "Curly" Apted, the company's first display manager, helped organize the early processions and, for more than three decades after 1927, Jack Brockie, who was display manager for the Toronto store, served as the parade producer.[48] Being responsible for the presentation of merchandise, display managers were obviously attuned to visual spectacle and to emerging forms of commercial art. "It would be difficult to underestimate how great an influence colour has on our emotions … whether we are aware of the fact or not," one internal discussion of Eaton's display strategies stated.[49] They were, in other words, perfectly positioned to create fantastic and colourful parades by drawing on many forms of popular and consumer culture.

If the style of the parades synthesized several international trends in display and performance, their fantastic and storybook vocabularies drew on shifting trends both in Christmas and in amusement. Santa Claus and Mother Goose shared in a process of Victorian reinvention, so twentieth-century department stores inherited a series of tame but miraculous icons ripe for systematic commercialization. From the early nineteenth century, when images of Santa were heterogeneous, author-itarian, and not entirely respectable, St Nick was tamed by the triple Victorian processes of standardization, domestification, and commer-cialization. Illustrators steered Santa's early visual variety into more standard and familiar modern symbols – chubby, white beard, and red coat – with Thomas Nast most famously capturing this trend with a series of woodcuts for *Harper's Weekly* in the early 1880s. Meanwhile, poems like Clement Clark Moore's "A Visit from Saint Nicholas" pre-sented Santa as a jolly figure, distributing good cheer to North American families, essentially stripping him of his authoritarian streak while re-taining his miraculous meanings. Santalore still promised no presents for the naughty, but it was more and more an empty threat, as Santa became a chance for parents to shower all their children with gifts.[50]

The result was an ambivalent figure. Critics often contrast Santa and Christ as symbols of the contest between commerce and religion at Christmas, but Santa himself, although not fully Christian, was not fully secular either. Penny Restad notes that the Victorian Santa acted as a "medium through which children and adults … acted upon spiri-tual principles … Santa issued from the realm of dreams, hopes, wishes and beliefs, not from the realities and compromises necessary to nego-tiate contemporary life."[51] This synthesis was never perfect. As much as Christian spirituality and Christmas magic shared romantic, anti-rational, and otherworldly impulses – both, at base, were premised on belief in what could not be seen – the compatibility of religion and the corporate fantastic can easily be overdone. After all, Santa's reinvention for mass festivity was partly premised on his desanctification: there is nothing explicitly religious about "The Night before Christmas," for example, despite Moore's own intensely Christian background, while Nast's famous images dispensed with any reference to Santa Claus's saintly past (he wore no robes, crosses, or other Christian symbols). Not surprisingly, Santa Claus did attract some religious critique, as in the denunciation of the vulgar materialism of Eaton's Montreal parade by the nationalist Association Catholique de la Jeunesse Canadienne-Française in 1934 or the Catholic Bishop of Calgary's lament, in 1949, that Santa Claus "was [so] blatantly over-emphasized that we could change the name from Christmas to Clausmas." Many more Christians probably just suffered in silence, avoiding rather than actively critiqu-ing the parade. Still, many of the most public religious laments came down to balance rather than outright rejection. "Where Santa remains as a spirit of kindness and charity, it is altogether desirable," Frank

Morley of the Grace Presbyterian Church in Calgary argued. "I believe there is more goodwill, more genuine friendship and cheerfulness at Christmastime than at any other time of the year, and in all this benevolence Santa Claus plays a part ... I'd hate to lose the old fellow."[52]

Eaton's planners appear to have dealt with these tensions by avoiding them. In every city and across the decades, the parades were consistently non-religious, apparently by design. In Toronto, Jack Brockie remained steadfastly opposed to addressing the religious basis of the holiday in the parade, despite intermittent public pressure and the company's well-known reverence for its founder's Victorian Methodism. In a typical letter, Mrs William Kingley wrote that the spectacle was wonderful but might recognize "the true meaning of Christmas" by featuring a float of "the babe in the manger, the shepherds, and the star." Eaton's officials always answered such letters politely, but normally pointed correspondents to the company's Nativity Window on Yonge Street.[53] On rare occasions, biblical symbols appeared in the parades, but they were normally recast to highlight colour, character, and even comedy. In 1920, a monkey sat on Noah's Ark "contentedly smoking a pipe," while four decades later a float of the same biblical story presented "a fully stocked menagerie" with Noah in a blue sailor suit being towed by "two frisky blue whales."[54] Neither was likely to please a devout Christian.

Santa's meanings remained rich and multilevelled. Jean Phillipe Warren argues in his study of Christmas in Quebec that as Santa rose to Christmas hegemony, he served not as a one-dimensional commercial icon but as a "total social phenomenon" that fused many symbolic meanings: fantastic, spiritual, magical, and material.[55] Paradoxically, as Warren and other scholars point out, Santa's non-commercial character made him an even more attractive promotional device. As a tame but fantastic figure, he was a perfect fit for marketers anxious to spin carnival meanings around their products.[56] Merchants even experimented with live Santas in their stores – Eaton's in 1903, only two years before sending him on his first trip through Toronto's streets. By 1910, the company had fully embraced the modern approach to Christmas displays, making Toyland into an elaborate and sumptuous "Place of Delight for Young and Old."[57] "That the good news be spread everywhere," announced one Eaton's ad in 1927, "that it be thrown to the wind so that all learn of it and come, Saturday, to the Toy City, the enchanted city, the fairy tale city, the biggest, most beautiful, most brilliant, most gay that ever existed. Oh! The toys ... Come listen to the burst of laughter and the cries of joy from a merry little world."[58]

In the Eaton's parades, as in the stores themselves, Santa Claus suggested abundance. His sleigh was huge, his body ample, his clothing colourful, his laugh hearty. His float was packed with stuff. In 1929, Calgarians could see that Santa had a big bag of toys "and those who remembered the bag last year claim it is much larger this year and think this is a good sign." "On the floor of his sleigh was a large red bag with dolls, trains, automobiles, skates, wagons, and many other toys bulging out of its immense mouth," the *Toronto Daily Star* echoed in 1931.[59] But the idea went beyond the specific displays: in its entirety, the parade flaunted abundance and brought to life an ideology of "more." Each year, it seemed, Eaton's made a spectacle that was bigger than the last. From a handful of presentations in the early years, the Toronto parade quickly grew to a mile in length, stretched across a six-mile route, taking at least forty-five minutes to pass a single point by the 1940s. The company bragged about it too, promising "Oodles of Scrumptious Christmassy things" in 1924 and "More Bands, More Fairies, More Story Book Friends, More Clowns, More Funnies" a quarter-century later. Even journalists got into the spirit of plenty, carefully enumerating the vast quantities of material required to mount the procession: "In the creation of today's extravaganza the producers used up such materials as 1500 pounds of plaster of paris, 2000 yards of fabrics, toy mountains of hooks, braid, about half a parade length of zippers and enough jingle bells to buckle a belfry."[60]

Indeed, the parades communicated abundance so effectively that they became convenient touchstones for counternarratives of poverty amid plenty. The *Toronto Daily Star*'s Santa Claus Fund, founded by newspaper baron Joseph Atkinson in 1892 to help poor Torontonians buy presents, frequently depicted families in the crowd getting their only look at Santa Claus that year. "We'd better get a good look at him now, because maw says he isn't coming to our house Christmas," an imaginary youngster said from the curb of University Avenue in one charitable pitch, only one of hundreds of poor kids who "sat in thread-worn overcoats, feet cold with lack of proper footwear, watching Santa Claus with fear in their heart that this was the last they would see of him." Seven years later, a similar charitable appeal told the story of a "thin, shabbily dressed" mother who dreaded bringing her "pale youngster" to watch the parade, fearing that "the scene … would arouse in him hopes and desires which could not be fulfilled Christmas day." As Santa passed, the child asked, "Will Santa come to our house this year?" The mother had no answer. This holiday discourse of poverty amid

WILL THIS BE THEIR LAST GLIMPSE OF SANTA CLAUS?

Will to-day be their only hope of a glimpse of Santa, as he rides majestically down the streets in parade? Will he never again go by? Will he return to their house on Christmas eve? Ten thousand— yes, twenty thousand, children are asking this question. Anxious hearts are beating fast as the days grow shorter and shorter and THE DAY draws nearer and nearer. The only hope that Santa Claus will come to thousands' of poor homes this Christmas is in The Star Santa Claus Fund. The only way tha fund can send out sufficient boxe to meet the need is for citizens t send money to 80 King St. W. fo that purpose. So that Santa Clau WILL return to the homes of th needy, will you not send a donatio. . . . to-day?

Poor children gaze at Santa, 1934.
Toronto Daily Star, 17 November 1934, 21.

plenty could also have political import. In 1941, at a meeting organized by the wives of soldiers in active service during the Second World War, Toronto councillor Fred Hamilton registered two complaints: that soldiers' wives were unable to clothe their children decently when they sent them to school and that they lacked the means to take their kids to the Santa Claus parade. Both claims spoke of socially defined and politically charged standards of living and decency. The meeting called on the federal government to institute a cost-of-living bonus for the dependents of service men.[61]

Even if charities expressed the contrast of abundance and poverty philanthropically and councillor Hamilton did so politically, everyone understood that the Eaton's parades were powerful forms of commercial speech that went to the heart of familial relationships. As such, they were not startlingly new. After all, the success of the Victorian reinvention of Christmas was partly based on the way it fused commercialism and domesticity. By the turn of the century, and even more after 1920, department stores, copywriters, and mass market manufacturers merely extended this notion by exploiting the advertising potential of children, aiming for images of wondrous innocence on the one hand and amplifying their pluck, desire and sass on the other – what historian Gary Cross calls "the cute and the cool."[62] In both visual and narrative terms, the Eaton's parade vocabulary aimed primarily at the cute: "To a child, anything that is out of proportion is funny," noted Brockie. "But we deliberately avoid anything grotesque or horrifying … We want to evoke the child's sense of wonderment, not to frighten him."[63] This carnival balance was based on experience as much as expertise. Company lore suggested that in early parades Eaton's employees had tried to frighten children along the route and that fairy-tale wonder, up to the 1920s at least, coexisted with a more morbid and grotesque sensibility. One early Winnipeg ad stated rather plainly that Santa would be drawn by a horse because his reindeer had drowned during his trip from the North Pole. In Toronto in the mid-1920s, the company's interpretation of Jack and the Beanstalk – which featured a dead and prone giant – was perhaps a bit too violently literal for a parade aiming at innocence and wonder.[64] Of course, fairy tales were originally quite violent and decidedly uncute, so whether a dead giant actually scared children is not clear, but the company worked hard in future years to keep the grotesque under control. "A papier-mâché horse might be scary," argued Brockie in 1953. "But if we put a rider on him, the kids know everything is under control. An alligator is fun, but one year we had one with jaws going up and down and it didn't go over well at all. We'll use it again, with his mouth closed and new look in his eye."[65]

In this sense, Eaton's reinforced and confirmed broader developments in childhood wonder. While fairy tales had originally been for adults, they were reshaped in the Victorian era by domesticity and commercialism, the same forces that had redirected Santa Claus to the parental aspirations of the emerging Euro-American middle classes. By the twentieth century, many commercial institutions were drawing on and extending this process of cultural selection, stripping the stories of their ambiguities and complexities and refashioning them into one-dimensional tales of fantasy and wonder. Walt Disney became the most powerful agent of this transformation, translating fairy tales into movies that were simple in story but rich in visual appeal.[66] This aspect of storybook characters was exactly what interested department stores like Eaton's. Christmas pageants bypassed the fairy-tale genre's rich history in favour of evoking its sense of familiarity, fantasy, and image. One issue was simply practical: in aggregate, the parades were long, but each individual presentation moved by quickly and needed to communicate its message succinctly, placing a premium on familiarity and visual impact. Yet even as it met this practical issue, Eaton's also engaged in a broader process of cultural selection and invention. Although based on storybook characters, the floats did very little storytelling. Eaton's used sounds and images to evoke a richer backstory, but (like Disney) privileged colour, sound, and dramatic effect over moral context and literary meaning. In the simplest sense, where once there had been words and story, there were now sound and image. "There was almost too much for little heads to remember," Jack Karr wrote in 1954, "so that it blended into a kaleidoscope of gay colours and bouncing music."[67]

The parade script reinforced these aural and visual tendencies. The company was often cavalier with stories, creating generic storybook worlds by jamming together different characters on the same float, juxtaposing traditional fairy-tale characters with new mass culture icons, and even reframing characters to give them different meanings from year to year. Just as organizers built biblical stories into floats of whimsy and colour, fairy tales could be reframed to serve the thematic and commercial needs of the moment. In 1954, with its corporate eye focused on the untapped consumption of Toronto's growing immigrant population, Eaton's adopted "internationalism" as its overarching theme and recast characters into national and ethnic categories:

Heidi represented Switzerland, Pinocchio Italy, Prince Valiant England, and so on. "Perhaps the whole thing will remind our New Canadians of the carnivals in which they've taken part in their homelands," Jack Brockie surmised.[68] The reframing of storybook characters was not always so cynical, but the effect could be similar. Eaton's presented a "mile of make believe" based on image, colour, fantasy, and wonder rather than story and meaning.[69]

In its total effect, this mile of make-believe was broadly consumerist but not explicitly commercial. Eaton's articulated the underlying impulses of consumer society – excitement over deliberation, desire over discipline, sensation over contemplation, emotion over rationality[70] – but usually left the relationship to actual buying implicit and indirect. To be sure, the company promoted the spectacle heavily with elaborate full-page ads, lengthy press releases, special colouring books featuring each float, and (most obviously) the route of the procession, which after 1917 led spectators to the various Eaton's stores.[71] Still, initially, the company brand was not deeply inscribed into the spectacle itself. Indeed, the word "Eaton's" barely appeared before the 1950s, generally only a simple sign ("To Eaton's Toyland") near the front. Nor did the parade explicitly implore consumers to buy, and even when it dipped into new forms of mass culture, the company preferred characters, like Yogi Bear and Mickey Mouse, who updated the "traditional" storybook theme. Indeed, even the specific commercial benefits of gathering a large crowd often seemed dubious to Eaton's officials. Organizers did not seem anxious to have crowds follow Santa into the stores, for example, so in many years, Toyland didn't actually open to visitors until the following Monday. In Toronto, the company discovered at a 1945 meeting of its Mothers Council that most members left Christmas shopping until December, which they claimed was more fun because of the larger crowds and more elaborate decorations.[72] The Santa Claus parade was a spectacle of capitalist non-realism, then, tied to the underlying emotional impulses of a commercial order but eschewing many obvious and explicit forms of promotion.

But if the specific effect was not commercial, the parade remained profoundly and deeply corporate. Eaton's was well aware of – and explicitly exploited – the public relations benefit of the event. In every city but Toronto, parade traditions were initiated as soon as the local outlet opened: in Winnipeg in 1905, Montreal in 1925, and Edmonton and Calgary in 1929. Throughout its history, moreover, the spectacle

Ad for Santa Claus parade, Winnipeg, 1934.
Winnipeg Free Press, 16 November 1934, 24.

remained one key pillar of the company's image building, something that made Eaton's more than a corporation, more than a profit-making enterprise. "Eaton's is part of the Canadian outlook," one souvenir company history announced. "Children learn the name when they see their first Santa Claus parade, remember it through their lives as a symbol of Canadian enterprise, a reflection of the Canadian way of living."[73] But the corporate character of the parade had an even deeper institutional and organizational meaning as well. The Santa Claus parades were, quite literally, the property of the company, organized from front to back by employees who inhabited a national corporate structure and who, through their professional activities, built links with similar experts in other big metropolitan centres.

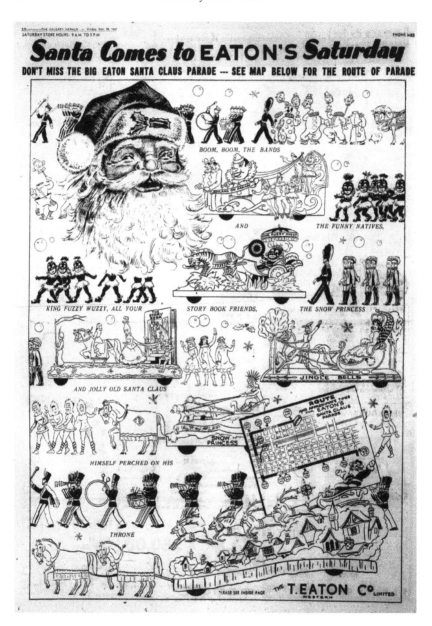

Ad for Santa Claus parade, Calgary, 1947.
Calgary Herald, 26 November 1947, 28.

"Paraders with spectacles – taboo"

The Eaton's parades were singular and company-controlled. In all the cities, the parade was under the primary jurisdiction of the local display department, which undertook a meticulous and highly organized production process. "The annual parade," the *Winnipeg Free Press* noted in 1933, "is the result of months of work and planning. It may be likened to an ambitious stage production, requiring scores of unusual costumes [and] unheard of scenic effects. It presents problems in design, draftsmanship, costuming, acting, carpentry, and outwitting the weather … Shortly after each year's parade, a meeting is held to discuss plans for the next year … Ideas are submitted, discussed, finally rejected or approved after weeks of consideration. Then sketches of the various floats and characters are drawn … and handed to a small army of carpenters, painters and others, who work out the details."[74] Similarly, in Toronto, Jack Brockie and his staff produced the parade from front to back in their corner of a company warehouse north of the city, and notwithstanding periodic intracorporate negotiations about budgets and an intuitive awareness of consumer reaction, they were left alone to fashion the parade.[75] In a year-long process, entries were sketched and modelled, colours were coordinated, detailed press kits prepared, and Santa's salutations scripted. No detail was overlooked: one year, Brockie's parade post-mortem simply noted, "paraders with spectacles – taboo." The company's design vision even extended to the background. At one meeting in the early 1940s, parade staff pledged "to eliminate the presence of so many drab, gray outfits from the reception stand … movie operators, etc. should wear red blazers or windbreakers – anything that would pep up the appearance."[76]

Corporate organization shaped the nature and character of participation. The public was invited to appear, but always on the company's terms. In Toronto, the company's Junior Council and Junior Executives, with representatives in many schools across the city, became one key way to recruit children for the parade. Council members were instructed to look for marchers of a certain age and size. The company also received many direct applications, but even those refused were sent a free ticket to the company's annual Lunch with Santa.[77] Participants, once enlisted, served assigned roles. Marching order did not represent any broad social principle beyond the aesthetic agenda of the parade designers: "It is an extremely difficult job to keep the Parade picture so plotted that a pleasing flow of colour results, and a clash of opposing colours does not meet the eye," noted Brockie.[78] Children were categorized by objective not subjective criteria, by size and shape rather than personality, enthusiasm, or theatrical flair. "On acceptance, each student is indexed according to height, weight, and other statistics to facilitate the fitting of costumes … the cards are sorted and the applicants assigned to each of the sections. Duplicate copies are sent to the costume room where they are then matched with corresponding costume size and held in readiness for parade day." On parade day, participants moved through a chaotic but efficient assembly line from parental handoff to costumed character. In churches near the parade route, students arrived at 7 a.m., changed into costumes and checked clothes (which the company transported to the end of parade), passed through make up-department, and got assigned papier-mâché heads, all before being loaded onto floats a few minutes before the start. Once the parade disbanded at Eaton's store, marchers picked up their clothes and paused for free coffee and hot chocolate.[79]

This process reflected the visible hand of managers with considerable experience coordinating large groups and complex multi-staged projects, but it left little time or space for public dialogue. At the time Eaton's mounted its first Christmas procession, most large-scale public events (even ones organized by elites) took in a wide range of social groups and required some sort of negotiation and accommodation to different interests and agendas. H.V. Nelles's history of the Tercentenary of Quebec City (1908) describes the way imperialists, nationalists, the clergy, business, and others tried to assert their own plans, but no single group succeeded in controlling the events. Similarly, Robert Cupido notes that while nationalist elites tried to impose their sense of order and meaning on Canada's Diamond Jubilee in 1927, the actual performances left room for ethnic groups and civic organizations to insert their own ideas at the local level. Both of these events were larger and better organized than most annual marches, which relied heavily on volunteer labour, placing an even larger premium on organizational openness and community involvement. Even ostensibly simple matters, like marching order or manner of dress, were often subject to intense negotiation and conflict, not only because such matters were endowed with social significance (the order of march, for example, might signal relative importance), but because the relatively open organizational politics allowed, even required, balancing multiple agendas. These behind-the-scenes questions were not just incidental or institutional, since the organizational politics of a parade determines its syntax and influences its overall meaning.[80]

To be sure, Eaton's meticulous organization did not always work out. Children were cute, but often unpredictable. Even before the parade began, they showed up with the wrong clothes, without mittens, at the wrong place, or (worse) wearing their glasses. On floats, children would be placed precisely for maximum effect only to shift position out of a desire to be seen, while others facetiously thumbed their noses at the crowd and a few simply fell asleep.[81] Adults were only slightly easier to control. Despite being shown movies of previous parades, some performers refused to stay where they were supposed to be – leaving formation to shake hands with spectators was particularly popular – so timing and spacing were a chronic problem.[82] Few entries were more frustrating than bands, however, which moved at their own pace, played regimental music rather than Christmas carols, or simply stopped playing altogether.[83] As a result, Eaton's Santa Claus parade became a massive and precise disciplinary project. School teachers were recruited as parade marshals and provided pages of detailed instructions. By the 1950s, the company appointed two designated "greeters" for each section and reminded marchers to *Leave the shaking of hands to them.* Children were sometimes strapped down into seats on floats and Santa was given scripted "salutations to be spoken during the parade."[84] Even these efforts failed on occasion: marshals, for example, drew frequent complaints, as some seemed out of touch and unsure of their responsibilities, while others became too "officious" and insisted on yelling at the children. These disciplinary dynamics probably reflected an inevitable clash between the non-professional performers and the precision of the parade makers' design. But if complaints about misbehaving children, confused marshals, and uncooperative bands filled Brockie's post-mortem notes, these were disciplinary failures not invitations to the public to discuss or create.[85]

Meticulous organization and fantastic style reflected the professional equipment of the company's display, merchandising, and advertising departments. In Toronto, Brockie, who took over the job in 1928 and served at its head for more than three decades, was merchandise display manager for the Toronto store, responsible for the design of price tags, special exhibits, fashion shows, the Christmas Toyland, and street-level window displays. Unlike many parade designers in the United States, however, he was not a professional artist, although he became a member of the American Graphic Arts Society through his work at Eaton's and, at various points in his life, he was involved with amateur theatre in Toronto. Indeed, Brockie had a traditional background. He joined the company as a teenager in 1914 after graduating from business school, eventually landing a permanent job supervising the correspondence and secretarial staff. Hoping to build esprit de corps, he mounted a series of successful plays and revues for Eaton's employees. This "flair" earned him a transfer to Merchandise Display, where he soon found himself at the helm of the Santa Claus parade. Brockie's skills, then, were perfectly suited to the corporatization of wonder. Combining business training, organizational proficiency, and a natural (rather than formally taught) artistic sensibility, he was the man in the grey flannel suit with an eye for colour.[86]

Over time, the parades relied on permanent staffs of professional artists, sculptors, designers, and tradesmen. In the early days, Toronto's parade was built in a hectic three months before parade day, but by the 1950s a full-time staff of ten year-round carpenters and artists took charge, supplemented by summer students from the local art college and, on parade day itself, massive numbers of paid staff and volunteers (at least forty dressers and twenty make-up artists, largely women, staffed separate boys and girls dressing rooms). In Edmonton and Calgary, it appears, the process relied more heavily on assigning staff to the parade for a few months leading up to it.[87] Throughout this process, key staff did long service. Reginald Collins oversaw construction in Toronto from 1915 to 1950. He joined the company as artist-decorator in 1913, having studied art and apprenticed as a decorator in Scotland before doing mural work on private contract for a year in Canada. His first job with Eaton's was doing fine decorative painting at private houses and businesses, but he was soon assigned to fix up the four small floats that made up the Santa Claus parade at the time. He was less than impressed by the art involved – Mother Goose, he remembered, was "made of wallpaper and had a stick for a neck" – but by 1915, Collins was overseeing the parade's construction. He remained in the job until 1950, when Jim Carmichael took over and stayed for twenty years. Costume designer Margaret Morrison started in 1932 and continued for more than four decades. Continuity reigned: even when Brockie relinquished his duties in 1963, his replacement, Jack Clarke, who had been connected with the parade since the early 1940s, took over the Santa Claus duties as part of his new job as Toronto area display manager.[88]

Corporate structure, staff continuity, and shared display aesthetics gave to the parades stability over time and continuity across space. Certainly, changes did occur, but mainly in emphasis rather than underlying approach. New characters were developed, new materials adopted, and slight philosophy changes introduced. Under Clarke's leadership, for example, UFOs, astronauts, and even "psychedelic colours" like "chartreuse, cerise, electric blue and shocking pink" entered the Toronto parade, exactly the kind of features Brockie had explicitly rejected on several occasions. "When space ships and superman come in, I get out," Brockie told *Canadian Business* magazine in 1955.[89] Similarly, some aspects of the racial exotic (particularly blackface) had disappeared by the 1970s. Nonetheless, the basic aesthetic foundation of the corporate fantastic remained largely the same over time: fantasy, wonder, colour, and child-centred good cheer. Continuity across time was mirrored by similarity across space. The whole promotional structure of the various parades ran in parallel, using radio broadcasts in advance, advertisements, and other promotional schemes. Even the timing of the parades was similar, with all the outlets mounting them in mid- to late November (Toronto, Winnipeg, and Edmonton generally on the third Saturday and Calgary and Montreal on the following weekend), a schedule set for the most part by the Christmas shopping season rather than by a more logical criterion like the local weather. Channelling the parade idea through local display departments meant that each spectacle flowed from a similar set of narrative, aesthetic, and promotional influences.

This shared approach was reinforced by Eaton's national corporate structure. Avenues of communication between branch stores were many and deep. Eaton's display personnel corresponded and met frequently, comparing notes on a wide variety of programs and ideas – from Toyland and window designs to mannequins and price tags – and even coordinated action where appropriate. Christmas plans always figured prominently in such conversations. "For the benefit of the Eaton Stores and Branches which are inaugurating a Santa Claus Parade," noted the minutes of one meeting, "many points in regard to construction costs, length of Parade, and feature floats were discussed." At another discussion, Toronto announced that it would distribute its parade strip – the basic visual outline of the spectacle and the reference point for all the artists and workers assembling the floats and costumes – to other branch stores, "in order that ideas may be pooled." In the 1940s and 1950s, Brockie corresponded frequently with his Montreal counterpart, Emile Lemieux, laying out parade plans and exchanging pleasantries like genial corporate acquaintances. "Had a little mishap, sprained my left ankle, reminds me of Ross Jenkins, Winnipeg," Lemieux wrote to Brockie in 1944. "The joke is really on me after all the fun I made at his expense in Winny."[90] In mounting local parades, the various branches also engaged in direct exchange of material and personnel. Montreal literally built its parade from the raw material of the Toronto production: beginning in 1925, floats were loaded onto flat cars and shipped to Montreal for use the following week, replacing the earlier practice, which saw the Toronto floats burned on the local CPR tracks after the parade.[91] Some material was also exchanged between Toronto and Winnipeg, particularly oversized papier-mâché heads, and Brockie borrowed Winnipeg's Ducky Dandy costume at one point, though Toronto–Winnipeg exchanges seem to have been less common than those between Montreal and Toronto.[92] Regardless, all the local organizers incorporated many new promotional ideas emerging from the Toronto head office, like Punkinhead and the parade colouring book. Another vector of intracorporate influence was staff transfer. L. Scott Brewster, for example, joined Eaton's Winnipeg Display department in 1928 after training as an artist at the Toronto Technical School, the Winnipeg Art School, and the Banff School of Fine Arts. Seven years later, he moved to the Edmonton store as head of the Display Department before returning to Winnipeg (again as head of display) in 1947. Throughout his Eaton's career, Brewster lent his "excellent understanding of the art of stagecraft" to the Santa Claus parades in both cities.[93]

All of this stopped well short of complete central organization and uniformity. Indeed, the surviving minutes of display and merchandising meetings suggest a hybrid of national consensus and local organization, a sort of corporate federalism that embraced local initiative within loosely defined limits and within a shared sense of priorities. By the 1940s, head office approval was required to mount a parade, but the spectacles themselves were not organized from the centre, an idea that was brought up on occasion but never seriously considered.[94] "There was a decided feeling at the meeting that each Store had its own particular problems in construction and planning," the minutes of one meeting noted, "and that the populace of any one place had to be considered, the Store catering to the type of presentation that would be most favourably received."[95]

These "particular problems" included a range of issues from cultural to practical. In Montreal, linguistic and cultural difference shaped the spectacle in many ways. The basic elements of the parade were shipped from Toronto, and some of the characters would have been unfamiliar to francophone audiences, but the spectacle was hardly a straightforward anglophone import. Promotions were bilingual (both newspaper ads and radio broadcasts) and the parade itself grafted several bicultural elements onto the basic form imported from Toronto, including both the Union Jack and French Tricolour at the front, adding bilingual signage and some locally designed floats, and even shifting the meaning of the Toronto presentation. In 1954, for example, when Toronto organizers recast the standard characters into ethnic categories, Montreal used the floats but without the ethnic spin. Bands and marchers were an especially easy place to insert local content. So, in 1961, Montreal spectators could sing along with the band of the Black Watch or dance along with the majorettes of Les Ambassadrices de Shawinigan. In other years, minor changes like using a different Santa float or having Mother Goose on foot gave the Montreal parade a slightly distinctive look.[96] Montreal officials seemed to view the Toronto parade as a sort of menu from which they could order their favourite items. In 1955, for example, they informed Brockie that they didn't need Cinderella, Mother Goose, Mary Mary Quite Contrary, and Queen of Hearts (though why they rejected those floats in particular is not clear).[97] The total effect, however, was never strikingly different, as Montreal parades continued to be filled with fairy tales, clowns, nursery rhymes, and floats shipped from Toronto. Indeed, when the idea of Montreal organizing its own parade was raised in the 1940s, the idea was explicitly rejected, owing to the extra expense.[98]

The popularity of the Eaton's parade in Montreal clearly spanned the linguistic divide, serving as one example of the way French and English – though geographically separate in many ways – nonetheless found numerous "moments of contact … in stores [and] public places."[99] The spectacle garnered glowing coverage in both French and English newspapers, and press reports also indicated crowds coming from east and west to shout "hello Santa" and "bonjour Père Noel" as the old saint passed. Some of the characters – particularly the British nursery rhymes at the core of the corporate fantastic – would have been unfamiliar to francophone audiences, but by 1925 Québécois consumers were well adapted to the selective use of anglophone consumer institutions. Many francophones shopped at Eaton's and the company's mail order catalogue was widely used in Quebec even before 1928, when it was finally translated into French. It didn't hurt that the parade – like the catalogue – was at least partly a visual medium. Indeed, many cultural differences in parade character and script were no doubt cloaked by the wide appeal of the basic visual ingredients of the corporate fantastic. Dream worlds, Orientalism, the racial exotic, the distortion of scale, and the circus were widely popular across all of western Europe and its settler colonies.[100]

These cultural forms were articulated and reinforced in Quebec's consumer culture by francophone department stores. Dupuis Frères, the most important and innovative of these companies, essentially translated these key elements of consumer carnival for the Quebec market, using exotic and wondrous displays extensively, refracting the language and symbols of international consumerism through the company's patriotic interest in family, faith, and nation.[101] Dupuis Frères even used Christmas promotions like radio broadcasts by Santa, featuring all the typical narrative devices: a journey from the North Pole, meeting "les esquimaux," getting hit by a storm, and delivering news of his pending arrival at the store.[102] In the store itself, moreover, the company put Père Noel in a "Ville des Jouets" in the basement (later renamed the "paradis des enfants" and moved to the fourth floor) with child-friendly features like gnomes, a miniature train, and so on.[103] And, finally, in 1950, Dupuis Frères began to mount its own Christmas procession, picking up the essential features of the corporate fantastic pioneered by companies like Eaton's. That year, Santa arrived at Dupuis Frères in a helicopter, accompanied by "Santa's elves," a style further elaborated over the 1950s. In 1956, Santa landed his helicopter in Parc Lafontaine and paraded to the Dupuis Frères store in classic fantastic style. The presence of Little Red Riding Hood, Cinderella, and Puss 'n' Boots would remind children of their favourite fairy tales, *La Presse* noted, while the "thousands of toys heaped around the legendary figure" would only intensify the excitement.[104]

In this sense, the style and the appeal of the Eaton's Santa Claus parade in Montreal seems quite in line with what Lorraine O'Donnell describes as an "essentially English" company that made efforts to forge connections to francophone consumers, including everything from hiring bilingual employees to undertaking significant advertising in newspapers like *La Patrie* and *La Presse*.[105] Still, as O'Donnell points out, the fact that consumer culture could resonate across linguistic lines should not cloak the broader inequalities at work. Eaton's efforts remained structured by the web of social, economic, and cultural hierarchies embedded in the linguistic divide. Early in the century, Eaton's made it clear to mail order customers that it preferred correspondence in English, and stories abounded of disrespectful and snobby treatment of francophones by Eaton's employees in the Montreal store. Though float signage was translated, many of the images in the ads for the Montreal parade retained English labels, even into the 1940s (an advertising approach quite common for anglophone companies operating in Quebec).[106] Nor was the public impact of Christmas spectacles in Montreal reciprocal. While francophones crossed the spatial divide to shop at Eaton's and to watch the company's parade, francophone spectacles made nary a dent on the anglophone public sphere: the *Gazette*, for example, simply ignored the Dupuis Frères parade, at least until Simpson's complained that its timing conflicted with the Eaton's-defined beginning of the Christmas season.[107] Eaton's bilingualism, then, was a practice of the dominant.

Differences with Toronto shaped parades in other cities as well. While all the parades embraced "playing Indian," for example, organizers in Alberta occasionally invited actual indigenous people to appear. Some parades in Calgary and Edmonton included members of the Tsuu T'ina nation,[108] who travelled from their nearby reserve to escort Santa Claus to the Eaton's stores. In 1930, the presence of these First Nations people became a prominent part of the parade's promotion. Ads claimed that the Tsuu T'ina had offered Santa shelter on the way to the city and had adopted the old saint into the tribe, naming him "Chief White Beard."[109] Of course, actual indigenous people were common performers in mainstream spectacles in the west, so the Tsuu T'ina were probably just considered a logical addition to a popular annual event.[110] Surviving evidence does not make clear the terms of this participation, or the Tsuu T'ina's own views of the matter, but it does seem clear that their presence was treated quite differently than the standard image of exotic difference. The Tsuu T'ina were actors, not background, in the story of Santa's journey south to the parade. The *Edmonton Journal*'s 1946 story certainly constructed them as visual spectacle – noticing the beads, the feathers, and the moccasins – but the report struck a more noble than exotic tone: "Santa Claus shared the spotlight with a band of 50 Indians. Situated midway in the parade, they drew as much interest as any of the parade features. Many of them were on horseback and the men wore colorful costumes comprising feather headdresses, leather coats and breeches and moccasins showing beautiful headwork. The women carried their small children papoose-style on their backs while the older children walked along with them."[111] Moreover, Eaton's own story actually named the Tsuu T'ina leader, Edward One Spot, one of only two people considered noteworthy as real personalities, the other being the Eaton's display manager, who organized the parade.[112] Of

Tsuu T'ina in Calgary parade, 1931.
Glenbow Archives, NA-3992-49.

course, playing Indian and inviting the Tsuu T'ina were both colonial practices – the aim in both cases was essentially theatrical and neither approach sought real understanding – but they were also different registers of representation. Actual indigenous people required a different framing than the standard exotic of the Eaton's parades.

There were other forms of difference between various cities as well. Winnipeg embraced modern and futuristic displays, something that Jack Brockie explicitly rejected in Toronto. A rocket ship float appeared as early as 1934, while postwar elements played on other space age images: Superman imparting "a modern note" in 1949, Marvo the Man from Mars in 1952, and Punkinhead riding on a "moon rocket" in 1954.[113] The promotional schedule of local parades could be slightly different as well. In the 1940s, Toronto used Santa Claus broadcasts to highlight many Christmas promotions, including the parade, and used them right up to Christmas, while Winnipeg's broadcasts were keyed to the parade itself and ended once Santa arrived in town.[114] The Toronto/ Montreal and Winnipeg parades were much larger, and their art more professional and expensive, than their counterparts in Edmonton and Calgary. There were, moreover, a whole series of practical differences that flowed from local context. While it often rained in Toronto in late November, requiring designs and building materials that could stand wet and wind, Winnipeg was usually bitterly cold, placing a premium on costumes that allowed bundling up. Winnipeg paraders even wore special "ice creepers" on their shoes to walk on icy roads.[115]

The dual impulse to standardization and variety played out at a still larger, continental scale. After all, in their backgrounds, inspirations, artistic approaches, and professional networks, Brockie, Brewster, Clarke, and their staffs operated in a North American commercial context. Not only did they borrow ideas from a mass culture that was North American rather than local and national in scope (amusement parks, radio, movies, and later television); they also consciously cribbed from other, similar parades. In 1948, Eaton's developed its Punkinhead character to respond to Montgomery Ward's successful invention of Rudolph the Red-Nosed Reindeer.[116] Even the design of the new bear flowed from the continental networks of commercial art and design. Punkinhead was designed for Eaton's by Charlie Thorson, a Winnipeg native who had worked on the Eaton's catalogue in the 1930s before heading to the United States, where he put in a decade at big studios like Walt Disney and Warner Brothers.[117] For other ideas, both Brockie and Clarke collected images and newspaper clippings of the Rose Bowl parade, Macy's Thanksgiving parade, and similar processions by Bamberger's of New Jersey and Hudson's of Detroit.[118] This continental context fit the broader corporate history of Eaton's. Though widely perceived as a Canadian icon, from the beginning Eaton's was mainly a local expression of broader developments in North American and European retailing. Company founder Timothy Eaton, a hard-working Victorian Methodist who revolutionized the local retail scene, would have fit nicely alongside more famous American department store entrepreneurs, and his successors kept their eyes on international developments. The company operated buying offices in New York, London, and other global commercial centres, and company representatives travelled widely to investigate new retailing ideas (to New York, for example, to investigate the self-service system during the First World War).[119] "It is most essential that members of the staff pay an occasional visit to New York to check up on types of displays in stores," one memo noted in 1944.[120]

In this sense, each Eaton's parade was a particular version of a North American culture of commercial processions. This dynamic offered a new slant on the long-standing continental character of Canadian popular culture. Scholars long ago gave up on imperial analogies to describe the influence of American culture in Canada, turning instead to concepts like "appropriation" and "reinterpretation" to explore the subtleties and nuances in the reception of American products.[121] Christmas parades represented a different pattern. Ideas flowed across the border, but these transnational influences were more a function of metropolitanism than Americanization. Brockie was not just a cultural broker transferring ideas from American metropole to Canadian hinterland, nor was he simply "reinterpreting" or "appropriating" American concepts for local consumption. Instead, Brockie and his staff were active and important participants in a broad network of corporate parade makers in large cities across North America. The flow of ideas was circular and reciprocal. Some American department stores made their debt to Eaton's clear. In the 1920s, Hudson's in Detroit consciously borrowed the parade idea from Eaton's, while Macy's contacted Eaton's for help, though a plan to borrow floats did not work out.[122] Eaton's parade officials even travelled to New York to watch Macy's first parade.[123] Over time, broader, deeper, and more systematic links were formed. Key Eaton's staff often attended American Christmas parades, sought out explanations of the "inside workings" of the events, and wrote reports, while American officials visited Toronto and did the same. Reports included notations on the most interesting floats, hand-drawn sketches of noteworthy presentations, and overall assessments of an event's effect. Friendly notes followed, offering thanks for hospitalities that had been extended by local officials to out-of-town visitors. These yearly travels forged both formal and informal relationships among metropolitan parade makers, a network in which courtesy and borrowing were common and expected.[124] "In general, my approach to the parade for the past several years has been in line with your thinking," one Macy's official wrote to Brockie, "namely that it is a fantasy ... and construction has been based on more use of Dream Puff and Crystal Tear Drops and other imaginative materials which give, as much as possible, the fantasy effect."[125]

The result was similarity not homogenization, as Brockie and his colleagues adapted more than copied international ideas. Indeed, Eaton's officials took an almost disdainful attitude towards many American parades. Reginald Collins depicted Macy's first parade in almost comical terms, with officials yelling at kids to cheer and a hungry elephant stubbornly parking beside a bread truck and refusing to move. Stephen Fernie, one of the Eaton's parade designers in the 1940s, also remembered his visits to the Macy's parade disdainfully, dismissing the New York spectacle as "terrible," with dull blow-up dolls and employee marchers rather than "enthusiastic kids."[126] Moreover, observers often noted, and Brockie often highlighted, the distinctiveness of the Eaton's parade. "Parade planners are determined their Christmas welcome to Santa will never become the chorus-girl, commercial television-slanted circus which some American cities present," the *Globe and Mail* reported in 1959. Macy's and the Santa Claus Lane parade in Los Angeles relied heavily on celebrity participation for promotional punch. In 1950, comedian Jimmy Durante served as grand marshal and Bert Parks as master of ceremonies in New York, while various floats featured other celebrities from TV and film.[127] By contrast, Eaton's parades relied on local children, teachers, and only a few company employees to fill ranks of marchers and characters. Brockie and his staff were hardly hostile to mass culture, but they consciously eschewed the hyper-celebrity, overt commercialism, and rocket-ship futurism of American parades. "They took the idea of the parade from us," one Eaton's official declared in 1951. "But we took our idea from tradition: we kept to happy, dreamlike scenes that have illuminated the childhood of people for more than half a century."[128] Yet such statements tended to exaggerate national differences, since not all American parades were identical. Copying Macy's, Bamberger's initially experimented with large animal balloons, but soon gave up on the idea and returned to oversized papier mâché characters. Several American parades, moreover, did not use celebrities nearly as extensively as Macy's.[129] Each department store parade, then, offered a local interpretation of similar narrative and aesthetic strategies, different versions of the corporate fantastic.

"A bit juvenile"

It is tempting to argue that, as a spectacle with a wondrous surface and an underlying business structure, the corporate fantastic expressed a contradiction between emotion and rationality. "My family think I am a bit juvenile when I start to plan settings for fairies, gnomes and storybook characters," Brockie wrote to a Paris colleague in 1949, "but then as the old saying goes – 'There's more ways than one of earning a living.'"[130] The comedic tension flows from a sense of contradiction between the world of adult employment on the one hand ("earning a living") and childlike wonder (fairies and gnomes) on the other – between reason and emotion, bureaucracy and wonder. Why would a mature man, a department head at an iconic and powerful company, read fairy tales? How could he hold meetings, write memos, form committees, build institutional continuities, and forge links to wider commercial networks, all in the service of childhood fantasy? And how could a parade so full of fairy tales, so full of colour, and so full of Christmas wonder – all to sanction a certain sense of whimsy – be produced by such a company man? Yet the corporate fantastic was more an expression of capitalism than contradiction. As Eaton's built its Christmas spectacle in the middle decades of the twentieth century, the corporate synthesis of art and commerce was widespread, animating consumer culture and Christmas in particular. Santa was no longer the multi-levelled and potentially grotesque pre-Victorian figure; he was genial and generous, dispensing presents and good cheer to North American children. Department stores like Eaton's represented only one slice of this powerful thread of consumer culture, building dream worlds through their stores, their displays, the catalogues, and their spectacles. Of course, actual products needed to be at least partly functional, but this wasn't Santa's, or Brockie's, concern. For Eaton's, the parade was an opportunity not so much to get people to buy particular products as to construct a magic and fantastic spectacle that would excite the desire and wonder that lay at the foundation of the culture of consumption.

Brockie was good at his job. For more than three decades, he organized one of the most popular public events in Toronto – indeed, Canadian – history. Full of childlike wonder, the parade dazzled by embracing colour, distorting size and scale, using sound and motion, showing the unusual, the fantastic, and the exotic, sanctioning a certain sense of whimsy, and, most importantly, juxtaposing all these elements to play on notions of abundance and plenty. In this sense, the parade was not entirely new. If Eaton's pulled together the basic script from well-known children's stories, they built the spectacle on familiar forms of street performance and commercial display. The parade's real novelty lay more in its underlying organizational politics. The corporate fantastic was stunningly singular, the product of meticulous planning by an emerging group of experts in performance and display, who built links with colleagues across Eaton's national structure and with like-minded parade makers in metropolitan centres across North America. These connections never produced homogeneity. Brockie hated rockets, Winnipeg had UFOs; floats that played well in Toronto needed to be adjusted for Montreal; farther afield, Macy's had great blow-up balloons and Los Angeles was filled with celebrities, a feature that Eaton's organizers looked on with disdain. Each local store and company worked its own magic in designing the precise content, but everybody – from Eaton's branch stores to competitors in New York and Boston – operated within the broad aesthetic principles of fantasy and wonder. At its core, the Santa Claus parade was both corporate and fantastic.

2

Santa in Public

"Within the last day or two in this city there occurred the annual Christmas … parade of a well-known mercantile establishment," Toronto judge J.T. Garrow wrote in quashing Becky Buhay's vagrancy conviction in 1929. "Many hundreds of citizens, intent on getting to their places of business were impeded … Could those who take part in such a parade be successfully prosecuted as vagrants, or as loose, idle or disorderly persons? I very much doubt it."[1] Buhay, a well-known Communist, had been arrested in early September while giving a speech at the corner of Queen and Soho in Toronto's west end. The case itself was one of many instances of state harassment of Communist activists, but Garrow's ruling sidestepped Buhay's political views to confront the long-standing tension between speech and obstruction in urban space. The statement was mainly clever rhetoric, since Garrow had many reasons to quash Buhay's conviction. Still, since no one doubted Santa's right to parade down Yonge Street, it represented a striking articulation of the liberal public sphere, a clear assertion that public space should be open, equal, and accessible to all.[2] Facing ongoing police harassment for her political activities, however, Buhay probably had a different sense of Garrow's analogy. Santa Claus was not a single Communist activist but a ubiquitous commercial icon; since the content of Buhay's speech, not the obstruction it caused, was really at issue that day in September, her right of access depended on fighting legal penalty in court, while Eaton's staff simply secured a permit from city officials; Buhay was free to address some two hundred spectators at the corner of Queen and Soho while Eaton's was free to marshal its corporate resources to grab the attention of the entire city. Both Santa and Buhay could appear in public to communicate, but they entered it on quite different terms.

Santa Claus and Becky Buhay suggest another expression of the power of the corporate fantastic, but "public" is a slippery and difficult word. On the one hand, Santa's parade appeared out of doors – literally, in *public*. In the Eaton's stores, Santa sat in Toyland, a relatively accessible but nonetheless private space. A crowd assembled and a long line-up of children, waiting to deliver their Christmas wishes, snaked between the displays, but the store was corporately owned, governed by company priorities, and bounded from the city by walls and doors. Santa's parade, by contrast, followed a shifting route through relatively open downtown streets, theoretically open to Christmas elves and Communist activists alike. By doing so, Santa gathered a large crowd on the sidewalks and caused massive disruptions across the city. In this sense, Santa, during his parade, was in public. On the other hand, by parading through the city, Santa also entered – much more aggressively and prominently than his in-store cousin – a metaphorical public sphere where ideas formed, clashed, and circulated. Santa's purpose was not just to march through space or to literally appear, but to leave an impression, to garner good public relations, to make people think of Eaton's, and to shape the meanings of the season. While this public required real people and material technologies (like newspapers, radios, and televisions) to exist, it was not just a physical space but a realm of ideas where the event was processed and interpreted and its influence noted and assessed.[3] In this sense, to understand the power and influence of the Santa Claus parade is both to examine its physical presence in the city and to wrestle with something we might call the Christmas public. Through Santa, Eaton's joined with other groups in trying to define the meaning of the season.

Yet the public also had its own geography, social codes, and informal practices, all of which shaped the character and reception of the parade. To follow Santa into public, then, requires attention to several issues. It requires, first of all, mapping the shape of the cities that Santa was entering. These were not the compact and dense places that gave birth to North American parade culture in the Victorian era; nor were they, until late into the century, the sprawling metropolitan spaces that we know today. Spreading outward under the influence of several developments, Santa's cities nonetheless retained a festival focus on downtown, a dynamic reinforced by the parade routes themselves. Second, we need to examine the size and character of the crowd that assembled, a crowd that at once accepted the Eaton's agenda and seemed unrestrained, even chaotic, as it crossed social and urban boundaries and followed its own path. Indeed, spectators were much more active than the word "spectator" might suggest, but they were called together by Eaton's promotional machine and, in many ways, were shaped and structured by broader cultural dynamics. Finally, Santa in public requires an understanding of the contested and complicated definitions of the Christmas season itself. Almost everyone agreed that 25 December was Christmas Day, but no one seemed sure when the more nebulous Christmas season should begin. The absence of any clear calendrical or official definition, in the end, allowed the Santa Claus parade to define the beginning of the season. By appearing in public space, then, the Eaton's Santa helped to shape public time. Through Santa, Eaton's pressed its promotional priorities onto the season.

Santa in public reveals Eaton's to be an immensely powerful player. It could never dominate and control Christmas, but through the parade, the company pressed its corporate agenda onto the season to an unmatched degree. In this sense, the Eaton's Santa Claus parade was both a traditional and a novel event. Though commerce was not a new presence in parading culture – leading Victorian businessmen had often organized grand civic events and individual owners frequently contributed floats – businesses normally appeared in processions as one part of the imagined civic community.[4] With its Santa Claus parade, however, Eaton's extended its own private spectacle into public. Once there, it exercised increasing cultural power: when Buhay spoke, the crowd obstructed a small stretch of sidewalk; when Santa paraded, Eaton's set public time, gathered a massive audience, and disrupted the entire structure of urban space.

"Westward, too, marches Winnipeg"

By the time Eaton's mounted its first Santa Claus parades, urban residents were well used to watching. Opportunities for spectatorship were many and expanding in late Victorian Canadian cities. Urban residents had been well trained in observing the movements of the streets, a legacy of the Victorian era's lively public sphere. Processions ranged in style and content, from grand celebrations like civic anniversaries through respectable marches of fraternal groups to more boisterous presentations of circuses, but they all reinforced a fragile but widely held belief that streets should be open to many groups and uses, and simultaneously taught urban residents to see parades as a key form of communication, entertainment, and politics. By the late 1800s, many other sites – theatres, sports venues, rodeos, and exhibition grounds – formed a sort of semi-public middle ground between the domestic spaces of home and the open publicness of the streets.[5] In the twentieth century, respectable movie houses, cheap nickelodeons, indoor arenas, amusement parks, and many other sites opened even more opportunities for gazing and watching. Some sites assembled crowds that wandered informally and chose their own paths – what Gary Cross and John Walton call "the playful crowd" – while others controlled behaviour through assigned seats, formal rules, and so on. But they all regulated access with tickets, gates, and line-ups, separating themselves from the more unbounded public of the streets. So pervasive were these opportunities for watching that scholars used to call the twentieth century "a culture of the eye." This view probably exaggerated the triumph of sight over other senses, but it nonetheless spoke to the many ways that urbanites became trained to see in a particular way, as *spectators* – sometimes passive and polite, sometimes active and unruly, but always watchers of spectacles and events.[6]

By the First World War, as the Eaton's parades morphed from simple promotional events into sophisticated artistic and narrative presentations, urban structure was changing underneath these customs of spectatorship. Victorian parade culture had been sustained by a particular social geography: cities were compact; public spaces were dense and accessible; commerce, industry, and residences were mixed together. Central streets in most North American cities still bustled with many forms of activity. Urban dwellers would have come across parades fairly frequently just by going about their everyday life.[7] Over time, however, industrialization cracked the foundation of the socially mixed city, rapid population growth created new forms of social segregation, and new transportation technologies allowed the city to spread out. Horse-drawn trams, later electric streetcars, and finally gas-powered cars and buses pushed out the liveable boundaries of the city, serving as both cause and outcome of booming suburban living.[8]

Still, it is not entirely useful to see such developments in terms of a linear narrative of decentralization. Cities grew and spread out, but central areas remained important for many reasons. As residences trickled to the fringes, commercial and office space spread through the centre – creating a distinct "central business district" that drew in office workers, shoppers, and others. Streetcars had an ambivalent effect, promoting (in the words of J.M.S. Careless) "both central focusing and spatial outreach" by allowing populations to live on the fringes but converge on downtown for shopping and working.[9] This new urban geography was reinforced by other commercial decisions and cultural developments. The largest and most sophisticated sites of spectatorship gathered along main downtown streets. By 1930, the best movie houses lined main streets like Yonge in Toronto, Sainte Catherine in Montreal, Portage in Winnipeg, and Jasper in Edmonton. The big new arenas found similar locations. The Montreal Forum opened in 1924 at Sainte Catherine and Atwater, for example, while Maple Leaf Gardens opened in 1931 at Carlton near Yonge. The social power and cultural reach of "downtown" was made crystal clear by the way main streets served as festival spaces, natural and spontaneous attractors at moments of celebration. When crowds poured out of doors to celebrate Grey Cup or Stanley Cup victories, the end of wars, or other big events, they gathered on the main commercial streets like Yonge, Portage, Jasper, and Sainte Catherine, generally spontaneously and without conscious coordination. Until at least the 1960s, then, central business districts in Canadian cities retained some degree of hegemony, downtown remained a magnet, and main streets held cultural power.[10]

Department stores were key agents in these ambivalent developments. On the one hand, their huge stores and locational decisions disrupted the original social geography of city centres, while on the other they reinforced the social centrality of downtown. When Eaton's opened large stores in Toronto, Winnipeg, and Montreal, they entered the emerging rather than the traditional commercial centres of each city. In Toronto, King Street had long been the key commercial and cultural thoroughfare, attracting the best stores, the promenades, and other forms of vibrant urban life. By contrast, Queen and Yonge, where Eaton's and rival Simpson's both located in the late 1800s, was somewhat outside the city's centre of gravity at the time. No one would have made the same point by 1929, as Yonge Street moved to geographic and social centrality, the main street of the growing metropolis. In Winnipeg, the dynamic was broadly similar. When Eaton's arrived in 1905, it located its store outside the original commercial centre around Portage and Main. It was a wise choice, since, over time, the decision consolidated the shifting gravity of retail and urbanity. "Westward, too, marches Winnipeg," one reporter commented when the Hudson's Bay Company opened its new store along Portage in 1926, "and the business section of Portage Ave. will take on a new appearance of strength and activity."[11] In Montreal, Eaton's didn't open a completely new outlet, moving instead into the site of the old Gibson's department store along Sainte Catherine Street in 1925. By that time, the long-standing focus of commerce downtown – old Montreal – retained its administrative, financial, and wholesale hegemony, but with multiple department stores (Eaton's, Simpson's, Morgan's, Ogilvy, and, further east, Dupuis Frères) and several smaller specialty shops, Sainte Catherine had become the key retail and festival space of the city.[12]

In this sense, even as they disrupted the Victorian geographies that had given shape and focus to cities, department stores helped to make and reinforce the social centrality of downtown. To be sure, over time and with further urban growth, department stores found rivals in fringe areas – by the 1920s, Saint Hubert Street became a key commercial district for north Montreal, for example, while north Toronto strips were causing anxiety for Eaton's promotional staff by the 1940s[13] – but while these challenged downtown exclusivity they hardly cracked its hegemony. Department stores remained key anchors of central business districts and important magnets for shoppers from across Canadian urban areas. Even into the early postwar years, every major streetcar route in Winnipeg ran in part along Portage Avenue, the main commercial drag of the city that included Eaton's, the Bay, and many independent stores, while numerous routes brought Montreal residents from north, east, and west along department store row on Sainte Catharine.[14]

With the arrival of the Eaton's Santa Claus parades, the corporate fantastic entered this shifting urban structure, which shaped the practical and cultural meaning of routes, the nature of the crowds, and the effect of both on the wider city. Oddly, Santa's route often ran against the grain of the established festival geographies of downtowns. In many years, the company conspicuously avoided main streets like Yonge and Portage, which must have produced strange results. After all, could anyone imagine a space less conducive to festival and fantasy than University Avenue in Toronto, with its drab office buildings, huge hospitals, Boer War monuments, and high-speed traffic? But there were, for Eaton's, a whole host of pragmatic considerations. Bulky floats were difficult to control and manoeuvre, so the company preferred wide streets with few narrow turns or steep hills. Routes had to be long to stretch out the large crowds. The parade had to begin near a large facility or open space where it could be properly marshalled. Other considerations were more political. The large crowds often annoyed smaller merchants on busy commercial strips, so city governments sometimes urged Eaton's to find alternative streets. But if the calculations were pragmatic and political, the total effect of route planning was often to

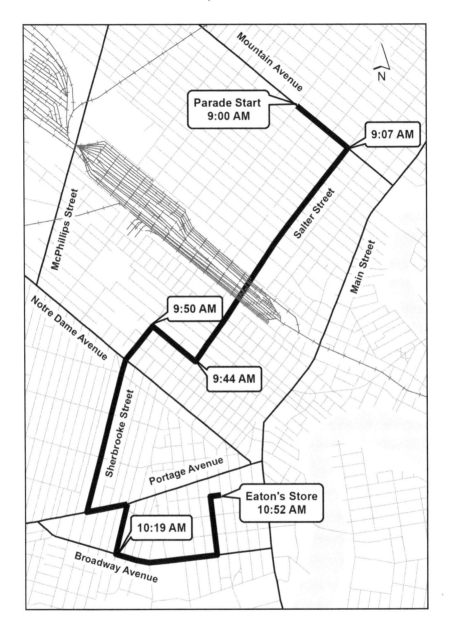

Winnipeg 1947

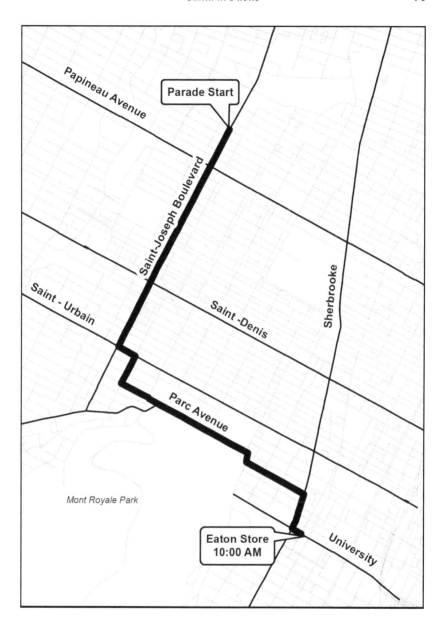

Montreal 1954

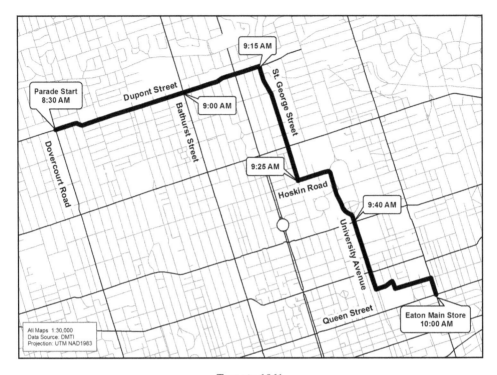

Toronto 1961

span urban geographies and to cross cultural boundaries. In Winnipeg, the parade usually began in the immigrant and working-class north end and crossed the train tracks while heading south to the Eaton's store. In Montreal, the route ran for many years from francophone east to anglophone west. And since, in every city, the ultimate destination was the Eaton's store, Santa generally moved from residential fringe to commercial downtown.

"My office is disarranged – how about yours?"

The crowds along these routes were enormous. "The streets were literally flooded with spectators," *La Presse* declared in 1930, a phrase typical of reports from every parade city across the century. "Thousands braved the cold today to welcome Santa," the *Calgary Herald* echoed in 1937, noting that spectators were three and four deep all through the residential section of the route and thickened as Santa arrived downtown. "There wasn't an inch to spare along the entire route," the *Winnipeg Tribune* noted in another typical report.[15] Precise numbers were harder to come by. Estimates of interwar crowds ran in the tens of thousands; in the postwar decades, numbers swelled to enormous proportions. In 1956, the *Toronto Daily Star* claimed that an astonishing one million spectators lined the route. But such figures were more art than science. The *Globe and Mail* offered a more modest total (500,000) for 1956. Four years later, Assistant Police Director William Minogue also estimated a half-million spectators, but Eaton's officials used a more conservative figure (300,000).[16] In the late 1960s, journalists attempted more objective mathematics that came up with much smaller totals.[17] Whatever the precise numbers, the crowds were very large, and most reporters contented themselves with generic references to "cheering thousands," "hordes of young fry," or "biggest ever." Indeed, the absolute numbers in the crowd seemed less important than their relative size. Everywhere, journalists claimed that the parade drew the largest or near-largest crowd of the year, surpassing or at least matching the biggest and most important local festivals, an especially astonishing accomplishment given the often inhospitably cold weather. "It was a record parade for Edmonton," the *Journal* announced in 1946. "The crowd was enormous on Saturday," *La Presse* echoed in 1967, comparing it to a "crowd of the Saint-Jean-Baptiste."[18]

Crowds didn't gather at an Eaton's parade, they *arrived*. Only a few spectators in choice residential areas experienced the parade as a neighbourhood event and few people just happened upon the spectacle while going about their daily rounds. Crowds streamed inward, intentionally, from the residential fringes and towns beyond. In 1930, the *Gazette* reported, "street cars from east and west were jammed sardine fashion, literally to capacity" with Montrealers on the way to watch the parade. Others came from farther out. "And the citizens came from many a mile to give their official greeting," claimed one Winnipeg report. "Not only city folk were on hand. Trains, buses and cars poured their human cargo from nearly every corner of the province."[19] Toronto's parade drew spectators from several nearby small towns, while Montreal's got visits from as far away as upstate New York, both reflecting the wide metropolitan influence of the two cities. "Mr. and Mrs. Warren Duprey and daughter, Joy, recently spent a day in Montreal, Que., where they saw the annual Santa Claus parade," the *Plattsburgh Press-Republican* noted

Crowds in Edmonton, 1934.
Glenbow Archives, ND-3-6893a.

in its report on the local goings-on in Chazy, New York (about ten miles south of the border) in 1952.[20]

For spectators, then, the parade started with a painful and hectic commute. Already by the 1930s, congestion was a key problem for downtowns across North America, but the hustle and bustle of normal city life hardly compared to the hyper-congestion of Santa Claus parade day. "From seven o'clock on Saturday morning," the *Montreal Gazette* explained, "parents and children squeezed themselves into overloaded streetcars, buses and automobiles to get downtown before all the choice vantage spots were taken." Indeed, everywhere, the crush was overwhelming. Traffic stretched for miles; parking was impossible; streetcars and (later) subways were packed. In 1951, one reporter went in search of the end of the traffic jam entering Toronto and "found himself

Deep lines of spectators, Toronto, 1962.
York University Libraries, Clara Thomas Archives & Special Collections,
Toronto Telegram fonds, ASC34679

driving for miles." Many families, stuck in a six-mile clog, missed the parade entirely "in spite of police efforts to break up the mammoth jam."[21] Getting back out was often as hard as getting in. In 1946, the *Star* reported that "an hour after it was over traffic still moved at a snail's pace along every main street" out of downtown. "If there ever was a traffic jam like this downtown before," complained one police official, "I never heard of it. This is the worst ever."[22] Making it downtown became an enormous act of planning and self-discipline. Many observers urged spectators to plan their schedules and their movements precisely. "If you want to see everything, you have to arrive two hours in advance," *La Presse* cautioned one year. "To the motorist who will be transporting children to the parade, I would suggest he park his vehicle ... facing away from the parade route," announced Robert Kerr, Toronto police service traffic inspector, in 1952. "This will greatly assist the motorist who is moving out of the area when the parade has passed."[23]

In drawing such crowds, the parade intensified and overturned the normal rhythms of the city. Even if decentralization was challenging the hegemony of downtown in the middle decades of the century, the central business district continued to be a Saturday shopping and working destination. For those who needed to be downtown, the parade had two distinct effects. On the one hand, the crowds simply overwhelmed the downtown infrastructure: restaurants were packed, walking the sidewalk was impossible, parking completely unavailable. On the other, the long route cut the city in half, making getting around a nightmare. In 1925, *La Presse* reported that the parade blocked all traffic near Saint Catharine West, while six years later a wedding party on Sherbrooke Street found themselves trapped by the crowd, "because they forgot to listen to the policeman and found their route blocked by the procession and an impenetrable cheering throng."[24] In Toronto, transit officials engaged in an intricate dance each year, pulling buses and streetcars off and on routes with assembly line coordination, rerouting streetcars at each intersection for a short time while Santa put on his show, and then quickly returning them to normal routes once it had passed. The *Star* summed up this operation with the headline, "Look What Santa's Doing to Our Trams." In the postwar period, automobiles became an increasing problem. By 1949, Winnipeg required over forty police officers to corral traffic and coordinate the parade; eventually, the city banned parking along the route, but police often simply begged drivers to avoid the downtown completely.[25]

Out of simple necessity, then, normal ways of doing things were suspended and the regular pace of the city altered.[26] Midday shopping was diverted to early morning. Work stopped for some, as Saturday office workers paused to view the parade, called in sick for the day, or simply never made it to work. Those who did found their workplace fundamentally altered. Office windows looking over the route were lined with children and parents; families looking for warmth took over the lobbies of buildings; even the Toronto police court (which overlooked the route) was opened to kids, introducing a relaxed and carnival atmosphere to proceedings. "Business was stopped," one Winnipeg reporter, stationed at Portage and Main, observed in 1916. "Windows were filled with employees of various establishments desiring to see the official arrival of Santa Claus."[27] Another year, construction workers building the new Mount Sinai Hospital in Toronto paused for half an hour to lean on their steel girders and watch the parade go past.[28] For others, work intensified, as retail businesses struggled to manage the rush of people and the increased threat of shoplifting. In 1975, when the Toronto parade was moved to Sunday, some press reports tied the decision to rumours that prolific shoplifting by youngsters had produced complaints from downtown merchants. Even without petty theft, however, police had a "monumental task on their hands" every year, as they struggled to corral the burgeoning crowds, deploying increasing numbers at street level to manage the crush.[29] In Montreal in 1952, police "formed chains in the downtown terminus area of the parade, holding back the tidal wave of humanity which rushed down University Street after the arrival of Santa." "Today is the day when old Santa arrives, the children are having the time of their lives," one Toronto citizen commented in poetic style, "at blocking the traffic and causing detours, my office is disarranged – how about yours?"[30]

In the streets outside of workplaces, many of the usual hierarchies and boundaries of urban space broke down against the onslaught of people. In 1930, *La Presse* observed children "on steps, on sidewalks, in windows, even on roofs," an observation echoed in countless reports from every parade city. "When we say [children] lined the route, we don't mean they just stood along the road in a trance," the *Star* explained, "they climbed things. Anything. Telephone posts, houses, porches, verandas, railings, roofs." Children literally took over the downtown, pushing aside the normal movement of the streets. In 1938, Toronto traffic "gave way before a mob of youngsters who stormed the parade. Children ran behind Santa's reindeer all over the roadways. Metro traffic just had to stop." In Calgary the year before, "boys and girls swarmed along behind, shouting and cheering as Santa tossed handfuls of whistles into their midst." But adults, too, joined the fray. "Signal lights are just being ignored by pedestrians," complained an exasperated Toronto police officer as he stood directing foot traffic at Bay and Queen in 1937. "They sure are having a picnic today."[31] Nor was the chaos confined to the parade route. Unbounded by gates and uncontrolled by assigned seats, the crowd spilled onto nearby streets. One year in Montreal, the crowd accumulated "snowball-fashion" as "some followed the procession along its own route, and others walked along parallel streets and lanes, like a devastating army in mass formation." Some experts worried, like the Institute of Child Study, which warned parents to keep children close, to educate them in traffic rules, and to forbid them from climbing trees, but much of this behaviour was officially tolerated. "It's the kids

Watching from balconies, Montreal, 1946.
BANQ, P48,S1,P13858, Photographer: Conrad Poirier

day," Police Inspector Page reminded frustrated drivers in 1950, urging them to stay clear of the route until well after the parade had passed.[32]

The blurring of boundaries, the alternative use of offices, and the whimsical spectacle of the parade itself all contributed to a boisterous atmosphere in the downtown. Merchants brought out decorations along the route and petty hawkers descended to supply balloons and noise makers, transforming normally drab November streets to a sea of colour and cacophony of noise. "Long before the hour set," as the *Montreal Gazette* put it, "they crowded along the curb, covered the sidewalks and stretched up on to doorsteps, window sills and galleries, turning drab grey streets into a gay riot of bright woolen caps, coats and scarves." "For the balloon vendors and souvenir sellers," the *Star* reported one year, "it was a thousand fairs jammed into one ... [A] mass of color assailed

Children watching from the top of a car, Toronto, 1935.
City of Toronto Archives, Fonds 1266, Globe and Mail Collection, Item 35337.

the eye."[33] University Avenue, where the Toronto parade travelled for many years, was totally transformed from a drab and stately institutional street to a lively pedestrian thoroughfare. Even cars, the source of considerable damage to public life and to congestion, got transformed on parade day. Many scholars have described how twentieth-century cities were re-made to accommodate automobiles, one part of a broader reformulation and regulation of street culture.[34] On parade day, the effect of congestion was more ambiguous: traffic both fed the crowds and battled them. Automobiles even became sites of spectatorship: one year in Toronto, a stranded truck driver threw open his back tarpaulin and allowed kids to scramble up to watch the parade go by. In other years, clever families arrived early, paid for parking in a lot along the route, and sat on top of their cars to watch the parade.[35]

The parade also created an alternative urban soundscape. Modern cities were loud. Factory noise, loudspeakers, honking horns, and the pounding of construction machines assaulted aural sensibilities, and cities often struggled to control the cacophony. In 1953, after several complaints in Toronto, the city struck an Advisory Committee on Noise Abatement with representatives from multiple groups (Board of Trade, Ontario Motor League, Local Council of Women, Health League of Canada, Home and School Council), which proceeded to make war on modern sound, writing a new comprehensive by-law and undertaking campaigns of public education. Yet even the most comprehensive forms of aural regulation (Toronto's by-law listed over a dozen categories of offending noise) freed up festival sound. The Toronto by-law allowed the Board of Police Commissioners to exempt the "use in a reasonable manner of any apparatus or mechanism for the amplification of the human voice or of music in a public park or other commodious space in connection with any public election meeting, public celebration or other reasonable gathering," including "any military or other band or any parade." Even efforts to control bands and noisemakers in front of hospitals – surely, on their face, uncontroversial – were put down. In 1953, Alderman Grossman presented a motion proposing that University Avenue be "rigidly maintained" as a quiet zone from College to Dundas (the so-called "hospital row"), "strictly prohibiting the playing of bands and the blowing of automobile horns or sirens; the use of noisemakers in parades or demonstrations." The Board of Control rejected the motion. Festival sound, after all, was not a normal nuisance.[36]

The sense of wondrous disruption had limits, however, and hardly approached moments of genuinely carnivalesque inversion. As a tame, family spectacle designed for children "eight to eighty," there were few hints of the real bedlam or disorder. Downtown was loud, streets were congested, normal routines were disrupted, but Santa's crowd was more cute than chaotic. The intention of the parade itself was largely hegemonic: even if consumer desire and childlike fantasy had been countercultural in the nineteenth century, they were hardly so by the middle of the twentieth.[37] If the spectacle and the spectators created moments of genuine irrationality and novelty in the city, the inversions were tame and respectable and the crowds ultimately posed few threats to the social order.[38] In the end, moreover, the arrival of bands, clowns, and old St Nick could have a disciplining effect. The Eaton's parade was a spectacle to be watched not a festival to be joined, though it was never clear just what the spectators were seeing.

"The best memories of their childhood"

Watching has a history. Scholars have made it clear that spectatorship has been shaped by historical forces. Shifting cultural norms, ongoing public debates, informal codes of watching, and numerous changes over time have all, in different moments, created what Russell Field terms "the culturally specific skills needed to be a spectator."[39] Decades of this audience research have dispensed with older (indeed, now very old) notions that spectators were passive receivers or pliable dupes of mass spectacles. Even when audiences were tamed – in amusement parks, by entrepreneurial efforts to construct a respectable, middle-class audience; in arenas, by assigned seating, variable pricing, and formal rules – the triumph of control was hardly complete and spectators rarely did as they were told. Yet changes did occur, as with the shift from the boisterous and active crowd of the silent-movie era to the polite and passive audience after the coming of sound. Similarly, Paul Moore's stimulating work suggests the many ways that movie houses transformed urban crowds into "attentive mass audiences."[40] The Santa Claus parades suggest a similar set of audience dynamics. Eaton's called forth the crowd by mounting a spectacle and advertising it, but watching was both active and social, if ephemeral. Eaton's had the power to promote its festival to draw people downtown, but it could not control the crowd that gathered along the route, and the spectacle hardly constituted the whole parade experience.

Watching was, first of all, hard work. As if the commute to get there wasn't bad enough, just watching the parade go by was an exhausting act of parental labour. Parents mounted their little ones on shoulders, jostled with other spectators, struggled to keep everyone patient, made runs to nearby washrooms, kept an eagle-like eye on children who seemed always ready to wander off, and even rigged up clever devices to make sure their kids saw the parade. "Long before Eaton's Santa Claus parade passed," the *Toronto Telegram* reported, "it looked like moving day for fathers. Kitchen chairs, high stools, stepladders, benches and boxes were pulled and hauled, then manoeuvred into position for the youngsters." Inventiveness reigned. For the twenty-nine years up to 1973, when a *Star* reporter found him at Bloor St. and Delaware Avenue in Toronto, Bert Hutchins set up two stepladders and mounted a plank between them, an impromptu, elevated bench for neighbourhood children to see over the thickening crowds. Indeed, getting a good view often meant being places you didn't belong. In 1973, one Toronto

Self-built seat on a pole, Toronto, 1963.
York University Libraries, Clara Thomas Archives & Special Collections,
Toronto Telegram fonds, ASC34664.

father used a ladder and "a big jump" to get two kids, lawn chairs, blan-
kets, and a thermos of coffee onto the roof of a service station "where
they all had an unimpeded view."[41] By far the most popular viewing
spot, however, was the shoulders of tall parents: "One mother missed
the parade. Dad, with two blue-coated little girls on his shoulders was
teetering precariously on a bench. Behind him, acting as prop to keep
him steady, was poor mother."[42]

   Theoretically, all this hard work was redeemed by the dual attrac-
tion of familial leisure and imagined childhood. Eaton's never did systematic studies of the crowd, but press reports make clear that it was

composed of clusters of family units, neighbours, school friends, and adults playing hookey from responsibility. "Whole families, including even father, were noticed among the spectators," the *Tribune* noted from Winnipeg in 1922. "The kiddies got the preference and made a row along the curb," a *Toronto Daily Star* reporter observed in 1928, "although they were outnumbered by the adults in a proportion of about three to one, the majority being members of the stronger sex, supposed to be working in their offices with their noses to the grindstone." The presence of children and the wondrous nature of the spectacle shaped the character and meaning of the whole crowd. Adults spoke of being transformed into children by the sight of Santa. "Hundreds of thousands of children appreciated this parade," *La Presse* reported in 1925, "[and] thousands of adults also appeared very happy to relive … some of the happiest memories of their childhood."[43] "I haven't missed one for twelve years," claimed one seventy-two-year-old spectator in 1947. "It makes me feel young again." Four years later, another Toronto resident made the same point more poetically: "A shout went up as he passed by/Time was forgotten then;/For captivated by the spell/I was a child again."[44] Returning to one's imagined childhood was evoked by the feeling of fantasy built into the parade and the sense of merriment around it, but also by the presence of happy children. In 1968, columnist Bruce West admitted the parade could be an exhausting chore – "standing there at the chilly curb with one youngster on your shoulders and maybe one in each arm" – but advised heading downtown anyway. "You'll be able to witness that increasingly rare and precious thing called wonder," he wrote. "The beautiful part of it is that it's contagious. No matter how old you may be it is still possible … to share in the wonder that is written on the face of a child as those magic Christmas floats go by. How pleasant it is to peek once more, even for a moment, at the land of color and glitter and make believe, through the eyes of a child."[45]

Vicarious wonder may have redeemed the hard parental work of the parade, but West's reaction was more constructed than natural. "By the 1900s, Americans were ready for a new image of the child," the American historian Gary Cross writes, "one expressed in the word 'cute.'" Even the word itself took new power, drifting from its nineteenth-century mooring in "acute" (shrewd and witty) towards the idea of "wondrous innocence," an impulse powerfully expressed by the conclusion of West's column. This definition of cuteness was an intensely modern, and adult, development, flowing on the one hand from the

The standard cute child with father photo. "Baby Betty Berslund
watches her first Santa Claus Parade," Edmonton, 1948.
City of Edmonton Archives, EA-600-1770c.

perceived hegemony of reason and disseminated on the other by print
capitalism and commercial culture. "Wonder was saved from rationality and progress when it was given to children," Cross writes, drawing on a survey of trade cards, newspapers, middle-class magazines,
department store ads, and many other mass media. On parade day, as
West made clear, wonder was also the counterpoint to frustration and
exhaustion. Of course, fairy-tale wonder and Christmas magic also had
adult appeal. Woody Register points to the importance of adult yearning for childhood play as an antidote to the sacrifices and challenges
of modern life, a condition that emerged alongside new commercial
amusements in the early twentieth century.[46] Santa Claus parades played

on exactly this sense of adult yearning. These modern developments paralleled the efforts of circuses and amusement parks to clean up their image, redefining and reshaping their customers in playful and respectable directions, partly by transforming "the crowd into family clusters focused on children and child-like fantasies."[47] The parade stirred genuine emotions, but they were authorized by broader cultural forces.

At Santa Claus parades, the rhetorical power of cuteness seemed to have few boundaries, sweeping aside not only frustration but social difference as well. Wonder was universal, at least in the minds of reporters and Eaton's officials. Even if, as the company often claimed, French Canadians treated the parade like a festival while Torontonians saw it as a show, everyone came together under cuteness and wonder. In Montreal, they came from "from Westmount and Rosemont, from Maisoneuve and Verdun," as the *Gazette* put it one year, so some shouted "Hello Santa Claus" and others "Bonjour Père Noel" along the route, but if reporters could be believed, boundaries of language and identity fell before the wondrous onslaught of the parade.[48] "Democracy reigned on the sidewalk where little ragamuffins, and little Rosedale people, confided in one another," the *Toronto Daily News* claimed in 1918. "There were olive skinned and dusky eyed children. There was even an almond eyed round faced little person from the Orient. In fact, every nation seemed represented in those tens of thousands of children who lined the streets."[49] "Every year I go along University Avenue and look at the expressions on the faces – white faces, black faces, yellow faces," echoed Brockie three decades later, "along together for their Santa Claus."[50] Such appeals to Christmas universalism could admit differences, but the narrative purpose was always to lead back to the universal cute and the binding power of joy.

In fact, at some fundamental level, there was no single crowd at all, but a mish-mash of different agendas and experiences. Confronted with Eaton's call to the cute, a few spectators advanced alternative agendas. Some children got scared. In 1949, the *Winnipeg Tribune* pointed to "one little boy at the corner of Redwood Avenue and Charles Street gave a cry of fright when the first grotesque clown passed and buried his head in his mother's lap, refusing to look at the rest of the parade." Others got cool. In 1933, a *Globe* reporter detailed the decidedly unmerry behaviour he had witnessed along the route: at Albert Street, a group of young "iconoclasts" fired snowballs at the parade; further along, a small girl loudly declared that she didn't believe in Santa. "Some youngsters fired snowballs into the route of the parade," the

Winnipeg Free Press echoed in 1965, "but most did not." Even adults asserted their own, less wondrous agendas. In 1968, an "elderly man in a black leather coat" informed the Toronto masses, "This is not a parade for God ... This is a parade for the devil" (to which one mother replied, "For crying out loud, will you shut up").[51] Still others got arrested. Quirky local activist Reginald Diddy showed up at one parade with a sign reading, "Down with Santa! Up with truth. Stop Lying to the kids! Santa Claus must be exposed as a fake!" all the while chanting, "Kids! Santa is a phony and full of baloney!" Several angry parents shouted at Diddy and he was charged with causing a disturbance. "Shouting 'There is no Santa Claus' at a Christmas parade is akin to calling King William a 'fink' at an Orangeman's parade," Diddy's trial judge told him before laying down a $50 fine. "Attacking Santa Claus is akin to attacking motherhood and apple pie and the results are predictable."[52] Other adults simply used the crowd for their own functional purposes. In 1978, reporters enumerated the various people who had descended to feed off the assembled crowd. Men in "blue blazers" did a marketing survey, others sought signatures for a petition against the neutron bomb, while overhead an airplane towed a sign urging Torontonians to vote for Tony O'Donaghue for mayor.[53]

The desire to see, moreover, often produced competition and stress as much as wonder and excitement. After a long commute, the annoying search for parking, and the hunt for a decent spot, the waiting began, a fact that promised frustration and conflict. There were no assigned seats, a clear invitation to crowding and competition, and the size of the crowd and the final excitement of the parade only added to the anxiety and potential for disorder and confusion. In 1906, the *Tribune* condemned adult behaviour at the Winnipeg train station, noting that "a lot of grown up people made vigorous attempts to secure the toys intended for the children, and in many cases were successful ... One woman was observed actually slapping the ears of a little girl for daring to frustrate her in her designs on a six inch doll."[54] In 1928, a Toronto reporter enumerated the "comments [that] flew from the curb," including "who d'ye think yer pushin'?" "Will you little boys let the little girl stand there?" and "Get offa me foot." The crush could be as dangerous and menacing as it was wondrous and carnivalesque. In 1976, at the end of the parade, the surging crowd produced "a shoving crying mass of people as children had their faces squashed against Eaton's Christmas windows." "This could be dangerous," one father declared, "Let's get the hell out while we can."[55]

Waiting, Toronto, 1963.
York University Libraries, Clara Thomas Archives & Special Collections,
Toronto Telegram fonds, ASC34665.

Watching was the subject, therefore, of various forms of discipline, from outright social control to softer forms of cajoling and even informal codes along the sidewalks. The first line of control, of course, was family. Parents struggled to corral their children and to manage their moods (not to mention their bladders), as the little ones occasionally seemed less than enthused to be waiting. In 1969, one four-year-old in Toronto complained, "I want to go home," to which his father replied "You can't go home. You'll watch the parade with me." Over time, Eaton's found it necessary to extend its disciplinary efforts to the crowd (using radio to remind adults "to let the children stand in the front lines along the curb") and even police got into the act, deploying increasing numbers at street level, who struggled to corral children and to control the selfish behaviour of adults. At the Winnipeg train station in 1906, one police officer "undertook to uphold the rights of the children and took several toys away from the grown folks." Along the route, police tried to move smaller children to the front. In 1927, Montreal police struggled to contain the crowd, "trying as much as possible to allow the smallest to be up front, to better observe the interesting parade." Fifteen years later, in Winnipeg, "the cry went up, 'here it is!' The policeman on point duty at the bridge moved the little watchers in front for a better view."[56]

Such efforts could go only so far. There were too many spectators and too few controls on their movements for outright discipline to work. In the end, watching was a social act, so the most powerful rules had to be worked out in the street. Scattered evidence suggests the emergence of informal codes in the audience – one year, for example, children spontaneously agreed to take turns at a prime viewing spot. Much of this sort of behaviour seemed governed by various forms of schoolyard morality: first come first served, taking turns, the shortest go to the front. But on the ground, even these well-understood rules often seemed in conflict. In 1980, Marjorie Babcock complained that her children's enjoyment "was almost marred when my husband and I attempted to place our children at the front along with other small children. One man commented that we were not going to place our children in front of him," a reaction that Babcock called "ignorant and obnoxious." But, in fact, the man – even by Babcock's own account – had been waiting there for an hour and a half, and one other spectator angrily came to his defence, pointing to the parents (like Babcock) who seemed to think they could show up as they pleased and place their children in front of families that had been waiting for hours. In a way, the problem was philosophical – what principle, first-come or children to the front, was most just?

– but it was also intensely practical, particularly when the anticipation and excitement of the approaching parade could sweep away even the most careful plans. In 1934, just the sound of the oncoming parade was enough to overturn the moral economy of the sidewalk: "Those first notes were enough. The barriers established by the first comers were broken. Mounted policemen, masters of the situation until then, were dissolved in the new ranks that formed and became mere spectators."[57]

But who knew what the spectators were seeing, or if they were seeing at all? "For me, the fun of the Santa Claus parade is always more in the crowd than in the floats, which I can't see anyway," Joyce Dingman wrote in 1966, "because my children have gone through to the front and I am left standing behind some man with a large child on his shoulders."[58] And children, even when they were paying attention, often followed their own agenda. "I most loved the man in the blue costume on the horse," one six-year-old told her mother in 1971, referring to a mounted police officer.[59] At another level, too, children in offices had a different sightline than those on the sidewalks – "From above, his eight faithful reindeer seemed to prance over open snow. From the street, these same reindeer seemed to lope through the crowds"[60] – while the parade itself was less a single event than a serial collection of theoretically identical performances. At an arena or theatre, spectators were gathered together, watching the same spectacle, but at the Santa Claus parade, the crowd spread out along an extended route. At their most extreme, variations in performance along the route could produce a startlingly different viewing experience. One year, spectators at Bathurst and Bloor in Toronto were horrified to see a child, sitting on a float, collide with an overhead wire and fall to the concrete, a fifteen-foot drop. His injuries were severe enough to warrant an ambulance. But while witness was a less pleasant role than spectator, others along the route remained blissfully unaware until they saw news reports later in the day.[61] Along the route, then, the experience of watching could be quite different.

Neither rude behaviour, diverse experiences, nor informal rules altered the more fundamental fact: jostling, giving way, lifting up children, and witnessing accidents were all rituals of watching; in the end, the common purpose of most spectators was to be entertained by the parade not to share space or see the city in a new way.[62] Having been called together by the promotional efforts of a large department store, the crowd had hardly gathered spontaneously and the purpose of coming downtown seemed clear enough. "There was still the occasional

Presents look bigger from the sidewalk, Edmonton, 1947.
City of Edmonton Archives, EA-600-1770a.

flake of snow floating down lightly … as I heard the music and saw the first figures coming down the road," Bruce West wrote of taking his daughter to the parade in 1955. "I knew I was standing just at the threshold of a very magic land, indeed." As West stood on the sidewalk with his daughter, his sense of magic was no doubt real, but it began when he heard the music and saw the parade, not when he stepped into his car or joined the crowd on University Avenue.[63] The lines of spectators at the margins of parade photos, so many looking inward at the floats and clowns rather than back and forth at each other, make the dynamic clear. The crowd may have been fun and social, but it had gathered to watch. And it dispersed when the parade was done, lingering only until Santa had climbed the ladder or entered the store. In the end, the crowd left few traces on the city, but the event had a profound influence in the public sphere.

Attention focused – the discipline of the spectacle, Toronto, 1932.
City of Toronto Archives, Fonds 1266, Globe and Mail Collection, Item 28637.

"Christmas cannot be far away"

Christmas was not a shy holiday. Before the Victorian period, the day was not universally celebrated, but in places where it was, events were highly public and often unruly. In many parts of North America, drunkenness, burlesque, costuming, "mumming," rough music, and generally loud and raucous revelry appeared with distressing frequency between Christmas and New Year's Day. Several scholars have examined these boisterous forms of celebration, and while Joyce Lewis found few examples of outright disorder in Ontario's nineteenth-century Christmas traditions,[64] there is no question that the emerging middle class across North America became invested in taming the festival through domesticity and respectability. Newspapers increasingly

Crowds dispersing in Toronto, 1946.
City of Toronto Archives, Fonds 1266, Globe and Mail Collection, Item 110062.

emphasized the family nature of the event, temperance advocates stressed themes of sobriety, and more professional police forces cracked down as much as possible on organized rowdiness.[65] This process of Victorian reinvention privileged domestic and familial forms of celebration (like visiting and walking) while more boisterous and public forms of sociability had been pushed to geographic or social margins (various forms of disorder and disguise, in particular, became much less common in urban bourgeois celebrations). This was not a linear or entirely one-dimensional process, but the Victorian efforts to tame Christmas laid a solid groundwork for a different sort of public holiday in the twentieth century.[66]

By the time Eaton's took Santa to the streets, the holiday acquired a new and different public momentum, with the proliferation of nativity scenes, municipal Christmas trees, and more elaborate decorations on streets and in shop windows. Even churches got into the act, embracing the sensual side of the holiday with crèches but also evergreen boughs, lights, and streamers.[67] By the interwar years, it had become standard for cities and business associations to cooperate on Christmas decorations or to pursue separate yet parallel projects with complementary effects. In 1930, Montreal's executive committee decided to place Christmas trees in several public parks, with Montreal Light and Power install- ing decorative lights on each. The following year, Toronto spent $600 for two large Christmas trees at City Hall, a practice that soon became a permanent feature of the civic Christmas. Such official efforts were supplemented by cooperative private initiatives. In 1930, Bloor District Business Men made plans for Christmas street decoration from Spadina to Lansdowne, aiming, so they claimed, to "stimulate the Christmas spirit," although the commercial advantages were no doubt prominent in their minds. Department stores took a key place in these efforts. The sensuous window displays and decorative lights of the department stores were spectacles in themselves, projecting light and colour onto the normally drab November streets. The total effect of these civic, com- mercial, and religious efforts was striking. "Brilliance reigns in down- town Winnipeg," the *Manitoba Free Press* commented in 1929. "Myriads of Lights Peep from Christmas Trees and Evergreen Festoons."[68]

Such efforts raised several implicit questions about timing. By the time the Eaton's Santa arrived on urban streets, calendars and clocks were well established as guardians of time, yet the holidays and sea- sons remained social questions.[69] Christmas evolved from a series of negotiations between official, seasonal, popular, and festival calen- dars. At the beginning of the Victorian era, New Year's Day remained an important gift-giving rival to Christmas and only a powerful, if sometimes haphazard, coalition of merchants and clergy turned the holiday focus towards December 25th. These two groups had differ- ent agendas, yet a festival focused on Christmas served the interests of both. Merchants saw a chance to leverage the day to stimulate com- merce and clergy to make spiritual meanings more central. The results were uneven, but by the time Santa took to the streets in 1905, there had a been a noticeable shift in most urban centres towards more in- tense and public Christmas celebrations.[70] But even after this creeping Yuletide consensus took hold, the broader seasonal question remained. Most Christians had settled on December 25 as Christmas Day, but the public lightings and municipal trees were intended to open a more nebulous "Christmas season" that had no clearly defined beginning.

When should the celebration begin? The question had a much easier answer in the United States, where Thanksgiving was fast becoming an important national holiday, located perfectly in late fall, where it was close enough to Christmas but still encouraged an extended stretch of Yuletide commerce. When American department stores like Macy's and Gimbel's initiated their own parades in the 1920s, then, they generally chose Thanksgiving as a "springboard for Christmas sales." But Canada had different Thanksgiving traditions, much more local and less homogeneous in the nineteenth century and beginning to focus on October by the twentieth.[71]

In the end, it was the Santa Claus parade that came to set Christmas time. Initially, the parade had no fixed date, roving about from mid-November to early December. By the early 1920s, Eaton's settled on the third Saturday in November for Toronto and Winnipeg and the week after in Montreal, Calgary, and Edmonton, where it stayed for several decades.[72] The reasons for this timing are not entirely clear, and several companies continued to follow their own promotional priorities for the start of the season. In 1906, Simpson's ran a series of newspaper ads that followed Santa on his journey from the North Pole to Simpson's, passing through towns, racing a Toronto streetcar, running alongside an automobile, and finally taking his place in the store's Toytown. In 1928, the company claimed that Santa arrived by airplane and, seven years later, by a magic carpet driven by Mickey Mouse.[73] The Hudson's Bay Company used similar promotions, filling the heads of children with Toyland dreams through storytelling ads that followed Santa's adventures. In Edmonton, the Bay even ran a Santa Claus parade in the 1920s, as did Gibson's of Montreal a decade earlier.[74]

All these diverse promotional strategies continued through the twentieth century, but as the date of the Eaton's parade settled into a regular position in mid-November, it began to mark the season itself. Downtown merchants waited to begin sales, set up displays, and mount decorations until the Eaton's Santa had opened the season. "There's a fairly definite unwritten protocol to observe," the *Financial Post* advised in 1955. "Stores in most areas agree not to have their Santas appear before the main arrival parade. (Toronto's Santas all climbed on to their respective thrones after the Eaton parade last week, for example)."[75] The impulse was widespread. "Time your biggest Christmas promotion push with Santa's arrival," the trade magazine *Home Goods Retailing* reminded subscribers two years later. "In this case it's Eaton's Santa Claus parade in three big cities, and business associations in smaller areas with their own Christmas parade. There's no better built-in Christmas merchandiser to start customers counting those dwindling shopping days until Christmas." Individual retailers often adopted such strategies. Winnipeg's downtown Kresge's advertised Santa Claus parade specials in 1964, while Sam the Record Man in Toronto offered a Santa Claus parade special on a *Sesame Street* record a decade later.[76] "Toy Town openings and Santa Claus parades make us mindful that Christmas cannot be far away," one downtown furrier declared in an ad that implored male consumers to "idolize" their wives with fine fur.[77] There was no conspiracy or coercion here – for store owners, playing off a popular public event was probably just good business sense – but the overall definitional effect was undeniable. Even some city councils and, more amazingly, Eaton's department store rivals bowed to the definitional power of the Eaton's parade. In Winnipeg, the city council and downtown merchants association set its official Christmas lighting to the night before the Eaton's parade, frankly admitting that the Eaton's parade would "tee off the big splurge" of Christmas shopping, while the Bay's Santa Claus display opened on the Monday morning after the Eaton's parade. One year, in Montreal, Simpson's even publicly criticized Dupuis Frères for jumping the gun on Eaton's paradigm-setting festival. "Santa Claus should be brought to Montreal by Eaton's," G.D. Thompson of Simpson's declared. "They've been doing it for 50 or 60 years." All of this reinforced – and was reinforced by – the widespread sense that the Eaton's Santa was the "real thing."[78]

The Eaton's-defined Christmas calendar did become more complicated, but was never completely undermined, with accelerating suburban development and retail decentralization after 1955. Widely separated from the downtown commercial atmosphere, suburban retailers at plazas and malls often put up decorations and Toylands early, and sometimes tried to construct their own Santa Claus spectacles. In 1956, one mall developer flew a live Santa in a helicopter for flash visits at various malls around Metro Toronto. In the mid-1960s, the owners of Winnipeg's Polo Park mounted a similar spectacle, landing Santa in the parking lot before marching him to his igloo at the centre of the mall.[79] Across North America, moreover, many smaller cities and towns began to compete by offering their own spectacles in the postwar years, often based explicitly on the Eaton's parade, offering a more local opportunity to set seasonal time.[80] Even into the 1970s, however, these alternative spectacles never really replaced Eaton's downtown parade as a symbol of the season's beginning, a point made clear when the company decided to hold the Toronto parade in the first week of November instead of the normal date later in the month. The company was inundated with complaints that it had started the Christmas season too early. In a 1978 letter to the editor, one clever suburbanite suggested that by 1980 the parade would be held on Easter, allowing for nine full months of Christmas advertising.[81]

The Watching Crowd

For spectators, the annual Santa Claus parade was at once spectacular and mundane, fantastic and frantic, an exhilarating carnival for the imagination and an exasperating struggle with urban life. Everywhere that Eaton's mounted Christmas spectacles, enormous crowds gathered, a reflection of the success of the parade and its ability to overwhelm the local downtown. People liked the parade – well, most did – but the event was doubly successful because it was never actually the whole story. The Eaton's event became a touchstone for childhood, family, and Christmas experiences, as thousands of spectators converged on downtown to greet the old Saint. Yet the spectators composed, in many senses, a watching crowd: cute, tame, respectable, neither totally passive nor entirely participatory. No doubt, the reactions on the sidewalk were genuine: whether the happiness of children at seeing Santa, the joy of parents at seeing their children see Santa, or the nostalgia of adults for their own sense of childhood wonder. Yet the culture that sanctioned such emotions was a historical development, one that owed much to the Christmas synthesis of commerce, family, fantasy, and wonder. In this sense, the joy in the crowd was both real and invented.

Regardless, Santa's power in public – really, Eaton's power – never came from controlling the crowd or creating passive spectators. Spectators were cute but quite active in pursuing their multiple agendas. But their activities were nonetheless part of a broader public where Eaton's remained the most powerful player. Eaton's power flowed, in the first instance, from its ability to call the crowd together through its promotional resources. In an era of growing cities where crowds had to arrive – often from afar – rather than spontaneously gather, Eaton's corporate structure gave it a huge advantage over other users of public space. Becky Buhay could address a small group of passersby at Queen and Soho; Eaton's could take over the whole downtown. At another level, the power of the Eaton's parade came from its ability to shape the season. The parade was ephemeral, but its wider influence endured. In this sense, the two forms of Christmas public – the material and the discursive – were, in practice, deeply intertwined. Santa's presence in public space was a powerful moment in the circulation of Eaton's message through the public sphere; that circulation of ideas in turn shaped the physical and material spaces of the city. It signalled, for instance, that the Christmas season had begun and that it was time to put up lights and decorations. Even if the parade itself was the focus, the public life of Santa lived as ideas well beyond that moment. In the end, then, the best measure of Eaton's power is not its ability to control the crowd or focus attention on its own event. It was hardly an omnipotent corporation controlling social life and creating passive spectators. Instead, power lay in the company's ability to overwhelm other players in the Christmas conversation (even its own department store rivals) and in its capacity to outcompete other users of public space. Simpson's could have its promotions, but Eaton's had the real Santa; Becky Buhay had the right to address the public, but Eaton's had the power to shape it.

3
The Mediated Santa

There must have been a lot of happy parents in Winnipeg on the third Saturday of November, 1954. It was Santa Claus parade day in the city, but for the first time since the event began in 1905, families could see it without enduring frozen feet and jostling crowds. The Canadian Broadcasting Corporation had recently brought television to the city, and for its first live public event CBWT would air the Eaton's parade. Local radio had been covering Santa's arrival for over a decade, but if you wanted to see it – and, after all, the parade was a visual medium – here finally was something approaching an ideal experience. It would all be so simple: the CBC would set up a camera outside its new studio and the parade would pass by, its image delivered to living rooms across the city, where viewers could enjoy perfect sightlines, warm air, comfortable seats, and (perhaps most importantly) the bathroom close by.

Not surprisingly, matters turned out to be more complex. CBWT was so new that it hadn't secured mobile equipment, so CBC technicians would have to set up a studio camera outside. But since the parade didn't normally pass the studio's location, the route had to be adjusted, jogging a block off its normal path. That hardly settled matters. The front of the studio faced the morning sun, a mundane architectural fact with enormous visual consequences. A camera pointing into the sun would produce an overexposed and almost unwatchable image, a big bright splotch with the floats and marchers too dark to see. The only solution was to take a camera across the street and film it from the other side. The morning of the parade, then, CBWT's technicians strung a 400-foot cable across Portage Avenue to connect the camera to the studio. "It's going to take a lot of people to get the old fellow safely on to Winnipeggers' TV sets," the *Winnipeg Free Press* summed up. "It's going to take a good part of CBWT's television personnel, a big department store, AND the city engineering department to do it." Eaton's bragged that the broadcast was a success (receiving "many favorable comments," according to the company's employee newsletter), but even then, the situation was hardly ideal.[1] After all, less than half the local population had a television – though Eaton's had added to the total by supplying some free of charge to local hospitals while many other residents visited lucky friends – and all of them were small-screen black and whites, not really suited to a parade built on scale and colour. From the beginning of the broadcast plans, complexity and difficulty reigned.

When Santa made his annual trek to Portage and Hargrave in Winnipeg, he entered a long-standing if contested tradition of occupying public space, but when he passed the CBC's camera in 1954, his image was broadcast through an emerging and still experimental electronic technology. At the time, this novelty expressed itself in essentially technical questions, but in the longer term the dynamics of broadcasting the parade – of creating a mediated Santa – were much more social and conceptual. While showing a parade on television allowed for an expanded audience – by 1969, for a national and even continental one – at the same time it challenged the company at the level of presentation, planning, and message. Capturing Santa's image required little more than setting up a camera along the route, but creating a media event to match the power of the live spectacle was a much more complicated proposition. While the parade was big, colourful, and designed for watching by large crowds on the sidewalk, television at the time was small, black and white, and reached distant audiences in their private homes. How could a street spectacle be translated to this new medium?

If these questions were new for Eaton's-Winnipeg in 1954, they have become more familiar to scholars of mass media in the ensuing years. Since the royal coronation in 1953 was televised on British, American, and Canadian stations, such media events have attracted considerable attention, with analyses focusing on the Olympics, big news events, and particularly moments of royal spectacle. The work of Daniel Dayan and Elihu Katz on "media events" (what they call the "live broadcasting of history") has been particularly influential, focusing on the forms of mechanical solidarity produced when diffuse viewers tune in to a common event being held at a symbolic centre. What happens when a live event gets broadcast beyond its local context? How do meanings get communicated? How do they shift? Can a live spectacle be translated for a new mass medium? In many ways, these questions fit the broadcast of the Eaton's parade, an event organized by an iconic consumer institution, built upon the assumed universalism of Christmas cheer and childhood wonder, broadcast from important regional and national metropolitan centres, and watched by widely dispersed audiences as one of the central events of the holidays.[2] Not surprisingly, however, many scholars have criticized Dayan and Katz, most notably for their lack of attention to power, difference, and the constructed nature of symbolic centres.[3] From this perspective, Eaton's did create a successful media event, but its move to television placed it within cultural dynamics and against powerful institutions that it could not fully control. Even in 1954, the success of the company's broadcast depended heavily on the technical knowledge of the CBC, and over time the relationships between company, broadcasters, and audiences would become more complicated and difficult.

This chapter explores some of these issues by probing the power and limitations of the mediated Santa, a term I use in two ways. First, in descriptive terms, the mediated Santa points to the increasing importance of the parade broadcasts. This television spectacle could reach distant audiences, but to do so required some revision in the production and planning of the parade. Second, in a more figurative way, the term signals the way the broadcast entailed new forms of mediation between Eaton's and the audience. In the street, the company could communicate relatively directly with crowds on the sidewalks, while television required dealing with different types of audiences and with new kinds of powerful institutions. Broadcasters had their own interests, their own codes of communication, and their own audiences to keep happy. This level of mediation inserted several complications onto Eaton's planning agenda. More than just a technological feat, then, the mediated Santa both signalled Eaton's tremendous cultural power and raised questions about the nature of the parade, its status as a public festival, and its place in the lives of its audiences.

"As important as the event itself"

In many ways, the mediated Santa reflected television's rise from experimental curiosity to common experience. In 1926, Scotland's John Logie Baird demonstrated a working model of a technology that could broadcast moving images as a signal. Developments in Britain and the United States moved quickly, with the first regularly scheduled telecasts by the late 1930s and a clear momentum towards dispersion and diffusion of the technology. This process was interrupted by the war, but with the return of peace, developments came in rapid succession. In the United States, twenty-four stations were licensed in 1946 alone, and one hundred by 1948, while in 1947 four networks began sending out regular programming to local affiliates. As TV stations spread, Americans adopted the technology rapidly and thoroughly. In 1948, less than 1 per cent of American homes had a television, but by 1952 the figure was over a third and by 1960 over 90 per cent.[4]

Canada took a different, and somewhat slower, path to a generally similar end. In Montreal, *La Presse* and its radio arm, CKAC, set up a one-off broadcast as early as 1931, but the low-quality signal impressed few observers, and the technology remained an experimental curiosity. Government planning for Canadian television commenced in earnest in 1946, but the plan wasn't approved until three years later, and actual stations did not begin broadcasting until 1952. The existing public radio network, the Canadian Broadcasting Corporation, was empowered to set up TV stations and to regulate broadcasting, setting out plans for a single station in each major market. These CBC stations would be supplemented by privately owned affiliates in smaller centres that would be required to offer the Corporation's "basic national service" alongside locally generated programming. By September 1952, the first stations appeared in Montreal and Toronto, with many more coming online in places like Sudbury, Hamilton, Ottawa, and Winnipeg over the next few years. By 1956, then, Canada had thirty-six stations spread from coast to coast, though the majority were in central Canada. Two years later, all these stations had been connected to the CBC's microwave network, making instant national broadcasts possible for the first time. Still, only nine of the forty-seven stations in 1960 were actually run by the CBC; the rest were affiliated private licensees who carried the CBC slate but retained some local autonomy. The arrival of a second, private national network (dubbed CTV), with its own coast-to-coast relay system by 1963, increased the depth and coverage of Canadian television.[5]

Meanwhile, as in the United States, ordinary Canadians adopted television with remarkable speed. Even before Canadian stations emerged, in fact, some affluent families near the US border had purchased sets, picking up the American signals that crossed the line and were within range of almost one-quarter of the population. The growth of the CBC after 1952 meant that more and more households could also pick up Canadian stations. In 1953, about one-quarter of the population was in reach of TV signals, but the figure had grown to over 90 per cent by 1960. At the same time, the technology itself proliferated rapidly: growing from only 10 per cent of Canadian households in 1954 to over three-quarters by 1960, with TV sets turned on an average of six hours a day.[6] Even then, the experience of TV had already spread further than actual ownership. Watching could be a social act among friends and neighbours, particularly for big events and important spectacles. The first televised Grey Cup, for example, was watched by Canadians in neighbours' homes, in bars, and even in store windows. In 1954, over one thousand Winnipegers travelled to Fargo, North Dakota, to see the game on American TV, watching not as isolated families in living rooms but as part of mixed crowds in hotels, bars, and restaurants. Similarly, in 1957, near Barrie, Ontario, Mrs Charles Kingsley collected neighbourhood children in her living room to watch a broadcast of the Toronto Santa Claus parade. "Some went a mile or more to watch the wonderful parade," she informed the company.[7]

Across North America, Santa Claus and television forged a quick and easy alliance. In New York, Macy's had already demonstrated the potential of the new medium with an experimental broadcast of its Thanksgiving parade in 1939 and more regularized local coverage beginning in 1945. Four years later, CBS began to feed its coverage to other American cities over its network. At a time when the United States had more than one hundred stations and almost one million television-equipped households, the New York parade could garner wide appeal.[8] As with television, the Canadian parade broadcast came later but spread quickly. In 1952, the Montreal and Toronto parades were televised on the newly minted local stations. Four years later, the Toronto parade aired live in eleven Ontario centres (as far north as North Bay, east to Kingston and Peterborough, and west from Winnipeg to about seventy-five miles out) and on a delay to Port Arthur, Regina, Brandon, and Lethbridge, while the Montreal parade reached audiences near the bigger cities in Quebec.[9] Indeed, it is striking how quickly the parades arrived on what was still an experimental and developing technology, following soon on the advent of TV in each city: in Toronto and Montreal only two months later and in Winnipeg after five months.

Documentation on the original decision to take the parade onto television is scarce, but this timing does suggest that the marriage was a relatively easy one, at least in the beginning. No doubt both Eaton's and the CBC had good reasons to forge a meeting of the minds: for Eaton's, with thousands of customers outside key metropolitan centres, television offered a new opportunity to reach a much more extensive audience; for the CBC, the parade represented a popular live event with established appeal that would fill time on stations desperate for content. In fact, spectacle television was a vital part of early line-ups and took a key part in establishing television as a popular medium. The CBC's broadcast of Queen Elizabeth's coronation in 1953 – a program even more logistically complicated than Eaton's Winnipeg broadcast in the following year – set the early standard for festival television. Sports were another staple of early broadcasting. In Barrie, Ontario, the very first broadcast on the new CBC affiliate was a World Series game, while the corporation's annual Grey Cup coverage was also popular. Even the regular schedule had a strong component of spectacle television: the iconic *Hockey Night in Canada* moved from radio to TV in 1952 and became a staple of Canadian Saturday nights.[10] In fact, the early Santa Claus parade broadcasts were run by the CBC Sports Department, the only division with the skill and equipment to cover extended, outside events. Compared to a football game, the parade was a dream: slow moving, composed of oversized floats and characters, and easy to capture on camera, it lacked the unpredictable dynamism of a sport event.

The Santa broadcast was also a logical extension of the existing uses of mass media around the parade. Early on, Eaton's exploited emerging media technologies to promote and broadcast the parade to wider audiences. In 1925, the company organized formal Santa Claus radio broadcasts every evening for days leading up to parade, telling the story of the old saint's travels from the North Pole, his adventures, and the characters he met along the way. By 1931, Montreal and Toronto radio stations began to broadcast live coverage of the parades themselves, a practice that soon spread to other cities.[11] Although it is not clear if these efforts were initiated by Eaton's or the radio stations, broadcasting became an important part of parade organization for the store. Film was another way to court distant audiences. In 1929, the *Toronto Daily Star* featured the parade in a special newsreel at Shea's Hippodrome, which also included footage of a rugby game specially flown in from Hamilton. Seven years later, Eaton's made a film of its Christmas parade and sent it to New York for the benefit of American children.[12] By the postwar years, Eaton's began to regularly distribute movies of the parade across the country to Eaton's branch stores, movie theatres, schools, libraries, and volunteer groups. In 1954, the Vancouver store used the parade film as an in-store promotion, shown through a TV set with the help of "angled mirrors from the moving picture machine." The following year, the Quota club of Winnipeg featured the film at its annual party for the patients of the Canadian Arthritis and Rheumatism Society, an event that included dinner, a musical reception, Santa handing out gifts, and a film of the Toronto (rather than the local) parade. The movies received international distribution as well, with Eaton's bragging that they were sent as far as Europe and South America.[13]

Obviously, neither radio nor film was ideal. Radio commentators tried to paint "word pictures" and stations made efforts to add atmosphere by, for example, placing microphones at street level ("you could hear the kids breathing," one CFRB radio engineer commented in 1950).[14] But the parade was a visual spectacle ill-suited to radio, at least as a primary medium. Adele Buckner wrote from Deep River, Ontario, that she was "bitterly disappointed in the broadcast" – having seen the parade for many years in person, she knew "how elegant it really is." Buckner suggested several improvements, including that "the broadcaster be a radio performer instead of an announcer" and that the coverage be written up as a story "in nursery rhyme form." "If this could be arranged," she concluded, "it would bring a much truer picture of the parade to the children of the air audience." Brockie approved, but informed Buckner that Eaton's "was not in too strong a position to do more than pass along the suggestion," since the stations were covering the parade "as a service, free of charge."[15] This was no small matter, raising a dynamic that would intensify in the era of television. The parade itself was under the absolute sovereignty of the company, but the broadcasts required mediation by other interests that Eaton's could not always control. Regardless, Eaton's promotions made it clear that the radio broadcast remained secondary to the live parade: as *La Presse* put it in 1935 (a sentiment echoed in countless early Eaton's ads as well), the broadcast was "for you who unfortunately will not be in Montreal to see the parade, and for all the others who are stuck in hospitals."[16]

As a visual medium, film seemed to offer better possibilities. With a camera placed high above the heads of the assembled crowds, sight-lines could be ideal. Like the parades themselves, film could be rich in colour. In place of the word pictures of radio, Eaton's substituted heavily scripted whimsical narration, canned sound effects, and spliced-in shots of children laughing and waving in the street. Sometimes, the films told stories. In 1953, the parade was framed by a moment of familial story time. While the father reads "A Visit from St Nicholas" to a well-behaved daughter, a June Cleaver–esque mother looks on. As the story ends, the screen fades to the parade.[17] Perhaps most ideal, since production was contracted and Eaton's was paying the tab, the company could control the content and style of the movies. Still, such films had their own limits. They lacked the immediacy (or "liveness") of radio and, despite the whimsical commentary, had a somewhat canned and artificial quality. They were also expensive to produce. Most importantly, perhaps, the films were not really a mass medium, reaching widely dispersed audiences but only in small bunches.

Television, then, combined many of the promises of radio and film without the key problems. It possessed the immediateness of radio and the visuality of film; it allowed for ideal sightlines, since it was easy to set up a camera along the route to look over the heads of jostling spectators; it could reach mass audiences instantly through broadcast or soon after through kinescopes (literally films of the broadcast made by pointing a camera at a television) and later video, which could be shipped to local broadcasters for replay.[18] Certainly, television raised production challenges. Even in the era of black and white, some colours showed up better on camera, something designers had to consider as they imagined floats. Not surprisingly, such questions became even more important in the age of colour, when blue and green became more common for the sake of TV image.[19] A live broadcast also raised new disciplinary challenges. Time had to be precise to meet the thirty-minute segments of the broadcast day, and the behaviour of participants had to be controlled in new ways. "The parade is being televised with cameras shooting north on James as well as mobile units on University Avenue and Albert Street," read the 1956 instructions for marshals in Toronto. "Please take particular care of your section at that time."[20] Marchers also received more direct reminders, in the form of signs leading up to the camera: "Smile, you're on TV," read one in 1968.[21] Yet none of these efforts were entirely new. Brockie's design and disciplinary efforts had always been most concerned with the flow of the procession and the sightlines of spectators: considering the pacing and spacing of marchers, paying attention to the relationship of one presentation to the next; limiting the mobility of participants so as not to block the view of children in the crowd. In this sense, the broadcast merely intensified the existing disciplinary challenges of the live parade.

As with the Grey Cup and *Hockey Night in Canada*, the Santa Claus parade broadcasts were instantly popular, and quickly became attached to the commercial and symbolic identity of the company. This point was made all too clear to Eaton's in 1957, when spotty coverage outside Toronto raised howls of protest from small-town viewers. "Saturday morning four little children lined up in front of our rabbit ear equipped

TV set to see the Santa Claus Parade," Janet Williams of Barrie, Ontario, informed the company. "They waited in vain. We can only receive our local station." That year, Eaton's received dozens of similar letters of complaint from viewers – most located, like Warren, in small communities a few hours north of Toronto – denied the chance to watch the parade on their local stations because Eaton's had declined to sponsor the broadcast. For Eaton's, the letters – piled almost an inch thick in Jack Brockie's files – made the consequences of this slight clear, but for historians, they offer a glimpse into the symbolic identity of the parade and the growing importance of the broadcast.[22] Many writers began with consumerist claims, offering up general lessons in retail geography alongside careful enumerations of recent purchases. "It is the people in districts outside of Toronto proper where no doubt a great deal of your business comes from," wrote Mrs Dan Turner from Midland, while a writer in Parry Sound noted that "people in our northern area purchase plenty from your store." Some correspondents went further, offering up exacting enumerations of items purchased: one claimed to have recently bought "a stuffed pussy cat and a doctor bag; yesterday through your order office a pair of toddler's rubbers." One correspondent noted – apparently without irony given her complaint – that she had recently bought a television set in addition to other big domestic goods totalling over $900. Apparently, consumers believed, "Eaton's did not think enough of our patronage to bring coverage of the Santa Claus parade" to local TV. Correspondents were equally willing to make the consequences clear: "As of now I will make no more purchases from Eatons," an anonymous correspondent from North Bay promised, while another pointed to the high quality of the Simpson's catalogue. "[I] have decided to shop at home this Christmas," Jennifer Cook of Barrie added. For these small-town residents, the Eaton's broadcast quickly became a tangible symbol of the "consideration" the company owed to consumers.

More was a stake than buying and selling, as consumerist practices blended with broader social categories and with folkloric notions of Eaton's place in Canadian life. Indeed, even narrow claims about shopping generally served to position a broader grievance, asserting a kind of modern moral economy of consumerism, where long-time patronage, the Christmas spirit, the parade tradition, or the company's Canadian ownership created an obligation of loyalty beyond any economic calculus. "What a pity there is such a lack of the real Christmas spirit in such action," Mrs John Clemens wrote from Parry Sound. "You may not know it, but Eaton's belongs to Canada," another wrote. "By that

I mean it is a Public Service in spite of being privately owned. Since Simpson's joined forces with USA, Canadians feel that it is a patriotic duty to support a Canadian institution and will do so more strongly as time goes on. But what you have done is to give people a slap in the face." Political language was deployed. One letter argued that Eaton's move was "a clear case of prejudice against the other stations along the CBC network," while another insisted that small-town viewers had "as much right as people living in Toronto to see it." By far the most common symbolic language, however, was familial. Most of the correspondents were mothers, who signed their letters with taglines like "mother of three very disappointed boys" and "on behalf of two very disappointed little kiddies" or painted vivid portraits of "broken hearted" children waiting for the broadcast. "I hope you will consider our children before next year's parade," advised Mrs N. Palmer of Sutton West. "[The] Santa Claus parade has become a tradition in our home," argued a mother in Parry Sound. "The children look forward to it as we adults do the Grey Cup game and it wouldn't occur to us that the game or the parade would not reach us by television." On the whole, the letters suggest that the broadcast was much more than a television signal – it quickly became one part of a broader web of cultural practices and discourses, a social event in a real sense.[23]

From the perspective of television history, the letters might also be read as powerful omens of the parade as media event, as artefacts of emerging forms of virtual connection between company and audience. Some letter writers that year saw the broadcast as continuing and reinforcing their own childhood experiences in the Toronto crowd, an opportunity to relive the joy and to pass it on to their children. "When I was a child in Toronto we never missed the Eaton's parade," one mother told the company. "Now my children have enjoyed it for years from a distance through the air waves. They were all in front of the set this year as usual waiting, when nothing happened." Yet many others noted that they had never seen the parade in person at all; their only connection was a form of "festive television," one that nonetheless held a powerful appeal.[24] "My children have not seen the parade besides on TV, nor have I myself," wrote one disgruntled mother, "so you disappointed many a child and adult." "I never got to Toronto to see the Parade when I was a child," wrote another. "It was just something we read about…[so] *it would be deeply appreciated if you would put the Parade over CKVR TV Channel 3 too in the years to come*."[25] In a very real sense, the parade's television age had begun.

"It's just not the same thing"

Delivering on the promise of such virtual connections raised several narrative, visual, and institutional difficulties that stretched well beyond design and production. Once the spectacle was removed from its specific urban context, the nature of audience and the terms of communication were fundamentally altered.[26] Crowds on the street and audiences in living rooms were watching the same parade, but they were hardly experiencing the same spectacle. A television's screen (until the 1970s, mainly black and white)[27] could not evoke the parade's scale or colour, its limited speaker could not convey the sound, and neither could provide the sense of carnival and excitement in the streets. Few observers believed the broadcast was ideal – as Winnipeg's Bill Trebilcoe put it, "it's just not the same thing."[28] Indeed, in the street, the full sensory experience of the parade extended beyond sight and sound, making it difficult for viewers to experience the sense of carnival or the physical sensations of cold hands on warm hot chocolate, expect perhaps by proxy. "I grew up in the late 60s – early 70s in Toronto and fondly remember the Eaton's Santa Claus parade," one Torontonian remembered. "I always watched it on T.V. with a mug of hot chocolate in my hand and a blanket wrapped around me. Just watching everyone battle the elements made me bundle up even though I was in the warmth of my own living room."[29] In this sense, as with any media event, the central challenge was not to *show* the parade – once TV spread to key Eaton's cities and mobile cameras were widely available, that was easy enough – but to *evoke* it, to create a television experience that was more than simply a series of images on the screen.[30]

Commentary became the key fulcrum of this challenge for Eaton's. The television spectacle required a mediating voice between parade and viewer, both to describe what was being seen and to communicate the broader excitement of the moment. Eaton's took a particular interest in this aspect of the broadcast, since the commentator had to do more than describe and needed a narrative style that evoked the emotional spirit of the parade. The company learned that comedians, hosts of variety shows, and children's performers worked better than news anchors, but whoever was chosen, commentary needed to balance clear description with a sense of whimsy. This was a difficult balance, and it led to considerable experimentation.[31] In 1955, the Toronto broadcast featured Elaine Grand and Dick McDougall of *Tabloid*, a news magazine show. In Winnipeg, Chuck Skelding, a long-time radio announcer who went on to host a jazz show, covered the parade for many years.[32] In 1957, CBC Toronto tried a child commentator, but reviews were not good and the practice was not repeated for many years.[33] Children's performers became increasingly common over time, at least as one part of a bigger team: the Friendly Giant in 1968, Miss Sara and others from *Romper Room* in 1969, and Mr Dress Up in 1973. CTV's childhood star Uncle Bobby began his whimsical street-level reports in 1965, becoming a staple of the annual parade broadcast over the following years.[34] While such performers were experienced in talking to children and skilled at evoking the emotional spirit of the parade, they were often balanced with the more descriptive voices of news anchors or game show and variety show hosts: in 1974, CTV's line-up included Betty Thompson of *Romper Room* in the booth beside Jim Perry of the game show *Definition*, while Uncle Bobby reported from the street. Genial news anchor Lloyd Robertson did the CTV broadcast for several years in the late 1970s alongside a number of more whimsical sidekicks. Gender balance, as so many of these examples indicate, was also important.[35]

Befitting their importance as mediators between street atmosphere and living room audience, television commentators were the magnets for (sometimes contradictory) complaints. In 1953, *Toronto Daily Star* columnist Gordon Sinclair declared Pat Patterson's TV commentary to be "graceful but dull." A year later, an "Irate Canadian" from Sarnia, Ontario, complained that the "telecast was almost spoiled for me at the close by the commentators hogging the camera like two inferior vaude-ville turns."[36] Obviously, some personalities were more skilled than others, but the two complaints suggest that all commentators faced a difficult set of balances. In his 1953 comment, Sinclair contrasted the inherent styles of TV and radio. "Mark it down to prejudice if you like," he wrote, "but Pat Patterson's TV chore was patently to let the pictures tell the story. She therefore said but little and kept what remarks she did make to a sort of cultivated deadpan level … Wally and Jeff, the CFRB [radio] team, let caution go hang as they whooped and hammed and giggled their way through the processional as uninhibited as kit-tens. Radio had triple the animation of TV." On the other hand, as the Sarnia correspondent made clear, aggressive commentary could over-whelm the event.[37] But if commentators needed to balance description and whimsy, Eaton's had to walk the fine line between scripted and spontaneous. Commentators were not entirely controllable – they were hired by the TV stations, after all – but Eaton's left little to chance. The company employed "spotters" to assist commentators on parade day and its public relations staff prepared detailed outlines, using whimsical rather than descriptive language to guide commentators to notable features of floats. Yet Brockie's post-mortem reports often complained that commentators didn't follow the script, and (perhaps most disturbingly) forgot to mention Eaton's.

This last complaint made it clear that broadcasting the parade beyond its local context raised additional problems of brand identity. Traditionally, as we saw in chapter 1, the parade contained few explicitly commercial elements. This approach worked well enough in local terms: in all five parade cities, Eaton's could mobilize an existing institutional and cultural infrastructure to bind the identity of the parade to the corporate personality of the company. Its long-standing connection to the parade, its iconic local image, and the route itself could remind spectators that this was an *Eaton's* event. Outside of these cities, however, the link was never as certain. Eaton's was certainly a familiar name across Canada, but parade producers did not assume an automatic link between the broadcast spectacle and its public relations effect. The move to television prompted more explicit references to Eaton's. Overall themes eventually included the company's name, so that typical 1950s "Parade of Merry Times" (1957) or "Santa's Carousel of Color" (1960) gave way to "At Eaton's Christmas Comes to Life" and "Let Eaton's Share a Special Moment with You" (1973 and 1974). Well before this, however, "Eaton's" was explicitly inscribed into the presentations, like the "animated nursery blocks" that spelled out E-A-T-O-N-S in 1953 or the opening float three years later, which featured perennial favourite Mother Goose, but included new signs on each side "to carry the wording that the Parade is sponsored by Eaton's. (Up until now we have not included too much commercial mention of Eaton's but TV coverage is becoming greater each year. This [is] being done to cope with [the] lack of mention of sponsorship by commentators covering the parade)."[38]

The challenges of branding were only one small part of a much broader problem. The whole idea of mounting a broadcast of a quasi-public, quasi-commercial event raised difficult legal and conceptual questions. Even if the parade was by nature corporate, it sought attention by marching in the street and by inviting everyone to gather on sidewalks, both relatively open public spaces. The broadcast was an electronic signal produced by television stations that owned the images they sent through the air (to audiences in private homes) but also had broadly public purposes to inform and communicate as well as entertain. If the parade was a public event, then, what was the broadcast? At

The television age: "Eaton's" brand name on a float.
York University Libraries, Clara Thomas Archives & Special Collections,
Toronto Telegram fonds, ASC34673.

a practical level, this unresolved dilemma expressed itself in the incon-
sistent administrative relationship between company and broadcaster.
Early arrangements varied: some years, the CBC televised the parade
as a public service (meaning that local affiliates were not obligated to
pick it up, though most apparently did), while other years saw Eaton's
sponsor the broadcast, but even in those cases actual air time was occasionally given for free.[39]

At another level, the question was more conceptual, philosophical,
and certainly more difficult. In the United States, CBS butted heads
with Macy's and Hudson's over plans to broadcast the New York and
Detroit Thanksgiving parades. The department stores had arranged
for two rival networks (NBC for New York and ABC for Detroit) to
televise their parades without commercials, with two toy companies
(Lionel and Ideal) providing exclusive sponsorship. But when CBS secured yet another toy company as its own sponsor, it announced plans

to broadcast the Detroit and New York parades alongside the Gimbel's presentation from Philadelphia. At this point, the problems began. The chairman of Ideal accused CBS of "piracy, poaching, and unethical conduct," while the department stores contemplated legal action. "Macy's and Hudson's have copyrighted the floats used in the parade," noted the *New York Times*. "Unauthorized telecasts of these features ... could be the basis of action against CBS." These were powerful corporations with teams of lawyers, but in a broader sense the issue was hardly legalistic. The parades had always balanced commercial and public meanings. They were organized by a powerful corporation, but unlike, say, a hockey game (with paid and controlled admission, where selling broadcast rights was just an extension of those long-time commercial customs), they were also public events. Santa marched in city streets to seek publicity in both the broad sense of gaining attention and in the narrow sense of ensuring commercial exposure for the stores. Indeed, the accessibility of the Eaton's spectacles had always been the basis of their power to gather crowds. But if department stores could copyright a public event and assign broadcast rights to particular interests, the commercial impulse might trump the public. "The Thanksgiving Day parades take place in the street," a CBS spokesman contended. "We're covering it just as a newspaper would cover a news event."[40] Such conflicts occurred in Canada as well, although there is considerably less detail available. In eulogizing 1950s CBC program director Stuart Griffiths, for example, Mavor Moore remembered him insisting "that Eaton's buy thousands of dollars worth of advertising spots if CBC televised its annual Santa Claus parade – threatening to offer the program to Simpson's if Eaton's declined, on the ground that once on the street the parade was in the public domain. Eaton's decided to sponsor the event."[41] That decision made strategic sense in the short term, but hardly resolved the broader conceptual issue – was the parade a promotional affair or a public event? Clearly, television stations and department stores had different answers to these questions.

In Canada, such problems were exacerbated by the dual nature of television. By 1961, two English broadcasters competed for attention: the public CBC and private CTV, though the word "public" ought to be read somewhat carefully, since the CBC had many features of commercial television (from popular and often American prime-time shows to frequent commercial interruptions) but in typical Canadian style preferred an angst-ridden and ambivalent approach to the matter of outright commercialism.[42] As one CBC executive noted, the Eaton's parade rode a "fine line between entertainment and outright merchandising." It was at once an hour-long, mile-long commercial for the company ("primarily to make known the arrival of Santa Claus at the downtown Toronto Eaton's store specifically and at all Eaton's stores across Canada generally," in the words of Marcel Ouimet at the network) *and* a popular spectacle of considerable public interest and entertainment value. Beginning in 1962, the CBC imposed significant limits on the promotional aspects of the sponsored broadcast, aiming to separate commercial messages from the program content. "Our pickups of the parade must *not* include audio references to Eaton's," one policy memo ordered, "and must carefully avoid video exposure of floats, banners, costumes, or other items bearing the Eaton name or trademark. Neither may any reference be made to Eaton's in the program title." Nor could commercial messages relate specifically to the parade, a rather subtle distinction that allowed Eaton's to advertise its "goods, services, and attractions" during the parade broadcast but say nothing of the parade itself. Nor could the regular commentators deliver commercial messages; different voice-overs were required to keep the commercials and the entertainment separate.[43] In 1970, the CBC was clearly horrified to discover that Eaton's broadcast plans completely overturned this nuanced set of policies, calling for "commercials delivered from the site by program commentators, interviews with Eaton's employees during program content, the use of the music from Eaton's commercial jingle as background music during the program, total integration of some commercial with program content, in-store coverage of Santa's arrival to talk to children etc." None of this was a problem for CTV, which lacked any publicly owned mandate and so dispensed with the CBC's anguished and contradictory approach to commercialism. Thus, in 1969 CTV's coverage opened with the slide "Eaton's Santa Claus Parade," echoed by an announcer stating "The Eaton 100 SCP ... brought to you by Eaton's ... Canada's Christmas Store for a hundred years." Over at the CBC, the opening slide simply read, "The Santa Claus Parade," though the announcer made the sponsorship clear: "The 1969 Santa Claus Parade ... brought to you by Eaton's ... Canada's Christmas Store for a hundred years."[44] Still, despite the angst and nuance at the CBC, these were hardly fundamental televisual differences.

The problems of commercialism highlight a still broader institutional problem. In Toronto, Montreal, and Winnipeg, despite perpetual grumbling about traffic and congestion, civic elites seemed to go out of their way to accommodate Eaton's: rerouting streetcars, assigning extra police, encouraging downtown workers to stay out of the way. And many organizations knew well enough not to compete with the parade, scheduling their events on some other day. The parades, after all, were enormously popular, probably the most anticipated and well-attended annual events in any of these cities. The broadcast was also popular – in 1966, over one million Canadians tuned in to the English broadcast of the Toronto parade – but it did require Eaton's to deal with powerful gatekeepers intent on protecting their own interests, those of their imagined audiences, and those of other, equally popular broadcast events. In 1956, the CBC interrupted its Canadian Football League (CFL) playoff coverage to show the Montreal parade before returning for the end of the game.[45] This was clearly not a satisfying long-term solution. When Eaton's considered moving the Toronto parade to Sunday in 1973, for example, the CBC objected, pointing to potential conflicts with its popular coverage of the CFL Playoffs. Lengthy negotiations ensued, revolving around a complex delay schedule, owing to the CBC's concern about competition from the CTV broadcast. At times, these complications seemed frustrating for Eaton's planners. "At this moment," wrote a staffer at Cockfield Brown, the Eaton's advertising agency, "I don't know of any other steps we can take to satisfy CBC (which seems odd, in view of the fact that we're the buyer) but that's the way it seems to go."[46]

All of this conflict and difficulty played out at a different level for spectators and viewers. Brockie sometimes expressed concern about the relationship between the live and the TV event, telling *Canadian Business* in 1955 that some might stay home to watch it "the easy way" but the parade's colour would bring them back to the crowded sidewalks. "But what colour TV will do to the crowds," the magazine reported, "he won't even estimate."[47] And it did seem clear that the priorities of the broadcast could shift the experience of the live, in-the-street performance. In 1979, the Lugowy family "realized too late" that they were standing around the corner from TV cameras, meaning the bands took a break. "Only two of the bands played as they passed us," Mrs Lugowy complained. "Nothing is duller than a parade without music."[48] Five years earlier, one particularly quiet band had told a frustrated marshal, "we only play for television."[49] On the other hand, viewers who had experienced the live event never seemed quite satisfied with the broadcast, complaining particularly about the commercial interruptions. In 1962, Nathan Cohen of the *Toronto Daily Star* complained that CTV's parade coverage "was interrupted with ferocious frequency by commercials," hardly appropriate for a broadcast aimed at children. Twelve years later, Mrs A. Irvine wrote from Limehouse, Ontario, to complain that on CTV the bands were constantly drowned out by Eaton's ads. Even the wife of one Eaton's executive agreed, offering some "rather pungent remarks" through her husband on the quality of both broadcasts: "She thought the CBC commercials were well done as they only did the overprint message without a jingle so that the parade was not interfered with. On the other hand she thought the CFTO commercials were highly overdone where they used the jingle, very annoying, and would turn anybody against our commercialism."[50]

Still, in the end, such complaints were mainly wrinkles rather than fundamental obstacles or unsolvable problems. Larger audiences on television ultimately had little effect on the sizes of live crowds. By the mid-1970s, the broadcast from Toronto was attracting over two million viewers a year in English Canada alone – and many more in the United States – but the normal estimates of crowds in the streets hardly declined, continuing to reach one million for the same period. There was even evidence that the broadcast created greater demand for the real thing: "It's their first parade," claimed Maureen Brochu of Montreal, discovered by a *Toronto Star* reporter along Yonge Street with her three kids in 1976. "They've seen it on TV in Montreal and they're so excited about seeing it here live."[51] In fact, from another angle, this Toronto–Montreal encounter was even more interesting than it first appeared, pointing towards a larger set of cultural and geographic problems. By 1976, there was no parade in Montreal for Brochu to attend; her children could watch the Toronto event on TV, but that broadcast was surprisingly controversial.

"Anglo-Saxon fairy tales"

Over time, the mediated Santa reinforced the centrality of the Toronto parade. At first, the broadcast geography reflected the inherent tension of Canadian mass culture between national developments and local realities. Early broadcasts were regional, a dynamic that seemed to reflect social geography rather than technological limitations. Certainly, the reach of the very first parades was limited by the slow development of television. In Winnipeg, for example, the first signals were limited to about seventy-five miles, and kinescopes were awkward to make and slow to ship. But the broadcasts remained regional even after it would have been technologically possible to reach farther. By 1956,

the flagship Toronto parade could have been easily sent over the microwave network from Quebec City to Winnipeg (indeed, a week later, the
Grey Cup was shown live in that range and on delay farther out), yet it
was not broadcast in Winnipeg until 1964, and even then it appeared as
a supplement to the Winnipeg parade not a replacement. The Winnipeg
parade was also shown across the prairies, perhaps reflecting that city's
own metropolitan status in the region. The dynamic was similar in
Quebec, where CBC and Radio-Canada stations continued to show the
Montreal parade in English and French until 1969. The pull of region,
then, made for a remarkably complex broadcast geography. With more
stations coming on line every month, each parade seemed to bring a
more convoluted television schedule: by the mid-sixties, Eaton's enumeration of local coverage ran to almost eight pages.[52]

Over time, however, the broadcast of the Toronto parade became
national in scope. When the parades were discontinued in Calgary
(1953) and Edmonton (1957), they were replaced by the broadcast of the
Winnipeg event. In 1967, however, Eaton's officials ended the Winnipeg
parade in favour of more "exciting attractions" in the Winnipeg stores
and more focus on promoting the Toronto broadcast as an alternative:
"The Eaton Santa Claus parade in Toronto, has been carried nation-
ally on television, in black and white, and for the first time in color
in 1966," the company argued in its press release, "thus providing the
children of Canada with an opportunity to view this traditional feature
of the Christmas scene."[53] Three years later, the company cancelled its
Montreal parade as well. Here, the logic was partly local. Amid violent
street demonstrations, city council passed an extraordinary by-law to
halt all public processions, although it explicitly exempted both Eaton's
and the Grey Cup parade (municipal officials explained the exemption
by saying that Eaton's had already secured a parade permit before the
ban). The company nonetheless abandoned the parade for good.[54] "I
talked to the Chief of Police," recalled store manager Pierre Witmeur,
"and he said, 'We cannot be held responsible for the protection of the
population,' so I made the decision to end it."[55] The Grey Cup parade
went ahead without incident (although two cheerleaders did unfurl a
"Québec libre" banner and were quickly removed from the parade by
police), but the threat of violence was credible. By the late 1960s, the
company's image had become wrapped in the intense linguistic politics
of the decade, becoming one of many symbols of anglophone domi-
nation. In November 1968, a small home-made bomb exploded in a
customer locker in the basement of the downtown store in the middle

of the night, the third of a series of bombs in the city over a thirty-six-hour period. The following day, the store was evacuated in the evening when the company received a telephoned bomb threat; eventually, police found and removed four sticks of dynamite from the main floor jewellery department. In this context, the end of the Montreal parade made sense. But in the longer term, the company was probably happy to rid itself of an expensive and complex undertaking at a time when television provided an easy alternative. In later years, despite the lack of bombs and even with intense pressure from francophone TV networks, Eaton's never brought the parade back to Montreal.[56]

If the local dynamics were different in Winnipeg and Montreal, the broader effect was the same. By 1969, the early regional geography of the Eaton's broadcast was replaced by a single event, a national broadcast of the Toronto parade. The result was ambiguous. On the one hand, the new broadcast regime reinforced the centrality of the Toronto parade in Eaton's national promotional schedule. On the other hand, Canadians were, for the first time, watching the same parade, a national media event that connected viewers from Newfoundland to British Columbia. By the early 1970s, the Toronto parade regularly reached almost three million Canadian viewers over more than sixty stations from coast to coast, an impressive tally in a country with just under twenty-two million residents thinly scattered across a vast geography.[57] "Television coverage has become as important as the event itself," one television reporter noted in 1973, "reaching millions more children across the country in places as far away as Prince Rupert, British Columbia and St. John's, Newfoundland." Indeed, by this point, audiences were continental in scope. Beginning in 1963, the American network CBS slotted Toronto highlights into its Thanksgiving Parade Jubilee, which was centred on the Macy's procession but also included the Gimbel's parade in Philadelphia and the J.L. Hudson parade in Detroit, opening all these spectacles to an audience approaching 40 million.[58]

The triumph of Toronto in the broadcast landscape raised several new challenges and difficulties. By the 1960s, Toronto had emerged as a cultural and media capital of Canada, so at some level it made sense to transmit this local event to a wider audience.[59] Yet the cognitive gap between producer and consumer – inherent in any cultural product – was blown apart by the increased scale. Eaton's was in no position to control coverage in the United States, where the parade was subsumed into the American holiday rhythm, shown as edited highlights in a broader Thanksgiving broadcast. "C.B.S. is taking license with the

Table 3.1 Year of final Eaton's
Santa Claus parade outside Toronto

Calgary	1953
Edmonton	1957
Winnipeg	1966
Montreal	1968

Toronto parade, which had nothing to do with Thanksgiving," the *New York Times* television correspondent mused in 1963. "Canada observed Thanksgiving on Oct. 14." Audiences too might notice the cross-border difference. "The Eaton's parade always featured storybook characters," recalled Linda Young of Cranston, Rhode Island, "including British ones that I'd never heard of except on the morning of the parade."[60]

But in a regionally and linguistically divided country with, at best, tenuous commitments to unifying national symbols, even the Canadian broadcast crossed significant cultural boundaries. In the 1960s, the increasing importance of television audiences intersected with growing nationalist sentiment in English Canada (driven in part by the lead up to the country's Centennial in 1967), and Eaton's became increasingly interested in making the Toronto event relevant to a "Canadian" rather than just a local audience. In 1967, a Centennial float headed the parade, featuring ten guards in historic costume, provincial flower banners and trillium girls dancing around a maypole. Eaton's also arranged for a float featuring Bobby Gimby, the official pied piper of the Centennial celebrations, whose popular song "Canada" in many ways became the unofficial anthem for the year.[61] The company created Canadian-themed floats and considered bands from other provinces to replace local union outfits. Dropping in a few nationalist symbols was easy enough, but integrating Canadian content into the storybook script remained elusive, since there were few uniquely Canadian fairy tales. "I had some trouble finding Canadian folk tales and Indian legends which are familiar to children," a Toronto librarian admitted in response to a company enquiry. "The Princess of Tombosoa is certainly well known and Paul Bunyan is very popular too." Her hand-written addition to her letter made the broader point explicit: "Incidentally, Paul Bunyan is really American but the setting is so much like our own that Canadians tend to claim him too." Integrating new mass culture characters from television also meant greater American content, since the most popular TV shows "with child appeal" in Canada were almost exclusively American in origin – cartoons like Bugs Bunny and sitcoms like the *Beverly Hillbillies*.[62]

Managing difference, moreover, was a crucial element in this nationalizing project. The Centennial float featured the newly adopted and still controversial national flag, but also included the Union Jack and the banners showing the flower emblems of the ten provinces and territories.[63] But since Toronto's metropolitan ambitions had always been resented in other parts of the country, even prominent provincial symbols could not cloak the regional tensions. When a group of firefighters rallied to save the Winnipeg parade – and for their efforts had to compete against two (English and French) national broadcasts of the Toronto parade – T.R. Caine of St James made the regional dynamics clear: "I don't think we will ever see the day that Toronto televises our parade on their local stations. Do you?"[64] The problem was even more intense in French Canada, where the broadcast had to confront the linguistic politics of the Quiet Revolution, the term applied to the period of intense ferment in Quebec after 1960. For many years, Eaton's had run a parade in Montreal, largely by shipping floats from Toronto, adding a few locally defined features, and sticking on signage directly translated into French. Meanwhile, the CBC and Radio-Canada (the francophone version of the Canadian Broadcasting Corporation) had televised the Montreal parade in English and French. But, by 1969, with the Toronto broadcast as the only Eaton's show in town, and with language issues now at the centre of national debate, storybook wonder turned out to be far from the universal message the company believed it to be. In 1973, Radio-Canada objected strenuously to airing a Toronto parade built around what network officials called "Anglo-Saxon fairy tales" and cartoon characters with names that "can not even be translated," citing three years of viewer complaints.[65]

The problems in French Canada were deeper than just managing audience in a generic way. On American television, slippages in meaning were hardly disturbing or dangerous, but British characters that were quaintly different in Rhode Island were culturally explosive in Quebec. In the dispute with Radio-Canada, moreover, the issue was not just about appealing to a particular audience but dealing with institutional gatekeepers who could speak in its name. In 1973, national broadcasting was technologically possible, but the structure of television reflected Canada's long-standing duality ("les solitudes télévisuelles"

A Mile of Make-Believe

The national broadcast: French sign on a Dr Seuss float, Toronto, 1970.
York University Libraries, Clara Thomas Archives & Special Collections,
Toronto Telegram fonds, ASC34676.

in the words of Denis Bachand and Pierre Bélanger).[66] Both English
and French Canada had their own public (CBC and Radio-Canada) and
private (CTV and TVA) networks, with Radio-Canada serving both a
large French-speaking majority in Quebec and the increasingly asser-
tive francophone minorities in other provinces. With a strong interest
in building francophone culture across Canada, the network pressed
its agenda on Eaton's.[67] In the long run, the private network TVA offered a promising alternative (five TVA stations picked up the Toronto
parade in late 1970s), but in 1973 concessions were made and compromises reached. Eaton's agreed to build a "French float" in the future
(it was already too late to add anything new that year) but apparently
baulked at the more onerous suggestion of remounting its Montreal parade. Radio-Canada agreed to broadcast the procession, using its own
video feed from Toronto and its own hosts, the children's puppets Nic
et Pic, stationed in a Montreal studio. With serious issues of binational

conflict at stake, no one apparently saw much humour in the multiple layers of mediation at play (a public broadcaster's puppets in Montreal describing a department store's parade in Toronto for francophone audiences inside and outside Quebec), but the negotiations themselves revealed the fundamental difficulties of translating a local spectacle for a wider audience.[68]

Mediation and Power

In the television age, the Eaton's Santa Claus parade became one example of a powerful new form of commercial and metropolitan spectacle that could reach out beyond its local context. In mounting its parade each year, Eaton's did more than just amuse spectators on local sidewalks – it used its corporate power and networks to create a Canadian tradition with considerable reach, first by creating regional broadcasts and later through its national broadcast from Toronto. The connections that were forged between audience and spectacle, moreover, went well beyond watching. The broadcast became part of a wider web of social practices for consumers and one element in Eaton's broader folkloric power. These social meanings sometimes placed obligations on Eaton's – to sponsor the broadcast in small markets, for example, or to nationalize the symbols in the parade itself – but the broadcasts also allowed the company to extend its power outward and to deepen its influence in cities without a parade. While successful in many ways, this project nonetheless created problems, contradictions, and tensions. The parade expressed the growing cultural hegemony of Toronto but hardly overcame regional and local differences. There was a national broadcast, but no unified national audience. Eaton's could try to Canadianize the parade to accommodate the larger scale, but finding popular images and characters remained elusive. The broadcasts increased Eaton's promotional power but placed it against powerful networks with their own agendas and priorities.

At a deeper level, however, these complexities were simply by-products of Eaton's power. Broadcasting a Toronto parade certainly exposed the cultural fissures in Canadian life, but the company failed to build a fully national audience precisely because it had the economic, organizational, and cultural resources to try. In this context, Eaton's own power was reinforced by its location in Toronto, an emerging cultural metropolis in English Canada and the centre of a growing mass media infrastructure. Compared to other groups, then, Eaton's was able to speak to a much broader audience and to participate in a much larger public, one connected by new communication technologies rather than by the common experience of a particular urban space. Few processions attracted national broadcast attention and few users of public space possessed the knowledge and resources to compete with Eaton's on this larger scale. At a time when mass broadcasting was loosening the bonds between the public space of the street and the public sphere of communication, this was no small issue. If North Americans continued to use parades for many purposes, department stores were playing in a different league.

4

The Civic Fantastic

Sudbury's annual Santa Claus parade was in its usual fine form. Wet snow was falling, but the streets were bursting with people and colour. At 10 a.m. sharp, the parade moved off from a local arena, winding its way on a somewhat convoluted path through downtown. By any standard, it was an impressive spectacle, stretching over a mile in length, taking nearly an hour to pass a single point, packed full of floats, bands, clowns, and cheerleaders. Characters ran the gamut from traditional to fantastic – from carollers to Martians – while one high school float, titled "Christmas in Transylvania," featured TV icons *The Munsters* as an "off-beat" interpretation of the parade theme, "Christmas around the World." Members of Nickel Belt Indian Club sat in a giant birch bark canoe, Elmer the Elephant encouraged traffic safety, and Boy Scouts wore uniforms from around the world. A majorette troupe called The Twirlettes had travelled from Sault Ste Marie for the occasion. Spectators, at least thirty thousand strong, were delighted, waving and shouting and cheering as Santa finally approached. The local paper declared that the parade was "the best ever."[1]

This was 1965, but it could have been any year in the decade or so after 1958, when the city had witnessed its first Santa Claus parade. Sudbury was Ontario's sixth-largest city, a growing regional centre at the gateway to the province's booming northern mining region. The city was at the peak of its prosperity, and the impressive parade was hardly a one-off effort. The Sudbury Junior Chamber of Commerce (colloquially called the "Jaycees") had kicked off the annual tradition in 1958, but by 1965 the event included many of the city's key community institutions. The Jaycees were still the main organizers, but participation reached wide and deep, as multiple groups marshalled hours of volunteer labour to the cause. The Sudbury Police Association supplied the traffic safety float. The Unemployment Insurance Commission advertised its Winter Works Campaign, imploring residents with a sign reading, "Don't Wait for Spring – Do it Now!" Johnson Cartage provided horses for cowboys and cowgirls to ride along the route. Skidoo Snowmobile offered up a Winter Wonderland scene. The region's largest union, Mine Mill Local 598, entered a float of "beautifully dressed geisha girls" in an "oriental" scene. *Sudbury Star* carriers – "togged out with their new bags" – threw candy to the crowd. Two hundred Jaycee members served as clowns. The Retail Merchants Association covered the costs, while the *Sudbury Star* offered thousands of dollars in free advertising, not to mention uniformly positive coverage. With many more service clubs, business associations, and individual citizens joining in, the parade represented a mobile census of community organizations.[2]

Sudbury's Christmas spectacle was only one of many examples of the proliferation of Santa Claus parades outside of large metropolitan areas. By 1965, the idea had been taken up by entrepreneurs, civic groups, and chambers of commerce across Main Street North America. At first gloss, these parades show remarkable similarity and uniformity across space and time: wherever and whenever they were organized, Santa Claus parades played almost exclusively on versions of childhood wonder and storybook fantastic. They may not have been as professional in design as the Eaton's or Macy's parade, but they shared a narrative emphasis on wonder and fantasy and an aesthetic commitment to colour and whimsy. But if the Eaton's parades blended fantastic vocabularies and meticulous corporate organization, parades like Sudbury's grew from a strikingly different organizational base. The Eaton's parade was tightly organized, exclusive, and meticulous; Sudbury's was open, plural, and cooperative. I call this style "the civic fantastic" to highlight the blend of whimsical spectacle and community organization, though the term should not imply entirely local, inclusive, or ideal. Parades like Sudbury's were subject to many broad cultural influences. Organizers forged their events out of a mixture of wider cultural developments and more specific community needs, so the civic fantastic expressed both the promises and the perils of local organization in a commercialized and connected society. Even the basic geography of the civic fantastic should make this point: far from a local development, it proliferated rapidly across a wide continental space, arriving in places like Sudbury along vectors of influence that were created by mass institutions operating at a North American scale. At the same time, as creatures of civic

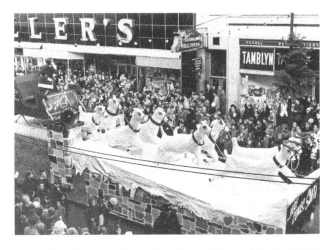

Santa Claus float, Sudbury, Ontario, n.d. (probably the 1960s).
Courtesy of the Sudbury Santa Claus Parade.

elites, the parades reflected the local cultures of power in which they were created. At the community level, the civic fantastic was shaped by a dynamic tension between inclusion and exclusion. Sudbury's 1965 parade, then, is best understood as a local interpretation of much wider developments and dynamics.

"Just about everything a parade should have"

Sudbury's parade came late to a long process of proliferation. Already by the 1920s, the Santa Claus parade idea was moving outside the department store networks that had created it. In some big cities, powerful institutions mounted spectacles that rivalled department store parades in scale and sophistication. In Pittsburgh, the largest newspaper, the *Press*, organized the city's first parade in 1928; in Chicago, the State Street Business Association mounted the city's first Christmas pageant in 1931. But smaller cities and towns formed the core of the civic fantastic. Parades emerged in the interwar years in regional centres like Windsor, Ontario; Youngstown, Ohio; Reading, Pennsylvania; Spokane, Washington; and San Jose, California. From there, the form proliferated widely and rapidly, with even small towns getting into the act in the middle decades of the century. Already in the 1930s, a few small towns around Toronto were mounting parades, but growth accelerated after the war, with Aurora, Newmarket, and even tiny Holland Landing greeting Santa in the streets. In the Nickel Belt, railway town Capreol organized its own effort, the first in 1961, often with participation of floats from nearby Sudbury. Farther south, Picton, Ontario (a town of only four thousand people) held several successful parades, as did nearby Belleville (population twenty thousand). Outside of Ontario, places like Minnedosa, Manitoba; Grand Rapids, Michigan; and Trois-Rivières, Quebec, also mounted regular annual parades.[3]

Over time, then, the form became a common-sense aspect of Christmas celebration across North America, spreading to absurdly ubiquitous status in both Canada and the United States. A brief survey of Ontario parades in the 1970s will make this point. In early December 1971, four communities west of Toronto, all within a twenty-minute drive, held parades on a single weekend.[4] Six years later, residents of southwestern Ontario could choose from a remarkable number of parades: in Windsor (two), Sarnia, Wallaceburg, Chatham, Ridgetown, Blenheim, Dresden, Thamesville, Bothwell, Tilsbury, Leamington, and Petrolia, all within a fifty-mile radius.[5] Many of these community parades reached impressive scale and style. By 1968, Sudbury's parade included nearly thirty floats, fourteen bands, 350 majorettes, cheerleaders from all fourteen of the area's high schools, and dozens of clowns, while nearby Capreol managed forty floats of its own, an impressive number that the *Sudbury Star* nonetheless claimed highlighted "quality over quantity." Perth's parade regularly comprised more than two dozen floats and several bands, drawing in spectators from several nearby communities.[6] The civic fantastic spread far beyond Ontario. By 1970, for example, the idea had travelled to at least a dozen Manitoba communities, while in 1977, the *Wilmington Star-News* surveyed what it called "the major Christmas parade season" in North Carolina, enumerating eight local events in a three-week stretch after Thanksgiving and noting that "while other area towns do not have regular parades scheduled for the season, most will have a special Santa Claus appearance."[7]

From the beginning, local organizers eagerly embraced the Christmas fantastic. Back in 1926, Youngstown, Pennsylvania's, first parade included Mother Goose, the Old Woman Who Lived in a Shoe, Little Jack Horner, Bo Peep, and Simple Simon. Reporting on the local parade in 1939, the *Windsor Daily Star* described a lineup that could have been found almost anywhere: "There will be soldiers, sailors, farmers, Mexicans, Christmas carol singers, dragons, animals, including cat, horse, bear, lion, tiger, and two monkeys. There will be ten blackbirds, there will be clowns, peasant girls, Indians, and just about everything a parade should have."[8] In London, Ontario, the 1961 parade similarly featured Jack Frost, Mother Goose, Banjo the Clown, and an animated music box, while that same year in Trois-Rivières, Quebec, spectators watched a dozen floats including "the Blue Fairy and Pinnochio, the Treasure Fairy, the Snow Fairy, the Toy Fairy, the Forest Fairy, and the Kingdom of the Fairies."[9] Naturally, Santa was always the mainstay and climax, but he arrived in multiple and varied forms of transportation: by plane, helicopter, parachute, fire truck, horse and buggy, and antique car. One year, in San Jose, California, the Retail Merchants Association offered local children a $5 prize for the best suggestion for Santa's transportation. The winner's idea was certainly novel and specific, "having Santa come in a specially constructed dirigible containing an inner ball of aluminum and an outer ball of treated rubber and mooring his blimp at the top of the Bank of America Building." The organizers did their best, although the blimp had to park at the Sunnyvale Airport before Santa toured the town in a cart pulled by Shetland ponies.[10]

None of these community parades were stunningly innovative in style. Marching bands provided the sounds almost everywhere, reflecting the hegemony of brass and drums in twentieth-century parade culture. Bands were supplemented, at times, by car horns, police sirens, and other easily available noisemakers. "With a tooting of horns and a shrieking of sirens, Santa Claus, in a private machine, led a procession of trucks, business and pleasure cars and delivery vehicles," one Pennsylvania report noted in 1925.[11] Similarly, the visual style mirrored the common approaches of the corporate fantastic: distortion of scale, vivid colour, and amusing juxtaposition were all standard fare. Whether "the big clown with … a tiny umbrella" in one Missouri town, the "retinue of monstrous characters" in Toledo, "les bouffons à tête de girafe" in Saint Maurice, or the "cavalcade of colour" in Sudbury, the civic fantastic had a familiar, and fairly standard, appearance.[12] Everywhere, it seemed, the parades embraced "Fantasy, Colour, Humor," as one *Sudbury Star* headline summed up in 1961.[13]

By 1965, then, North Americans hardly had to watch TV, turn on the radio, or travel to the big city to experience a Santa Claus parade. The form was widely available in local streets, kicking off the local Christmas season, and delighting children young and old. Huge crowds took advantage. In 1959, the *Sudbury Star* reported that the spectators were "more densely packed than for the Queen's visit in July," and by the late 1960s, estimates of local crowds reached fifty thousand, a figure that exceeded half of the city's population. Organizers lengthened the route to stretch out the crowds, but sidewalks remained packed, with spectators five or six deep in the busiest sections. But spectators along sidewalks in cities like Sudbury – while no doubt delighted by the fantasy, colour, and humour – were experiencing a spectacle quite unlike the larger Eaton's version. The presentation was familiar, but behind the scenes the civic fantastic was strikingly different.

"Young Men of Action"

Sudbury's parades were popular, but they were also decidedly unprofessional. Many floats suggested a talented hand, but there was no year-long design process, no experts in commercial art, no regular trips to leading American spectacles, no permanent parade staff, and no paid labour. The early parades were organized, coordinated, and mostly built by the Sudbury Junior Chamber of Commerce, a service club for young (eighteen- to thirty-five-year-old) businessmen who wished to perform civic action and community service. In the parade's first year, 1958, the Jaycees built most of the parade themselves, hammering out fourteen floats and wrangling up dozens of clowns in a little over a month. In subsequent years, other groups pitched in – several businesses and community groups built their own floats, for example – but the Jaycees remained the organizational and material core throughout the early years. It was hard work. "Jaycees have been working around the clock building floats," the *Sudbury Star* noted in 1959. "Starting with just an idea, 75 members have been busy with paste and paint for the past four weeks." In 1961, the group estimated that the parade had required over one thousand "man-hours" of organizational meetings and 1,200 "man-hours" of manual labour, supplemented by five hundred hours from other organizations.[14]

Sudbury's parade, while a product of local initiative and bottom-up enthusiasm, was equally an expression of the broad reach of the service ideal. The Jaycees were an international organization, founded in 1917 by a St Louis bank clerk named Henry Giessenbier. In 1916, he organized the Young Men's Progressive Civic Association, a group to "bring the young men of our great city together in one grand body with that great purpose of fellowship, advancement and everything which would make a good boy a better boy … and a good citizen a better citizen." The group quickly grew to 750 members and changed its name first to the Junior Citizens and then, in 1918, to the Junior Chamber of Commerce, reflecting a loose affiliation with the more senior Chamber of Commerce (itself founded in 1917 from the remnants of the Businessmen's League of St Louis). Speakers were invited to regular meetings, but from the beginning, the group emphasized action over talk. Early campaigns for the St Louis Jaycees included traffic, parks, litter, and transportation.[15] Giessenbier had wide aspirations. In 1920, he called similar groups from other cities to a convention in St Louis, where thirty separate organizations forged a constitution and a national body, which eventually established a steady pace of growth. By 1935, the Jaycees had grown to forty thousand members in 258 chapters across America. A decade later, these figures had more than doubled, reaching 105,000 members in 1,143 chapters. By this time, moreover, the Jaycees had set their sights on global growth, setting up an international body (dubbed JCI, for Jaycee International) and instituting annual world congresses, the first in Panama in 1945. Much of this growth occurred without Giessenbier, however, who was pushed out of the presidency in 1921 and eventually became embroiled in a long legal battle involving misappropriated bank funds (he was eventually cleared of the charges).[16]

Early on, the organization crossed the border into Canada. Much of the early Canadian growth flowed not from the global aspirations of the St Louis headquarters but from the natural continental connections of North American business life. The Young Men's section of the Winnipeg Board of Trade, similar in constitution to Giessenbier's original St Louis group, affiliated with the American body as early as 1923 – putting, as the group now claims, the "I in JCI."[17] By 1936, when a Canadian national organization was set up at a Toronto meeting, there were JC-affiliated groups in Vancouver, Calgary, Saskatoon, Moose Jaw, Toronto, Quebec City, and Montreal (two, in fact: one English, one French). Two years later, francophone groups in Quebec founded La Fédération des Jeunes Chambres de la Province de Québec, which split from the Canadian body in 1963 over linguistic issues and sought (unsuccessfully) independent recognition from the JCI headquarters. At the time, the Quebec group was larger than its English counterpart, but the International convention of the JCI refused them independent recognition and the conflict continued. The two groups remained separate until 1983. Such public tensions remained in the future in 1958, however, when the Jaycees – now twenty thousand strong in 266 chapters across Canada – arrived in Sudbury and, only months later, launched the city's annual Santa Claus parade.[18]

Jaycees Mother Goose float, Sudbury, Ontario, n.d. (probably the 1960s).
Courtesy of the Sudbury Santa Claus Parade.

Jaycee keywords – fellowship, advancement, citizenship – paralleled and reflected the service ideal that motivated many organizations in these years. In the early decade of the twentieth century, Jeffrey Charles reports, more than twenty national service organizations were founded in the United States, bearing names like Rotary, Kiwanis, Lions, Optimists, Sertoma, and Torch. In these early years, Rotary was by far the largest and most influential. It began in Chicago in 1907, founded by a young lawyer named Paul Harris. A native of New England, Harris found his legal business was suffering because he lacked local connections, so he started a group that held rotating meetings – hence "Rotary" – in the offices of like-minded businessmen, who could learn, enjoy fellowship, and exchange opportunities. By tapping into networks of travelling salesmen, Rotary grew quickly to many cities, but business opportunity proved a narrow basis for sustained organization. By 1911, Rotary's national constitution was changed to reflect a new emphasis on service to the community. The group never abandoned its base in free-enterprise ideology or its concern with business practice, but the emphasis shifted dramatically towards service and community. The Lions and Kiwanis were set up along similar lines during the First World War, forming the so-called Big Three service clubs that would dominate memberships and activities over the twentieth century. All three had been founded in large cities, but they boomed in the middle decades of the century as they found fertile ground in small towns and cities. By 1929, the Big Three had four hundred thousand members in the United States, 70 per cent of whom were located in counties with populations under ten thousand. After the Second World War, the Big Three spread to new suburban developments.[19]

As with the Jaycees, the Big Three spread quickly into Canada. Rotary was in Winnipeg as early as 1910, the Kiwanis were in Hamilton by 1916, and the Lions had spread to Windsor, Toronto, and Hamilton by 1920. In typical Canadian style, the growth of American clubs was supplemented by home-grown copies. In 1920, Hal Rogers of Hamilton wanted to recreate the feeling of male fellowship and the sense of service that he experienced in the military during the First World War but found himself shut out of the local Rotary chapter by its membership rules (each chapter could have only one representative of a particular occupation, a remnant of the original concept of exchanging business opportunities). In February 1920, he gathered a small group of friends for a dinner meeting, and the Kinsmen was born. The group was in nine cities when it held its first national convention in Winnipeg in 1926 and experienced steady growth in English Canada in the subsequent few decades. By the end of the Second World War, it had grown to 138 clubs across Canada and Newfoundland with 4,800 members, including its newest club in Perth, Ontario. Like the larger American Big Three, the Kinsmen did well in the burgeoning suburban communities after the war, expanding to 415 clubs and thirteen thousand members by 1965.[20]

Service clubs were a product of the age. Words like cooperation, fellowship, and service were ubiquitous in the early twentieth century, appearing in advertisements, business journals, political speeches, sermons, Community Chest campaigns, and reform tracts.[21] Service club organizers were certainly conscious of this context. "This is an age of organization and cooperation," one Rotary leader wrote to a potential member, "and the Rotary spirit is the idea of cooperation among gentlemen, bringing together those who would otherwise remain strangers, and turning the business of members and their friends into honest and brotherly channels."[22] Such words reflected a society that was rooted in liberal and individualist ideals but was struggling for more progressive forms of cooperative action. In this sense, Harris, Giessenbier, and Rogers were not ideological pioneers. Rather, they drew common liberal, progressive, and spiritual ideas into a potent mix that fell on fertile ground. As small businessmen, they were rigidly doctrinaire about

free enterprise. As progressives, they hoped for political consensus, for-
bidding political – they really meant partisan – debate in the clubs. As
liberal universalists, they sought to overcome boundaries of nation,
race, and creed.[23] As (mainly) Christians, though not always devoted
ones, they inflected their clubs with vaguely spiritual ideas, sometimes
through specific references to God (after 1947, the Jaycees' Creed declared that "faith in God gives meaning and purpose to human life")
but more often through vague platitudes and general ethical principles
(in 1924, the Kiwanis officially adopted the Golden Rule as one of their
Objects). At the first meeting of the Jaycees national body, Giessenbier
summed up the mix of business ideology, informal fellowship, and
civic action at the heart of such service groups. The aims of the JCs, he
argued, would be to

> increase and promote cooperation among the young men's business and
> civic organizations of the country ... to provide avenues of intelligent par-
> ticipation of young men in the study of city, state and national problems;
> to advance the character and business efficiency of its members along
> clearly defined constructive channels ... to secure cooperative action in
> advancing the common purposes of its members; to secure uniformity of
> opinion and concentration of action upon questions affecting the civic and
> commercial interests of the country; this proposed organization shall at all
> times be non-religious and non-political. It shall be an organization to ren-
> der service.

Words and study were important, but service always meant achieve-
ments. Work, practicality, and get-to-it-iveness defined club activity,
and propaganda held up action – what Paul Harris called "the eloquence of deeds" – as the purest expression of service and citizenship.
Indeed, the Jaycees called themselves "Young Men of Action."[24]

Not surprisingly, the dual emphasis on community service and practical action drove the Jaycees – and, secondarily, other service groups
– towards the Santa Claus parade. These groups organized an astonishing number of parades, from east to west and north to south, far
too many to enumerate. Certainly, the service ideal took clubs in multiple directions. Rotary funded hospitals, studied civic problems, and
cleaned up litter. The Lions took on the cause of blind children, a program matched by the Kinsmen's efforts for the mentally challenged.
In Sudbury, the Jaycees organized traffic safety programs (including
the cleverly named Teenage Road-e-o), get-out-the-vote campaigns,

leadership training workshops for members, an international pen pal program for grades seven and eight, and many other forms of civic action. Service groups poured hours of discussion and more hours of work into such programs, but there could hardly be an event better calculated to express the service club ideal than a popular, and highly public, Christmas event aimed at children. The parade provided organizational experience for members; it brought them together for late-night work and after-hours fellowship; it reflected their selfless interest in community action; it hooked into local boosterism; it expressed their ostensibly non-denominational Christian faith and sense of Christmas universalism; it leavened all these impulses with a family-inflected public consensus of good cheer. "Hundreds of people and animals ... are taking part in the parade," editorialized the *Oakville Beaver* in 1970, reflecting on a Jaycees-organized local procession about thirty miles west of Toronto. "They are doing it for one reason only, to bring the Christmas spirit to Oakville, especially to the youngsters."[25] It was no surprise, then, that the proliferation of Santa Claus parades and service clubs ran in parallel.

Service clubs like Rotary and the Jaycees formed the organizational core of the civic fantastic, but other groups also spearheaded community parades. Firefighters, police officers, Chambers of Commerce, Retail Merchant Associations (RMAs), Legion chapters, and special citizens' committees also organized parades in many different communities. These were not service clubs and might come to the parade from other directions, but they shared with the clubs a broad service ideal. Firefighters often took up parades as an extension of their philanthropic programs, including annual efforts in many communities to rebuild and restore old toys for poor families. Even the RMAs, who might have obvious commercial motivations, sprung from a folklore of retailing that put service at its centre – service to customer, to be sure, but also service to community. "In the matter of the building and maintaining of churches, it is the retail merchant who took the leading part," small-business activist W.L. McQuarrie declared in the midst of the Great Depression, "as he did also in sports and entertainment, hockey teams, baseball teams, schools, public libraries, swimming pools, skating rink, agricultural society, and practically every effort that goes to make up the social and recreational life of the society."[26] For their part, Chambers of Commerce also aimed to blend enterprise and service. Welcoming the Chamber idea to Hamilton in 1918, the *Spectator* predicted it would "create a civic conscience, aiming at certain definite objects, and achieving results impossible of attainment under ordinary hit-or-miss methods." In a revealing article three decades later, *Nation's Business* described Chambers of Commerce as the "365-day Santa Claus." "Its members have the Christmas spirit all year long," the magazine argued. "These fellows believe that it's more rewarding to *give* than to *take* … There are Chambers all over the country working hard to improve their communities, making them more enjoyable and profitable to live in. Chambers sponsor all kinds of civic projects – like conducting safety campaigns, improving the school, fire, police, sanitary and recreational systems, encouraging new industries to build, [and] solving traffic snarls."[27]

From the other side, moreover, service clubs were hardly opposed to commercial aims. Most had begun as business groups, after all, and even after they tilted their efforts towards service, they continued to marry such ideas to a small-business base and to free-enterprise ideology. In fact, there was considerable overlap between service clubs and Chambers of Commerce. In 1947, one American survey found that two-thirds of Rotarians belonged to their local Chamber of Commerce. Community and profit: for the service clubs, there was simply no conflict, so long as sociability was not coerced and business was conducted ethically. "He profits most who serves best," as the Rotary code put it after 1911. The Jaycee Creed struck a similar balance, asserting that "economic justice can best be won by free men through free enterprise … And that service to humanity is the best work of life!" The Lions, for their part, would "encourage service-minded men to serve their community … [and] promote high ethical standard in commerce."[28]

Not surprisingly, then, the civic fantastic fused commercial aims with service ideals. "During the last few years, many hundreds of people from Guelph and vicinity have been attracted to other cities by their Monster Santa Claus Parade," the Guelph Board of Trade wrote to its members in 1964. "This year the Junior Board of Trade … have offered to stage a Santa Claus Parade for the City. Your Board of Directors feel this is good business for the Guelph merchants to support such a project. This will encourage many hundreds from surrounding districts to our city and our stores."[29] A parade could generate crowds and show off the downtown, and many organizers simply declared the Santa Claus parade to be the "formal opening of the Christmas shopping season."[30] But it was rarely enough to simply generate crowds – that could get in the way of shopping as much as encourage it[31] – so some parade organizers tried to tie spectators to actual stores and real shopping. Santa

Mayor in "Shop Guelph" float, 1976.
Photograph appears courtesy of the Guelph Public Library Archives,
Mayor's downtown entry, [1976], F45-0-10-0-0-77.

flew over one Pennsylvania town dropping coupons redeemable in prizes (ranging from 10 cents to a bicycle) at local stores. Windsor merchants marked down prices on parade day in 1936, "to make it interesting for you, and you to do your Christmas shopping early. Make it a point to be downtown Saturday."[32] Some businesses used the parade itself as a rolling advertisement. In Gettysburg, Pennsylvania, the parade included the usual assortment of storybook and circus characters, along with floats and decorated trucks "designed by Gettysburg merchants and businessmen to furnish suggestions for Christmas gifts and exhibit the stock and quality of goods offered shoppers in local establishments."[33]

In this sense, contrasting the civic and the corporate fantastic raises a sort of paradox. The community parades were at the same time more aggressively and less powerfully commercial than their department store cousins. In so many ways, the Eaton's parades were defined by their corporate nature and by their connection to Eaton's structures and promotional priorities; yet the actual presentations muted the commercial pitch in favour of the underlying emotional premises of consumer culture. Indeed, until the television era, the word "Eaton's" was barely present at all, the company counting on its iconic status in each city to carry the parade's public relations effect, an agenda that was pursued with relentless singularity by the corporate employees who designed and built the Eaton's parades. By contrast, the civic fantastic flowed, first of all, from a service ethic enlivened with local initiative and enthusiasm; yet it often became, at least in part, an explicit sales pitch. Such presentations became especially urgent as Main Street merchants faced the increasing threats of mobile consumers, shopping malls, and, later, big-box stores in the decades after 1960. Guelph's Board of Trade, after all, was not just using the parade as a generic promotional opportunity, it was fighting to keep local shoppers, drained away by big events in other cities, at home. Yet commerce could never be the whole story, neither at the level of planning nor presentation, since the civic fantastic never represented the vision and agenda of one institution. It was, from the ground up, a profoundly diverse and multi-levelled event.

"A vast kindly web"

The civic fantastic was pluralistic. In Sudbury, the Jaycees initially built the whole show, but soon efforts spread across the city's entire institutional ecology. By 1965, the Sudbury event included a stunning range of groups: businesses, government bodies, schools, clubs, even the Mine-Mill union. This mix was absolutely typical of line-ups across North America, where organizational pluralism rather than corporate exclusivity was the rule. Sandusky, Ohio's, 1927 effort included a squad of local police, the Boy Scouts, the fire department, a high school band, several decorated floats sponsored by merchants, and even "a display of new cars by automobile dealers." In 1962, Kitchener-Waterloo's parade included floats sponsored by an electric appliance manufacturer, a carpet retailer, a hardware store, a radio station, the local newspaper, a group of university students, a service organization, the Kitchener Downtown Business Association, the Waterloo Retail Association, and the local Jaycees.[34] Similarly, Regina's 1954 parade, organized by the Lions Club, featured a radio station (offering free publicity), local theatres (including employees who worked for free to offer special post-parade kids' shows), the local mayor (who welcomed Santa at City Hall), Canadian Pacific Airlines (which provided free air transport for Santa Claus), Mounties (who escorted Santa to town from the airport), small businesses (that built floats), and even mothers who "give up busy Saturday mornings to bring the youngsters downtown for the parade." In a revealing phrase, the local paper noted that a "vast kindly web" made Santa's visit possible.[35]

This behind-the-scenes web was volunteer not professional. Budgets were often small, at least compared to the corporate-metropolitan version. Kingston's Jaycees had a 1960 budget of $1,500, while Regina's Lions Club got by on a meagre (and typical) $3,000 in the mid-1960s, with around one-third normally donated by city council.[36] All these figures paled against Eaton's spending, which reached $100,000 in Toronto alone by the mid-1960s. Yet even those small sums reflected an ongoing and frustrating imperative for organizers of community parades. Sometimes city councils or RMAs picked up all or part of the tab – often the source of interminable meetings – but in many cases, organizers sold tags on the street, held fund-raising fairs, and went door to door to canvas donations. In Newmarket, Ontario, the Canadian Legion regularly funded its parade through a summer fair. In 1952, the cost of Sarnia's parade was "borne entirely by the Sertoma Club from proceeds of their recent home bingo. The bingo cards were sold in all sections of Lambton County and, as a result, the club is extending an invitation to parents all over Lambton to bring their children to Sarnia for the parade."[37] In the end, volunteer labour remained the core of the civic fantastic. "This year's Santa Claus parade on Saturday morning is both for the people and of the people," the *Sudbury Star* argued. "Volunteers are … needed to ensure the parade will be a success."[38] Practically, these were massive efforts. "Year after year, the members of the Lions club … slave to get their parade ready," the *Regina Leader-Post* claimed in 1954. "We know. We've watched them work. We know the thankless hours spent in cold barnlike places big enough to permit the construction of a float. We know the hours spent away from their families each period in December when their help at home would doubtless be appreciated."[39]

On occasion, this plural form of volunteerism produced a somewhat less-than-meticulous organization. Boosterish local newspapers liked to emphasize the good order and business-like efficiency that lay behind the processions. "Few people realize … that the parade is a highly organized project, mapped out like a detailed blueprint weeks beforehand," the *Leader-Post* noted.[40] Committees were set up, divisions of labour defined, specific tasks assigned. The Regina Lions Club had a general chairman; two assisting co-chairmen; a Costume Committee of one chair and five others; a Floats Committee (chair plus nine members); a Theatre Committee (chair plus two); a Parade Committee (chair plus three); and a Parade Route Tag Day Committee (chair plus one), in addition to a person in charge of finances and one to assist with publicity.[41] Indeed, many parades did seem well organized, particularly considering the complexity and variety of activities involved, but the actual events sometimes belied such idealized descriptions and on-the-ground organization was often frayed and chaotic. Some organizers lost control of parade content: Minnedosa's 1951 parade had two floats of the Old Woman Who Lived in a Shoe; a decade later, London, Ontario's, parade featured two floats of Santa's workshop.[42] Parade sizes were unpredictable, particularly for inexperienced coordinators. One year in Sudbury, the parade was so long that "it met itself coming at the corner of Elm and Durban streets."[43] In other years, processions were unpredictably small. On one cold day in Lawrence, Kansas, organizers scrambled at the last minute to secure children to carry banners, and, still, the parade had only one band: "the Haskell Institute band braved the cold north wind and was the only musical organization in the parade. The Lawrence high school band and a clown band decided it was too cold to appear."[44]

Almost everywhere, events seemed on the brink of disaster. One year in Newmarket, Ontario, a drunken buggy driver lost control of his horse, which bolted from the parade and injured a young spectator. After an hour-long delay, police eventually corralled the animal and charged the driver under the Highway Traffic Act. In Owosso, Michigan, a well-meaning attempt to bring Santa by helicopter resulted in serial mini-disasters. First, the organizers couldn't secure the desired helicopter so opted for an airplane instead, which turned out to be too big to land at the local airport. Next, organizers decided to have Santa parachute into town, but area winds made it hard to land in a specific place, so a team of spotters had to be pulled together to follow Santa's route to the ground. Finally, the reception committee was delivered to Santa's landing spot and the whole crew was driven downtown to start the parade. The event, as far as the spectators were concerned, was a huge success.[45]

In many places, but particularly in small towns, parades had a non-professional, even participatory, feel. The biggest organizations in metropolitan centres might have considerable financial and organizational means, but most civic parades did their best with limited resources. "The parade wasn't impressive to adults," one Idaho newspaper noted, "the procession consisting of a police motorcycle, a Jaycee sound car playing 'Here Comes Santa Claus,' a city fire engine, two pickup trucks, and a police prowl car. But in the eyes of little children it was the best parade of the year."[46] Pilot Mound, Manitoba's, 1969 parade was composed primarily of "home-made floats, clowns, snowmobiles, and a tractor decorated as a train."[47] Many small towns were forced to fill out the parade with decorated cars, trucks, and delivery vehicles, or simply invited local citizens to join if they brought a costume or suitable Christmas equipment. In Buckingham, Quebec, the Lions Club asked that "any person with sleighs to spare is asked to bring them along to the Parade."[48] Sometimes, such participation was a necessary result of limited local resources, but in many cases, it was a genuine community impulse. Even some big-city parades were opened to bottom-up participation. In 1970, Winnipeg organizers declared that anyone with a costume could enter by showing up at the marshalling area before 9 a.m. Still, such direct invitations to participate were rare and most participation was mediated through community institutions. But whether intentional or not, open calls for citizen participation merely represented the most extreme extension of the community ethic at the centre of the civic fantastic.

The vast, kindly web operated behind the scenes, but it also formed one part of the vocabulary of the parades, shaping their meaning and the messages they sent to spectators. The corporate fantastic was a spectacle of consumer capitalism. Identities were obscured and content determined by the promotional and aesthetic priorities of department store experts. The civic fantastic had a similar visual style and pool of characters, but it was a spectacle of the community public where identity and affiliation were announced rather than obscured. "A parade is people," as the *Canadian Champion* put it in 1975.[49] Groups celebrated their identities and their place in local communities. "Among [the floats] was a group of Ukrainian children dressed in their native costume," one Youngstown paper announced in 1927. "Ethnic groups were among the many aspects of city life represented in today's Santa parade," the *Hamilton Spectator* echoed in 1961, including a photo of a Canadian Polish Congress float with children in native costume.[50]

Affiliation was also front and centre in the civic fantastic. Everywhere, spectators would know they were looking at the Lions, the Jaycees, a union local, or workers from the recreational centre. In Sudbury, the Mother Goose float literally and figuratively belonged to the Jaycees, and everyone knew it just by watching the parade go by. Politicians and civic leaders appeared as themselves, seeking recognition not obscurity. In Minnedosa, Manitoba, organizers in 1952 invited the mayors of six nearby communities, while St Hyacinthe's first parade, organized by the Chamber of Commerce in 1953, included a variety of local political figures. One year in Chilliwack, British Columbia, Canadian Prime Minister Pierre Trudeau – in town to campaign for re-election – rode in a car.[51] Newspapers, moreover, relentlessly named prize winners, participating groups, organizing committees, masked characters, make-up-covered clowns, honorary marshals, and Santa Claus himself. "The gracious Star Fairy accompanied Santa Claus during the parade," read a typical report from Quebec. "The fairy was played by Ginette Dufour from the hair salon Au Sommet de la Femme, which recently opened in Beloeil." One year, Milton's newspaper listed the names of the Three Little Pigs, even though they were masked and utterly unrecognizable to spectators.[52] Even for Santa, identity mattered. In Toronto, Santa was a nameless Eaton's employee; in Sudbury, he was a local celebrity. Wilf Salo, who played Santa for many years, had deep connections in the community. Born in 1907, he had arrived in Sudbury at the age of eleven, when his family migrated from Michigan. As an adult, he was an important figure in the local retail scene, both as floor manager at Silverman's for thirty-six years and as a small-business owner. He was also heavily involved in community and fraternal organizations like the Lions Club and the Shriners, and played Santa on a local television show for thirty-five years in addition to his lead role in the local Christmas parade.[53]

Theoretically, all these groups and individuals were woven together by more than good Christmas cheer. "Cooperation" was a service club keyword and bound together the organizational politics of community parades. The corporate fantastic was based on a hierarchical business structure. In Edmonton, for example, Scott Brewster was in charge, but answered to the store manager and assigned his display staff to build the parade. In community parades, pluralistic participation required cooperation across institutional rivalries and professional jurisdiction. The "Chambre de Commerce des Jeunes thanks ALL THOSE who made this Santa Claus parade possible," wrote Raoul Lupien in Valleyfield,

City of Sudbury float, Sudbury, Ontario, n.d. (probably the 1960s).
Courtesy of the Sudbury Santa Claus Parade.

whose capital letters drew clear attention to the plurality of contribution.[54] The following year, a report on Minnedosa's parade, organized by the Jaycees, similarly noted that "many organizations in town are co-operating to make the event a memorable one for youngsters. The Canadian Pacific Railway is supplying a special train … the Manitoba Dragoons will provide uniformed flag bearers. The Elks lodge is entering a float, and the ladies' auxiliary to the Dragoons will decorate Santa's throne. The Senior Chamber of Commerce has canvassed residents and merchants for finances. The army has thrown open the armories for constructing the floats and children from both schools will take part."[55]

In the civic fantastic, cooperation was both a practical and ideological impulse. With so many organizations and agendas involved, and with so little money to mount a parade, people simply had to join together and get along. But as Jeffrey Charles points out, words like cooperation "assumed a nearly religious intensity" in service clubs, and their constant repetition signalled more than their practical importance.[56] For the clubs, the most important guardians of the civic fantastic, cooperation between different groups and people was the foundation of service. Standing somewhere between individual liberty and group coercion, free enterprise and fellowship, cooperation promised

Santa arrives in Saint Raymond, Quebec, 20 December 1959.
BANQ, Fonds Paul-Émile Duplain, P322,S3,D01-17,P005.

exactly the form of liberal sociability and democratic community spirit that moved service clubs and underlay the civic fantastic – a middle way between government regulation and unrestrained individualism. "Cooperation is the keynote of happy community life," Rotary founder Paul Harris declared, whose group built the idea into its own Code of Ethics, which stated that the "genius of Rotary exists more in cooperation than in competition." It was a sentiment echoed over and again in service club and community meetings, rendered both in grand rhetorical flourishes and in more basic calls for progress through practical action. "If the cooperation of all the aldermen is necessary for achieving these constructive projects," the mayor of Nicolet, Quebec, told the local Chamber of Commerce, "the cooperation of an important body like the Chamber of Commerce is also a necessity."[57]

In practice, sewing together the plurality of participation and multiplicity of messages was probably too much to ask of a single keyword like cooperation. Rivalry, conflict, and controversy plagued the civic fantastic. In London, Ontario, the Jaycees diverted the parade from downtown streets after a dispute with the Merchants Association about funding; the parade appeared in the east end instead, a secondary and more downscale commercial strip on the working-class side of the city. In Cambridge, a city formed from the amalgamation of three geographically proximate but socially independent villages (Hespeler, Galt, and Preston), organizers initially worked out a rotational system, but this compromise was shattered when Hespeler merchants decided to mount their own parade.[58] Disagreements over specific content also drove controversy. Some organizers proudly rejected commercial content in their parade. "This event is strictly a community affair planned and managed by the *Press* and has no commercial aspect," the *Pittsburgh Press* announced in 1928. "No floats, trucks, or decorated cars of business houses will be permitted to appear in the parade."[59]

Explicitly anti-commercial content was often more controversial. In Windsor, the Coffee House committee of the Young Christian Workers designed a float with an edgy religious critique of commercialism. Huge money bags and gaudy Christmas gifts were surrounded with signs like "This year tell her you care with … Only $1,995.00," "Buy your child a Super Shooter Gun, $9.95," and "Get a photo of your child with Santa, $5.00," all under the main banner reading, "Where will Xmas end and Christmas begin?" On the morning of the parade, the marshall rejected the float. "The minute I saw it I knew it wasn't fitting," said organizer Elio Delcol. "It wasn't in keeping with the parade. It was my decision. I felt that it didn't conform with the theme of a Santa Claus parade for children." Delcol hardly rejected the idea behind the protest, but didn't think the parade was "the place to make it." Jaycee president Mike Brown agreed, arguing that the entry "wasn't in keeping with the theme of the parade, An Old Fashioned Christmas." The Christian Workers weren't surprised by the decision. "We were fearful the Jaycees wouldn't let us in," said one member of the group. "We were told 'don't try to get in the parade either, we'll put you out of there.'" After the Jaycee decision, they considered forcing their way into the parade, or moving to city hall to sing Christmas carols while the rest of the parade passed the reviewing stand, but decided they didn't want to cause trouble and quietly withdrew. "We didn't want to hurt the kids," said Ron Smith, one of the builders who had been up since 4:30 a.m. putting the finishing touches on the float. "The kids wouldn't understand it that much."[60]

Such disputes are analytically interesting, but easy to exaggerate. It is notable that the Windsor Jaycees were more concerned about traditionalism and children than any inherent conflict of religion and commerce. Such explicit controversies were, moreover, exceedingly rare. Indeed, it was easy enough to embrace both Christian and commercial messages in the same parade, since service club ideology and Christmas cheer both had spiritual and commercial inflections. Nativity scenes were common, as were other Christian symbols with serious religious content. In Picton, Ontario, the Catholic Women's League featured a Nativity scene on their float, while the Salvation Army entry depicted a house built on a bible with a banner reading, "Build the Home of the Bible."[61] The Three Wise Men were another popular entry, as in Swift Current, Saskatchewan, in 1959. Sometimes, the whole parade could be built around a Christian theme. Floats from both public and parochial schools formed the core of Ludington, Michigan's, parade in 1952, each "representing a scene from the story of the nativity."[62] In Waynesburg, Pennsylvania, seven years later, the Jaycees pulled together a number of religious and civic organizations under the parade theme, "Keeping Christ in Christmas."[63] Even in more typical fantastic parades, organizers often embraced flashes of Christian messages, sometimes using special prizes to encourage religious content. In Minnedosa, one float depicting a nativity scene sponsored by St John's Anglican Church of the Bethany won first prize.[64] In Springfield, Washington, organizers awarded prizes to best floats in three divisions: non-commercial, commercial, and Nativity.[65] This Christian-fantastic-commercial synthesis was perfectly expressed in Pittsburgh's 1934 parade, where "the scared note of Christmas, with the bearded hooded wise men bearing their gifts to the Christ child" sat amid a "caravan out of the Land of Make Believe."[66]

In this sense, the Windsor controversy – and the broader debates it represented – can be understood at two different levels. It was, first of all, a battle over content. The civic fantastic was a cluster of meanings – commercial, symbolic, familial, spiritual – bound together by impulses like cooperation, service, and Yuletide good cheer. With so much plurality in organization, such widespread geographic proliferation, and such a rich mixture of ideas, it is hardly surprising that the synthesis was never perfect and that community parades were multivalent and complex. The civic fantastic was frayed and strained at the edges, and

Nativity scene in Fergus, Ontario, 1976
Photograph appears courtesy of the Guelph Public Library Archives,
Fergus Santa Claus Parade, [1976], F45-0-10-0-0-255.

when tensions were made explicit, cooperation could not fully contain the debate. At the same time, the structure of the debate seemed as important as the content. Windsor Jaycees banned a Christian float, but such censorship would never have been necessary in the Eaton's parades, which were controlled by the company and designed behind the scenes. When people got angry at Eaton's, the result was consumer complaint not public debate. This organizational dynamic connects the civic fantastic not just to Christmas and family but to an entire project of liberal governance.[67] There was no hierarchy to contain or control the discussion. All the various organizations that spearheaded the community parades – what we might call the vanguard of the civic fantastic – inhabited a similar and broadly equal place in their local political culture. Service clubs, Chambers of Commerce, citizens committees, branches of the Legion: these were the institutions of civil society. Their efforts were sometimes endorsed or funded by municipal councils, but governments almost never actually organized Santa Claus parades. Even public sector workers like firefighters and police officers normally undertook parade organization through their associations rather than the official departments. These groups embraced commercial purposes because those were the basis of a healthy community life; they aimed for community fellowship as the basis of democratic engagement. They saw in Christmas a chance for service, fellowship, and universal good cheer. To mount the parades, they recreated their ideal form of democratic citizenship.

The "soul Saint"

The civic fantastic, with all its rhetorical sops to cooperation, citizenship, and community, reflected the social base and social imaginaries of its organizers. Fire departments, police associations, and branches of the Legion could have humble memberships, but the core of the service clubs, the Chambers of Commerce, and the citizens committees were small businessmen, independent professionals, and a few middle managers – what one Kiwanis member called "the articulate representatives of the great middle class."[68] Club and Chamber members were generally white – in the United States, often explicitly so – and exclusively male. Some service club leaders hoped for racially integrated clubs as an extension of their service universalism, but few were willing to court the wrath of local chapters by forcing the issue. The various central offices were much more militant about gender exclusivity: officially, women were not allowed to join any service club, and a local chapter that bucked the trend could expect instant discipline by the headquarters, at least until local militancy, court orders, and declining memberships forced the issue in the 1970s and 1980s.[69] Before this, women – generally, the word meant wives – were shunted off into auxiliary organizations like the Jaycettes and the Lionettes. These groups performed important tasks. For parades, they sewed costumes, packed candy, applied makeup on clowns, raised money, and did many other much-needed jobs.[70] But in parallel with their auxiliary status in the clubs, women almost never served as the main organizers and their roles in parade organization were clearly secondary. One year in Englehart, Ontario, this hierarchy was made crystal clear, with men chairing the various committees and women listed as "helpers."[71] As much as this patriarchal division of labour reflected the masculine ethic of the clubs, it also reinforced the gender division of labour at Christmas, which assigned to men the holiday's public face and to women its more hidden emotional connections.[72]

On race, the record was more uneven. In the main, community parades reflected and reinforced the dominant whiteness of civic elites and local popular culture. The civic fantastic leaned heavily on racial imagery. Outright racism mingled with Orientalism, blackface, and playing Indian. Sudbury's first parade featured a wagon labelled "Bob's Washer Service," with a Jaycee member dressed as a mammy (or Aunt Jemima-type) character, complete with blackface and curly wig, leaning over a tub scrubbing laundry. In Newmarket seven years earlier, "Black-faced Earlby Ruthven, with the help of black-faced Delbert Gibney and Charlie Crone of Sharon, performed unbelievable back-firing feats at the wheel of his fresh air model A sedan, equipped with locomotive whistle siren and bell." In a photo caption, the local paper referred to one of these black-faced participants as "Coon-skinned Crone." That same year in nearby Milton, the Dale Brothers float featured "a bevy of Ku Klux Klan men in their white garbs."[73]

After the 1960s, local black communities on both sides of the border became more aggressive in complaining about such presentations, though such images did not totally disappear. In London, Ontario, in 1989, the Dutch Heritage Language School entered a float featuring Black Peter, accompanied by "some white children with blackened faces and curly wigs, supposedly the helpers of Black Peter." Black Peter was a long-standing Christmas symbol in Holland, originally a punitive figure who delivered lumps of coal to naughty children but, over time, had evolved into a more comical Christmas icon. London African Canadians were aghast and began gathering signatures on a petition demanding an apology from the Jaycees (who organized the parade) and the school, noting Peter had been banished from US schools at least two decades before. "I'm surprised to see [Black Peter] surfacing now in London," Lorna Martin, secretary of the London Urban Alliance on Race Relations, commented. "It is very offensive to the black community. It's saying to little children that black is bad." "We are sorry that the Dutch community is not in tune with the spirit of our multicultural society," argued Parents against Racism, which was organizing the protest.[74]

No one apologized. Indeed, many local residents defended the float, arguing that it expressed rather than violated Canadian multiculturalism. "As it is obvious that [the leaders of the protest] were totally unaware of the history of Black Peter before pointing accusing fingers," a letter to the editor responded, "I think it is the Dutch community of London, and indeed Dutch people everywhere, who are owed an apology."[75] "In

Canada are we not doing everything possible to allow francophones to preserve their culture?" wrote another. "Did we not see Polish dancers performing traditional dances in Hamilton for Lech Welesa when he was there? So why are the Jaycees apologizing to the black community for allowing this float in their parade? Black Peter is part of Dutch folklore, part of their culture that goes back centuries."[76] Refuting such multiculturalism with a vengeance, one resident of nearby Wallaceburg pointed out that the local parade (sponsored by the Canadian-Belgina-Dutch Club) had featured Black Peter for many years, walking alongside St Nicolas in a black suit and beret. What set black Londoners off, she argued, was obviously "not Black Peter himself but the children who were on the float with black faces and curly wigs."[77]

At times, community parades could admit racialized groups. Sudbury's Indian Club float was filled with actual First Nations people, the club itself being an early expression of cultural revival in local indigenous communities that would eventually lead to a network of First Nations Friendships Centres. In Hamilton in 1964, seventy-six-year-old Chief White Gull of the Ohweken Indian Reserve marched in "his native costume" with two of his grandchildren.[78] Many American communities actually encouraged so-called "Negro" participation, even initiating separate prizes for black bands, floats, and entries, though sometimes the dynamics of such efforts showed all too clearly the "included but unequal" dynamics at play. One year, in Spokane, Washington, organizers offered a $40 prize for best float in the parade and a $5 prize for best Negro float. That year, the "entire Tom R Rogers family of 10" appeared under the auspices of the Calvary Baptist church to represent "Spokane's negro population. Mr. and Mrs. Rogers and the baby, age 2, will be in costume, and possibly some of the others, but all expect to participate … Mr. and Mrs. Rogers, as 'Mr. and Mrs. Santa Claus' and the baby are in the contest for the $40 cash first prize offered by the *Chronicle* for best Santa Claus representative. If they do not capture one of the three major awards, they still will be eligible for the $5 award for best negro Santa, and for several of the other special class prizes."[79]

The civic fantastic, moreover, was ultimately a flexible form that could be embraced and remade by multiple groups to suit the needs of their communities. In 1969, Jesse Jackson and Operation Breadbasket organized an alternative festival on Chicago's South Side, under the theme Dreaming of a Black Christmas. The two-and-a-half-hour parade featured "some 50 colorful floats representing black business and services and scores of school marching units and bands," led by the "soul Saint," a Santa-like figure played by a three-hundred-pound truck driver. The Saint donned a black beard and "a colourful African dashiki of black velvet trimmed in gold, red, and green, the colors of Ghana" and distributed candy from a bag labelled "Soul Power."[80] As with all the civic parades, aims were commercial, symbolic, whimsical, and community-based. Jackson hoped the parade would help replace "a white, fat, power image" with a "strong, black, positive image," but also aimed to increase sales at black businesses. "The idea of the Black Christmas parade is … primarily designed as a reminder to the black community of its moral obligation to support black business as a matter of enlightened self-interest," the *Chicago Defender* (which entered its own float) editorialized. "Despite its financial paucity, black business is the backbone of the black community … Thus in creating the Black Christmas parade, the Rev. Jesse Jackson … shows an uncommon insight into the need of the black community and the urgency for turning dreams into practical realities."[81] By 1970, the Chicago parade had taken on a much more political edge. The parade theme was "Bacon for Christmas," an overtly political though cross-party march that aimed to pressure the city government to appoint Warren Bacon as president of the school board.[82]

In many ways, however, the presence of racist imagery, the participation of actual racialized subjects, or the invention of alternative spectacles in a black metropolis were less striking than the overall – indeed, relentless – whiteness of the civic fantastic. Everyone "knew" Santa was luminously white, that fairy-tale characters were white, and that racial others best served comical or exotic roles. This knowledge was usually tacit, just a common-sense and probably unthinking assumption about the "true" nature of popular characters. On rare occasions, particularly when that tacit knowledge was challenged, the racial logic could be made more explicit. "We felt that a black face would be incongruous with the traditional Santa image," a Cincinnati department store official argued in response to demands from civil rights organizations for black Santas in local stores. "It just doesn't fit the symbol as kids have known it." In Bloomington, Indiana, organizers dealt with objections to a black Santa, entered by the National Association of Coloured People, by declaring that future parades would permit only one Santa, controlled by the parade organizers – the unspoken assumption, of course, was that he would be white.[83] In Toronto a decade later, after school trustee Pat Case suggested the parade might better reflect Toronto's ethnic diversity, T.M. Brown mocked the idea in a comment dripping with racial sarcasm: "It's almost laughable. What would … she like? For the parade to have a black Santa, or maybe an East Indian?"[84]

Ideas about Santa's whiteness, floats like Bob's Washer Service, and women's auxiliary status were drawn from widespread and popular cultural assumptions, but they did not represent a contradiction of the democratic and cooperative ethic of the parades. Male fellowship and service were inherent in the common sense of the organizers, who assumed that public life, and the parades, ought to be the purview of male service clubs and a masculine civil society. They didn't oppose the membership of women in their organizations simply because they wanted to keep their wives out of public affairs; their notion of fellowship was constituted by their masculinity and they wanted to preserve a particular form of male fellowship and service. Similarly, they "knew" racial integration would undermine the informal and friendly fellowship that undergirded the service consensus, but in some communities organizers also saw that community pluralism and holiday good cheer might allow a few "Negros" to appear in these once-a-year Christmas events, so long as their participation was an addition rather than a core element (like Santa). These social views made service club fellowship and built the social consensus underlying the civic fantastic. They reflected and reinforced dominant forms of popular culture, but they also flowed from and constituted the sense of fellowship and the structure of the local civil societies at the heart of the civic fantastic.

"We do not find it practical to carry a live Santa Claus"

Three years before the Jaycees arrived in Sudbury, Alderman Ralph Connor tried to mount what would have been the city's first Santa Claus parade. "Sudbury is almost alone among large Canadian cities which do not hold an annual Christmas parade," he complained in the fall of 1955. For Connor, this was a missed opportunity. "My idea of such a parade visualizes floats contributed by business and industrial concerns, service clubs, labor organizations, and other groups. It would be sparked by available local bands, clowns, and, of course, Santa himself."[85] Yet his efforts led him first, not to local service clubs and civic groups, but to Eaton's. Perhaps, he suggested, the Toronto parade could make a stop in Sudbury? Eaton's was less than enthused. W.E. Gooderelle, who worked for the company in Sudbury, wrote to the Toronto head office that "it is not desirable to run a Santa Claus parade in a city of this size, as the local facilities are not sufficient to create a parade that would have a satisfactory standard, and, also, the considerable expense must be considered as another factor."[86] Connor never did mount his parade, and the first parade would wait for the Jaycees' efforts three years later, but his dual effort – one eye cast on the corporate fantastic in Toronto and the other on the local public – fits well with the broader history of the civic fantastic. Far from a self-contained local event, Sudbury's parade – like those in so many other communities – was the product of a mass commercial society and was deeply implicated in larger cultural developments. These influences took many forms: the direct and indirect influence of department stores, borrowing from broad forms of mass commercial culture, and the power of different forms of screen capitalism.

Parade makers across North America eagerly embraced the direct and indirect influence of department stores. Eaton's parade files are riddled with letters from local organizations asking for advice and material or simply inviting the company to send the whole spectacle: the Cornwall Jaycees hoped Eaton's parade might stop in that city on its way from Toronto to Montreal; the Business and Professional Association of Stayner, Ontario, wanted to buy "items … that have been discarded" from the Eaton's parade; the Brandon Jaycees wrote to Eaton's to have the parade appear there.[87] Even the Sudbury Jaycees, struggling to put together their first parade in 1958, contacted Eaton's for help. In these cases, the company's response was polite but uneven. Brockie often offered advice to local organizers. Indeed, the Sudbury Jaycees were invited to Toronto "for luncheon some day soon" so that Eaton's officials could deliver the voice of experience.[88] In such cases, Brockie was an expert offering advice to amateurs, not a colleague exchanging courtesies with like-minded professionals; nor is there much evidence that Brockie established ongoing or reciprocal relationships with local organizers. Nor did the company show much interest in taking the lead in parades outside of the big metropolitan markets, though it did occasionally mount mini-spectacles – mainly Santa in a single car – to mark the opening of the local Toyland and it sometimes lent material, made small monetary donations, and even entered a float in some local parades. In circumstances that remain unclear, some of the floats from the Winnipeg parade made an appearance in Portage la Prairie in 1947, but the idea was never repeated.[89]

The civic fantastic also reflected the indirect influence of the bigger metropolitan spectacles. Local organizers in small cities kept an eye on the bigger events, either through direct travel, media reports, or television broadcasts. Screen capitalism spread the corporate fantastic widely and rapidly, a fact that reports of local parades often recognized and even celebrated. "Santa's retinue of monstrous characters – the kind often seen in Mardi Gras newsreels – are being imported," the *Toledo News-Bee* noted in 1934. Two decades later, organizers in St Petersburg bragged that their parade for the first time would feature "those giant balloons you have seen in the newsreels and on television in the annual Macy's parade in New York."[90] In 1988, the Cambridge, Ontario, Santa Claus committee ran its parade at night, an idea inspired by the broadcast of a Walt Disney parade on television.[91] As a result, the civic fantastic contained many corporate characters (like Mickey Mouse and Darth Vader), but also many that sprang from the department store spectacles themselves. Punkinhead, for example, appeared in many civic parades, and oversized balloons (typical of Macy's parade) were another popular addition. In 1964, after the Jaycee floats were destroyed in a fire, Sudbury organizers rented an entire parade from a Windsor company, composed of oversized balloon characters including a thirty-five-foot candy cane, a fourteen-foot kangaroo, and twenty-eight-foot automobile, and of course Santa's float at the end. Promotions for the parade eagerly embraced the outside influence: "For their sixth annual Santa Claus Parade, the Sudbury Jaycees, together with the Downtown Retail Merchants Association, are staging the kind of parade usually seen in the larger cities in the United States – floats that are more often seen at the Mardi Gras parade in New Orleans, the Rose Bowl parade in Pasadena, or the Macy's parade in New York."[92]

Another vector of commercial influence, then, was entrepreneurial. Sudbury's 1964 balloons were supplied by a Dynamic Displays, a Windsor, Ontario, company in the business of delivering props, costumes, and full balloon parades to local communities. Several other companies supplied parade content, from entire spectacles to specific features. Jean Gros Ltd, a Pittsburgh-based company, specialized in renting out parade material to communities of all sizes. Gros himself was a well-known puppeteer in the 1920s, but when an ill-conceived marionette opera plunged him into bankruptcy during the Great Depression, he cast about for a new theatrical idea. Eventually, Gros copied the famous Macy's parade by producing several large rubber balloons (clowns, kangaroos, totem poles, and "toyland creatures"), papier mâché heads, and other figures that could be rented to smaller towns that couldn't afford to create their own parade. By 1949, he had three parade units on the road, appearing in one hundred communities across

Cartoon characters on float, Regina, 1955.
Saskatchewan Archives Photo R-C5184.

North America, including several in southern Ontario. Another large operation was Thatcher, Keir and Adams of New York, which began operating in the 1920s, supplying real reindeer and Eskimos along with storybook characters to cities and towns from Michigan to Florida. In many ways, companies like Gros and Thatcher were extending the old travelling circus idea, even aping standard circus practices by sending advance men, having semi-permanent crews to assist in local set-up, and using railway networks and later trucks and so on.[93]

As with earlier circus networks, other companies worked smaller, more regional routes. Benjamin Matlock produced a Santa Claus parade that ran in several Ontario cities in the decade after the Second World War. Matlock began as an interior decorator before spending a decade as the "head animator" for displays in a Detroit department store, a position he left in the late 1920s to start his own business. Early work included an animated cow for a local dairy and a replica of the town of Leamington, complete with "small animated figures." In 1947, he scaled up his operation by putting together a rentable Santa Claus parade, clearly based on the larger department store versions, with oversized figures, fairy-tale characters, and other colourful displays. He began with mockups and presented them to the Windsor Retail Merchants Association, which quickly raised a $3,500 fee. On that basis, Matlock secured a $5,000 bank loan and sent notes to various nearby cities, offering his parade for anywhere from $400 to $3,500. His first year, he secured sixteen reservations, mainly in southwestern Ontario, and mounted his first parade in November 1948. From his initial six floats, Matlock soon expanded to twenty-two, which he piled into nine trucks to move from town to town.[94] Further west, in the Prairies, J.J. Dalke, a Saskatchewan farmer, "brought Christmas cheer to thousands of persons in cities across Canada and the United States," taking part in parades with "his trained reindeer, along with four dogs and three bears." From 1948 to 1955, Dalke toured Manitoba, Saskatchewan, and Alberta with his show, appearing occasionally outside the prairies as well, most famously playing a small part in the Hollywood film *The Road to Utopia*.[95]

Whether borrowed from department stores or rented from travelling parades, these outside parades still required considerable local effort and enthusiasm. Money had to be raised, meetings held, permits secured, and promotions undertaken. Travelling companies like Matlock's typically assumed that communities would inject local content into the parade. "We do not find it practical to carry a live Santa Claus," Jean Gros's promotional material stated. "In addition, most communities have a traditional local personality who always appears each year."[96] Typically, as well, local groups, bands, and other marchers filled out the basic pre-designed floats.[97] "Because of the difficulty of bringing together an entirely local parade, Newmarket businessmen voted to hire a ready-made parade" in 1951, but they added "the indestructible taxi" piloted by two local men, a popular feature of previous parades that was, in fact, only partly local, having been borrowed from the blackface clowning of Amos 'n' Andy.[98] In Sudbury's 1964 parade, the Jaycees arranged local floats, bands, and clowns – including the Police Association's Big Nickel float and the Boy Scout's Big Apple – to supplement the imported balloon displays. In many ways, this hybrid form – combining broad continental influence with local initiative – almost perfectly captured the organizational spirit of the service clubs and business organizations at the heart of the civic fantastic. The Jaycees, after all, were an international body that emphasized local action.

"The Christmas bandwagon"

In 1966, the Sudbury Jaycees abruptly pulled out of the Santa Claus parade. The Retail Merchants Association, which normally paid the tab, had decided to spend money on improving decorations in the downtown, and lacking an immediate source of alternative funding, the Jaycees withdrew. For a moment, it looked like no parade would be held, but soon a citizens committee, composed of ten local men, stepped forward. They quickly divided their efforts – one man arranging heavy equipment, another floats and publicity, another cowboys and Indians, another finances. The committee chair took a week's vacation and coordinated the whole operation from a temporary office in the Nickel Range Hotel. There wasn't much time. Even three days before the parade date, the route had yet to be confirmed, the parade marshal still fretting that the large cranes and trucks could not negotiate the tight turns and steep grades. In the end, the parade had "a lot of unprofessional aspects" but was declared a roaring success and "a triumph of last minute organization," taking the usual "hour to pass any one point" and drawing "tens of thousands of Sudbury district resident to the downtown streets." The citizens committee continued to organize the local parade in future years. The parade had been saved, but the incident points to a broader theme: the tension, at the heart of the civic fantastic, between fragility and resilience.

The civic fantastic was a fragile tradition. Dependent on volunteer labour, it offered no guarantee of continuity or ongoing organizational experience. Money and labour were quickly taxed, and enthusiasm never sure. In Anson, North Carolina, the Chamber of Commerce held a meeting to decide if the parade should continue, and the debate enumerated all the possibilities and perils of local organization. Opponents of the parade argued that it killed business on parade day, tied up traffic, relied too heavily on contributions from the same few merchants every year, and (from a slightly different direction) opened potential for "misbehaviour of bystanders who throw objects at Santa Claus and other participants" and hurl "catcalls at costumed girls." Proponents countered that the parade was a good way to "officially" open the Christmas shopping season, that it put everyone in a festive mood, that it brought "more people into town than any other single event," that it represented a show of appreciation by merchants to past and future customers, and that it was a parade for children that was enjoyed by all.[99]

No doubt, the debate made explicit ongoing conversations occurring elsewhere, but in the long term, disagreement was often less damaging than creeping apathy and exhaustion. Lacking any power of compulsion, organizers sometimes expressed frustration that merchants could reap the benefits from the increased exposure and traffic downtown without actually contributing money or sweat to the parade, something the *Windsor Daily Star* called "hitchhik[ing] on the Christmas bandwagon."[100] Individual miscreants might be subject to moral suasion – in Windsor, organizers put special banners on participating stores – but general apathy was harder to address. In Barrie, the local paper pointed with envy to the parade in nearby Aurora and suggested that the city needed a Jaycee group to undertake such an important project. In Dauphin, Manitoba, the Chamber of Commerce called a public meeting to discuss arrangements for a Santa Claus parade, but only four people showed up.[101] In 1982, Sudbury's organizers – who had managed only forty-seven entries including floats, bands, and clowns – complained that neither downtown merchants nor the wider community had offered enough support. "We could have better support from the business sector," the parade committee spokesperson grumbled, noting as well that the whole parade committee amounted to fewer than ten people.[102] By this time, Sudbury was hardly booming, and downtown businesses suffering the depths of recession were not anxious to spend precious money and energy on a parade with unclear economic value. Often, however, lack of initiative was not the problem – the energy remained but got targeted in some other direction. "Sarnia's business section this week is scheduled to be decorated for the Yuletide under the guidance of the Retail Merchants Association," one 1950 report announced. "Cooperating with a special committee of merchants in the project are the Sarnia Collegiate, Y's Men's Club, Hi-Y-Club, R.L. Sands and the Junior Chamber of Commerce. Street decorations are being substituted for a Santa Claus parade. For the past two years the merchants have sponsored a gigantic parade and no doubt there will be a number of youngsters disappointed by the lack of repeat performance."[103]

Rooting the civic fantastic in the local civil society, however, had a paradoxical effect. At one moment, the unprofessional and volunteer nature could be a source of weakness and fragility; at another, it could be a source of strength and resilience. In Petrolia, the volunteer fire department organized the first parades, but then ceded control to the Jaycees in the mid-1960s. Over time, however, the local Jaycees declined, bleeding members until the national headquarters disbanded the chapter. Facing the end of a popular tradition, former Jaycee Henry Tenk took it upon himself to sustain the parade. "I used to knock on doors collecting a dollar here and a dollar there," he recalled. "The first year was tough. Some of the merchants questioned who gave me the authority to take on the Santa parade." But he managed to pull it off and eventually found much more community support. By 1977, the merchants did fundraising and "people bend over backwards to help me."[104] Similarly, in Perth, Ontario, the Lions Club bowed out in 1977 but "other service clubs rallied to save it," despite the pessimism of original Lions Club organizers. Across North America, the result was a narrative of neither triumph nor declension, but of an ongoing tension between fragility and resilience. Parades came and went, organizers started and stopped, and revivals could come after long delays, often dependent on idiosyncratic local factors and in-the-moment influences. Windsor had a parade in the interwar years, then again from 1947 to '63, organized first by the Retail Merchants Association and then by the service club Sertoma; the Jacyees then revived the parade in 1969.[105]

From St Louis to Sudbury

Early in the history of Santa Claus parades, the form began to move outside the corporate networks that created it, as various local groups adapted and adopted the basic idea to their own local circumstances. To do this they borrowed liberally from department store parades and from other kinds of mass culture, but refracted those forms through their own forms of civic organization. This blend of continental cultural forms and local organization is, in many ways, not that surprising. All the groups that made up the vanguard of the civic fantastic, after all, were local in focus but continental (even global) in connection. Service clubs, Chambers of Commerce, and chapters of the Legion focused considerable attention on their local communities, but all of them forged ongoing links to bigger institutions. The Jaycees had been founded in St Louis not Sudbury, and local members remained rooted in civic action that was tied to the larger global structure of the organization.

The result was a kind of reverse co-optation. We are used to thinking of big companies going on the lookout for local cultures that can be spun into corporate forms. In the civic fantastic, by contrast, local organizers marshalled and enlivened their own community networks by adopting and adapting wider forms of commercial and corporate culture. The result was a civic fantastic that had many of the features of its larger department store cousin but that mobilized volunteer labour in the name of service, cooperation, and civic pride. Some of these parades were decidedly unprofessional in look and style, while others reflected a dedicated and even talented artistic hand. But the building blocks of the civic fantastic were as much identity and affiliation as papier mâché and chicken wire; its lifeblood was not money and corporate expertise but middle class service and volunteer labour. In this sense, the civic fantastic expressed all the possibilities and limitations of non-metropolitan civic organization, at once open to public engagement and largely closed to women and racial others. Bob's Washer Service could be as much a part of the civic fantastic as the plurality and democracy of participation. The result was sometimes fragile, but in another way, the rise and proliferation of the civic fantastic point to the limits of corporate power. By the 1980s, the civic fantastic, not its corporate cousin, had become by far the most ubiquitous form of Santa Claus parades.

5
Casualty of the Times

It was a glorious press conference, filled with backslapping good cheer, but Al Zwegers was not amused. At the front of a conference room at the Sheraton Centre in downtown Toronto, Zwegers's daughter, Amber, was being held aloft by the president of McDonald's Canada, who had just announced that the city's Santa Claus parade would not, after all, come to an end. A week before, on 12 August 1982, Fredrik Eaton had announced that Eaton's would no longer organize its Toronto parade, an odd and abrupt announcement that caught nearly everyone off guard. Eaton's had ended Santa Claus parades before – Calgary in 1953, Edmonton in 1957, Winnipeg in 1967, and Montreal in 1969 – but in most of those cases there had been some alternative. Television allowed the company to bring its parades to almost all Canadians, so even as the local versions ended, the reach of the corporate fantastic had actually increased. But the Toronto parade was different. It was the flagship event, broadcast from a cultural capital to a wide audience. It was also the last surviving Eaton's parade in the country, so with it would end the company's contribution to Yuletide good cheer. The event, more-over, continued to be massively popular, drawing tens of thousands of live spectators in Toronto and tens of millions of television viewers across the continent every year. People were shocked, and they told anyone who would listen – newspaper editors, civic leaders, even the Ontario government – that something had to be done. Six-year-old Amber Zwegers's contribution was a letter to Santa Claus, sent to Paul Godfrey, the chair of the Metropolitan Toronto government. "Dear Santa," it read, "don't stop the parade, please!" So, when a "citizens committee" of business leaders managed to pull together twenty sponsors, who each pledged $75,000 over three years to save the parade, they tracked down Amber, invited her to their press conference, blew up her letter to massive size, and held her aloft to announce the redemption of childhood wonder. "We found Amber," declared George Cohon of McDonald's. "You don't have to cry anymore." It was great news all around, but at the back of the room Al Zwegers introduced a hint of complication. "It's a little ironic, isn't it?" he asked a *Toronto Star* reporter. "G.M. is giving $25,000 and they've just laid me off."[1]

Zwegers's comment signals the ambiguous legacy of Frederik Eaton's mid-summer announcement. On the one hand, it was the end of an era. For seventy-seven years, Eaton's had run Santa Claus parades in Toronto, and the event had long since come to play an important civic and emotional role for the city and, to a degree, for the country. Eaton's had helped pioneer the Santa Claus parade, which over time spanned five cities and a continental broadcast and came to mark seasonal time and to define the real Santa. But by 1982, the corporate fantastic was in decline. There were hundreds of Santa Claus parades that year, but only a few were run by department stores, which themselves were far from the hegemonic commercial institutions they had been at mid-century. Eaton's was already in deep trouble, well into the downward slide that would lead to its 1999 bankruptcy. So if Frederik Eaton's announcement brought an end to the company's long-standing Christmas tradition, it was only one of many problems for Eaton's and the department store form. Still, for the many Torontonians who saw the Eaton's announcement as an opportunity to make the event into a genuinely civic festival, not much had changed. The new parade stripped away the Eaton's name and replaced it with the innocuous title, the Metro Santa Claus parade, but as Al Zwegers's comment suggests, the new event retained both corporate leadership and its status as a promotional vehicle. Even though the Eaton's announcement had begun a vigorous discussion of alternatives, the result was more a plural version of the corporate fantastic than a genuinely communal spectacle. In the end, the events of August 1982 were less a clear-cut end of the corporate fantastic than the beginning of a new relationship between the promotional intent of the parade, its public meaning, and its metropolitan aspirations.

Tracing the shift from one set of corporate agendas to another requires attention to several issues. First, we need to parse why Eaton's would come to believe that a popular parade was no longer worth the expense. This decision was partly the result of several economic and business developments that had undermined and diluted the company's power and resources. Indeed, in some ways, the continued public appeal of the parade – as one aspect of Eaton's broader symbolic power – had for a long time helped to cloak the company's underlying structural problems. At the same time, we can see that the parade itself was losing some of its shine by the 1970s, as criticisms about timing and excessive commercialism became louder and more public. Second, we need to understand that the criticisms – though loud and often vociferous –always represented a minority. Many Canadians were shocked by the Eaton's announcement and struggled, in public and private, to come to terms with the end of such a popular event. The discussion became a moment to lament historical change, to express inter-generational connection, to remind the company of its moral obligations, and to assess the character of Toronto society. Third, we need to understand the fate of the parade in Toronto. Laments became the starting point of an energetic conversation about alternatives to the Eaton's-organized event. Many ideas were suggested during an intense week of discussion and effort, but the event that hit the streets that November leaned heavily on business organization and know-how, a spectacle with a civic gloss but an underlying corporate structure. In this sense, the Metro Santa Claus parade represented the triumph of one imagined future for the procession.

"It was really mismanagement"

By the 1970s, all was not happy in the world of department stores. For much of the twentieth century, they had been the largest and most powerful retail institutions on the continent. They had helped to create modern consumerism and to develop new forms of selling. Their buyers circled the globe, bringing products from near and far to consumers in many cities. Their enormous downtown stores had embraced spectacular display and helped to define urban modernity. The biggest Christmas parades – powerful new spectacles that department stores had pioneered – attracted enormous crowds in their respective cities and, by the 1960s, reached continental audiences through television broadcasts. In Canada, the Eaton family was akin to royalty, enjoying a lavish lifestyle and undertaking highly visible projects of civic improvement and philanthropy. The Eaton company itself was enormous and retained considerable iconic power. In 1969, at the company's one hundredth anniversary, Eaton's had forty-eight department stores, 352 catalogue sales offices, a global network of buying offices, and (with over fifty thousand workers) was the fourth-largest employer in the country.[2]

Yet size and symbolism cloaked several underlying problems, both general to the department store form and more specific to Eaton's. By 1969, the Big Stores hardly served as good symbols of progressive retail or urban modernity. Still large and powerful, they nonetheless appeared slow and tradition bound, not quite relics but certainly symbols of the past. Eaton's increasingly appeared as a lumbering giant rather than as the economic force it had been at mid-century. Indeed, in a more basic sense, it wasn't even well run.

In strictly business terms, department stores faced attacks on two fronts. On one side, the proliferation of various specialty shops undercut some of the department store's core business. In several key areas, from toys through furniture to fashion, new chains and specialty stores (often located in regional shopping malls) offered service and specialization at the middle and upper ends of the department store market. By the 1970s, such stores had emerged as significant threats. Specialty chains in women's fashion, for example, saw their revenues increase by 104 per cent between 1971 and 1976, reaching the princely sum of $519 million.[3] At the same time, consumers began shifting their spending to areas where department stores were weak. Do-it-yourself renovations became increasingly important in consumer behaviour, but most of this market went to a burgeoning home improvement industry rather than traditional department stores. Lumber yards in particular reinvented themselves to meet this new demand, and by about 1960 a mature industry had come together to sell wall paper, tools, and other building supplies to consumers interested in tinkering and minor renovations. It was a large market, but one that largely bypassed traditional sellers.[4]

Meanwhile, at the bottom end of the retail market, discount stores presented an even more difficult challenge. These retailers traced their origins to the so-called bargain houses that emerged after the Second World War in big North American cities, selling cheap durable goods to budget-conscious consumers. In Toronto, Ed Mirvish began selling women's dresses from a small store at Bloor and Bathurst in 1947, but over time he expanded his operation by swallowing nearby properties and broadening his products to multiple lines. Like many discount sellers – though Mirvish disliked the term – he bought large quantities of cheap goods, focused on products that would "move," and eschewed expensive marketing and fancy store fixtures. Mirvish admired the big department stores, but in practice his approach might be described as anti-Eaton's. "While the department stores were offering wide aisles, specialized departments, alluring display cases, sales clerks, free delivery, refunds, choices in style and size, and credit cards," he recalled, "I kept bucking the trend." Mirvish took cash only, permitted no refunds or exchanges, and generally offered no service or frills. This approach allowed him to offer rock-bottom prices. "What we saved in the usual services," he recalled, "we could turn over to the patrons at reduced costs." Honest Ed's did excellent business – almost $2 million annually by the late 1950s – but a one-off store out of the central business district was not about to undermine a big company like Eaton's.[5]

In the early 1960s, the discount idea spread beyond one-outlet entrepreneurs like Mirvish, attracting emulation by existing mass merchandisers. Woolworths and Kresge's, two of the largest retail chains in the United States, both set up discount arms (Woolco and Kmart, respectively) in 1962. Such outlets represented a version of, but also a threat to, the existing department store model. Like department stores, Kmart and Woolco had large premises, high turnover, and department-style organization. Indeed, at the time, they were often called "junior department stores." Like bargain houses, their retail style was stripped down and basic, eschewing expensive add-ons like Toylands, parades, display fixtures, and extensive service, aiming for budget-conscious consumers with low prices and well-stocked shelves. Yet where Mirvish had chipped away at the bottom of the Eaton's market, chains like Kmart and Woolco mounted more dangerous attacks by finding excellent locations on busy suburban strips and by marshalling systematic business expertise. By the early 1960s, the main American chains had crossed the border into Canada, where they joined homegrown versions like Sayvette and Zellers. Rapid growth followed: according to Statistics Canada, juniors represented less than one-third of department stores and less than one-fifth of sales in 1966; a decade later, they made up almost 60 per cent of stores and one-third of sales.[6]

Discount chains and specialty shops were both a cause and symptom of bigger changes in consumer culture. As a mass marketer, Eaton's had always aimed for the broad middle of the consumer market, helping to define the social meaning and cultural categories of the new age of modern retail. Indeed, the very notion of the consumer (someone who would spend rather than save, want rather than need, and shop as a form of leisure) came together in parallel with the rise of department stores in the late nineteenth and early twentieth centuries. By the 1960s and especially by the 1970s, however, all the standard consumer culture abstractions – consumer, middle, mass, and so on – seemed to

be dissolving, as segmentation, differentiation, and fragmentation became the retail keywords. "Why should there not be a mass-produced
consumer?" retail expert Morgan Reid, who had worked for Simpson's
and Eaton's, wondered in 1966. "Not so long ago the large-volume
retailer ... drew assurance from his market evidence that there was a
growing, dominant market of middle-income people who would mainly want the same goods ... [but] the mass merchandiser who wishes to
improve his competitive position in the future must meet the demands
of an increasingly fragmented market."[7] In fact, the mass market had
never been as fully united as such thinking suggests. Even Eaton's
had served various micro-markets through its bargain basements and
annexes (which emphasized cheap goods for lower-class customers)
and the College Street store in Toronto (which aimed for the carriage
trade). But where Eaton's could aggregate different social groups under one company banner, discounts and specialty shops drove a spatial and brand wedge between these different clusters of consumers.
Department store owners and managers well understood this trend,
at least rhetorically. "It is no longer practical," an Eaton's marketing
report stated in 1975, "to be all things to all people."[8]

Such statements simply begged the question. It was all well and good
to flag fragmentation in after-dinner speeches or internal documents,
but if you couldn't be all things to all people, what should you be? And
for which people? Should the big stores follow affluent consumers up
the style and service ladder or chase bargain hunters down? The answer was hardly obvious, and department stores across North America
struggled to adapt. Some added distinct boutique sections, presenting
high-fashion items in separate sections within their existing outlets.[9]
Others opened stand-alone specialty stores, like Woodward's two fur-
niture-only outlets in suburban Vancouver. Many of the big stores also
flirted with the discount model. In 1972, Eaton's set up a distinct discount chain, called Horizon, which grew to thirteen outlets over the
next three years. Four years later, the Bay took a more direct route to
discount expertise, buying the established chain Zeller's. At the same
time, department stores responded to the new retail era by modern-
izing their operations, aiming for tighter and more efficient corporate
systems. Simpsons-Sears installed a powerful computer in 1962, using
it to track credit and inventory, while Eaton's followed suit three years
later. Both companies also centralized many buying functions in their
Toronto head offices, a trend that was not always greeted with enthusiasm in the branch stores.[10] Finally, department stores responded to

the new retail environment through accelerated growth. After 1964, they moved more aggressively to open branches in suburban shopping malls and, by the 1970s, became core features of downtown redevelopment schemes. As one government report put it, the rise of discounts had shaken the big stores out of their postwar lethargy.[11]

Few of these solutions addressed the broader problem. Branch store growth, for example, raised sales figures and dollar volumes but also produced a crowded retail geography. By the mid-1970s, marketing experts noted that most areas were "over-stored," with too many outlets chasing the same dollar. "Canada's great retail expansion bulge of the 1960s and early 1970s is over," Harvey Secter told the *Globe and Mail* in 1978, "with the result that retailers will have to keep a sharp eye on costs and productivity if they want to remain in business."[12] Indeed, in a broader sense, the raw growth of department stores did not halt their overall decline. In 1976, the department store share of the retail market was at about the same level as in the 1930s, but the sector included many more companies and many more stores.[13] Predictions of crisis and a round of consolidations and bankruptcies followed. Dupuis Frères closed its doors in 1978, despite efforts to find a saviour investor to keep it running, while the Bay bought Zellers and then Simpsons-Sears.[14] All of these problems were exacerbated by the economic crisis of the 1970s and, even more dramatically, by the deep recession of the early 1980s. With unemployment in the double digits by 1982, and high interest rates forestalling credit buying on big items, dollar volumes stagnated. Indeed, sales at Canadian department stores actually fell in four of the first six months of 1982.[15] "There have been serious casualties among both traditional department stores and junior department stores," one Statistics Canada study noted as early as 1979, "as both have fought over the shrinking retail dollar."[16]

Every department store chain had to confront the new context, but Eaton's had its own problems. After all, the Bay – which became the largest Canadian retailer in late 1976, with over $1.5 billion in sales – weathered the economic storm fairly well, modernizing its stores and internal operations, and getting bigger through growth and acquisition. Meanwhile, Eaton's stagnated and declined. Its share of the department store market had dropped to about one-tenth by 1977,[17] and in retrospect we can see that the company was already on the downward path to bankruptcy. As early as 1962, the company did a revealing internal survey that discovered the average store manager was in his mid-fifties, had served the company for more than twenty-five years, and had a high school education; not surprisingly, the stores were not well positioned to face a decade of rapid economic and demographic change. Higher up, middle management was hopelessly bloated, and executives seemed to spend more time on personal manoeuvring than coherent management. Yet the "whiz kids" hired to modernize the company in the mid-1960s achieved only partial success. It's not that Eaton's made no changes in this period – the company grew to malls in the 1960s and undertook modernization efforts like centralized buying and computerization – but that it did so slower, later, and less competently than other department stores. The introduction of computerized credit in the mid-1960s was a complete disaster, and when the company tried to update its marketing a decade later, the new strategies alienated traditional customers without gaining many new ones. One ad campaign featured a scantily clad woman and was widely condemned by traditional customers. Similarly, the company's efforts to compete with discounts absolutely failed. The Horizon chain never amounted to more than a dozen or so outlets and was abandoned by 1977.[18]

In many ways, all these problems flowed down from the top. Even with new managers, computerization, and more aggressive suburban growth, the fact remained that the Eaton family ran the company as a personal fiefdom. There was no doubt that, by the 1960s if not before, family ownership blunted the full force of internal change. John David's four sons – widely called "The Boys" – didn't offer much more hope, running the company through the late 1970s and 1980s in disinterested and even apathetic ways. They spent time with their horses, yachts, marital affairs, and broadcasting ventures, but none had any apparent aptitude for retailing in the new age. Yet non-family management was never seriously considered at any point in the company's history, except as a stopgap measure while sons and grandsons were groomed.[19] "It was really mismanagement, more than anything else, that killed Eaton's," retail consultant Robert Herber declared after the company's bankruptcy in 1999. "Even as early as the 1960s and '70s, the stores themselves were only breaking even. The only profit they were making was from their real estate and credit card operations."[20]

The company's iconic status nonetheless continued. The company was the target of considerable criticism throughout its long history,[21] but its powerful mainstream appeal continued well into the 1970s, even when its structural and management problems should have seemed clear. The company celebrated its one hundredth anniversary in royal style in 1969, and when Eaton's dropped its money-losing catalogue in

1976, the move was greeted with great sadness and even anger across Canada.[22] Then, in the midst of the early-1980s recession, the sluggish giant laid off several workers, a further chink in its paternalist image. At the same time, looking to cut costs across the board, the company cancelled the Santa Claus parade. "Cancellation of the Santa Claus parade by T. Eaton Co. is the latest signal of how badly Canada's department stores are being hit by the current recession," declared the *Toronto Star*. The parade was "a casualty of the times."[23]

Of course, by this time, the parade itself was losing some of its shine. Though it had never been totally free of complaints – drivers grumbled about traffic, Christians complained about commerce, a few spectators expressed disappointment about the quality of a particular parade – it is striking how few of these problems attracted sustained public debate. In general, complaints remained isolated and never came together into fundamental general disgust. In the 1970s, however, criticism became louder and more public, particularly around scheduling. In 1975, Eaton's finally bowed to official pressure to move the parade to Sunday. In the public mind, the move seemed to throw off the balance of Christianity and commerce. "It is very disappointing to see this decision by a store that, just a few short years ago, kept the blinds of its store pulled so people could not window shop on Sunday," Sue Harrison wrote to the *Toronto Star*. In fact, the company had tried to head off such complaints by consulting with church leaders and by holding the parade in the afternoon (so as to not interfere with church attendance), but few observers seemed interested in such explanations. "Santa Claus parade on Sunday implies that Santa is a more important person than Jesus," Jane Long complained, a sentiment echoed in dozens of letters of complaint to company president Fredrik Eaton. Few of these correspondents seemed interested in nuanced analysis or reasoned rhetoric. "History records the fact that desecration and commercialization of Sunday," one wrote, "have wrung the death knell to many nations."[24]

More critics emerged around timing the parade in November. For most of the century, the parade had been held on the third Saturday of the month, a customary schedule that was thrown off by a whole series of conflicts in the 1970s. Parents worried that mid-November in Toronto could be too cold for children, while veterans and their supporters complained that the parade date conflicted with Remembrance Day activities, which were normally held on the weekend after 11 November. "Though I am only 25 years old I cannot in good conscience support such disregard for Canada's veterans and war dead," one Ottawa resident complained. "I have therefore decided not to buy anything from Eaton's as long as your company interferes in any way with the veterans' parade."[25] Since a later date would only be colder, the company moved the parade to the first Saturday in November. If that timing started out early, falling on the fifth of the month in 1978, it became positively insane by 1981, when the parade ran on the day after Halloween. And since the Eaton's event marked the start of Toronto's Christmas season, the new timing fanned the flames of growing anti-commercialism. "As a life long Torontonian I wish to tell you of my great disappointment in Eaton's approach to the commercialism of Christmas," Lydia Watson wrote to Frederik Eaton. "Santa Claus arriving on November 5th among fall leaves and warm sunshine was just too much to believe ... The second or preferably third weekend in November is a much more timely date for Santa to appear, and we might even have the odd snowflake then."[26] The national broadcast served only to increase the scope of potential criticism. One resident of Greenfield, Quebec, who had spent the afternoon raking leaves, called the broadcast "an absolute farce." "The sight of band after band playing Christmas music in the warm sunlight along snowless Toronto streets was ridiculous," he wrote.[27]

The intensity and vociferousness of the criticisms were partly a symptom of shifting ideas of commercialism, childhood, and Christmas. In objective terms, 1 November was quite early for a Christmas parade and represented a clear change from the customary mid-November timing, but the nature and character of the criticisms suggested a new cultural context. The rise of the so-called "second wave consumer movement" had aroused a more critical consciousness towards key business institutions. After the mid-1960s, several institutions and activists across North America mobilized around consumer issues, pressing for new laws about advertising, marketing, safety, and consumer protection. Ralph Nader became the most famous of these new activists, but the movement was more diffuse, diverse, and multi-directional than any single figure. Several jurisdictions responded by passing new laws and appointing consumer watchdogs, with ambiguous results, but perhaps the most important shift was broader and more atmospheric. The key effect of all these efforts was not just specific laws and regulations but a more general shift in discourse, one that legitimized more public and vociferous criticism of commercialism and corporate practice. In 1980, to take one Yuletide example, the *Toronto Star* reported a survey about Christmas attitudes. When asked, "What is the first thing that comes to mind when you hear the word Christmas," 40 per cent responded "commercialism" (up from 16 per cent in 1953) while "religion/birth of Christ" was 10 per cent (down from 20 per cent in 1953).[28]

The new anti-commercial discourse was particularly intense around children. In the United States, a group of concerned "housewives" set up Action for Children's Television in 1969 and proceeded to do research, lobby government, and publicize their critique of over-commercialized childhood.[29] Canadians were ready to listen. By 1974, the CBC had banned commercials in its children's programming, while both the federal government and the CRTC investigated the question of children and advertising. In the end, they generally settled on various forms of voluntary guidelines, but in the process the investigations and hearings provided a high-profile sounding board for all manner of criticism.[30] As a central event of the Christmas season, one that combined corporate promotion, childhood wonder, and family leisure, the Santa Claus parade became a natural magnet for these shifting perceptions. Indeed, the intensity and language of the anti-commercial criticisms of the parade were striking. Jennifer Parry inverted the usual Santa–magic connection by suggesting Eaton's over-hyped and too-early spectacle robbed children of Christmas magic rather than served it up: "By setting the date of the parade so far in advance of Christmas, Eaton's is forcing on us the commercialization of the Christmas season and destroying the magic of this time for our children."[31] Critics often promised various forms of practical action. Alderman John Sewell asked the Toronto City Council's executive committee to request that Eaton's hold the parade no earlier than the first week of December. "I suspect the public can spend as much money in the three weeks before Christmas as it can in the eight weeks before Christmas," Sewell argued.[32] One parent threatened an organized boycott: "In the event that you do not return to the traditional time period for the Christmas parade, I consider it appropriate to explore the possibility of organizing like-minded parents to protest your disinterest in our children's development. A boycott of Eaton's toy department by parents who are concerned about the ever-increasing commercialism of the Christmas season might be effective."[33]

It is not a surprise, then, that by 1982 Eaton's officials seemed fed up. Squeezed by intense competition, battered by economic problems, and pounded by various forms of criticism, the company turned its sights on the parade as an expendable and expensive frill. Certainly, deleting a half-million-dollar expenditure of dubious public relations value in one stroke had to be an attractive proposition for a company struggling to stay in the black. "It has been a long and happy association, and I, with a lot of other people, have enjoyed it immensely," Fredrik Eaton declared at his surprise press conference. "Times are difficult, and it seems silly to be spending money on a parade when you are having to let people go."[34] It didn't help, of course, that the parade no longer held universal appeal. "The criticism is very difficult," Eaton complained. "It's supposed to be a positive event, but, when it creates negative reaction, you have to wonder." It was hardly a statement steeped in nostalgia for a long-standing tradition. Appeals to reconsider the decision had no effect. Protests from customers were answered with a form letter, and politicians like Toronto Mayor Art Eggleton and Metro Chair Paul Godfrey were rebuffed. Eaton's would not be moved. The parade would not return.

"Noblesse oblige, after all, is a bargain"

"Eaton's – neither the department store nor the family – never owed Toronto a Santa Claus parade," Christie Blatchford wrote in the *Toronto Sun*. "It was, in the store's early years, when such things were better understood, a gesture of corporate good citizenship and a clever public relations tool … That's what it was, you know – a gift, a present from a fine Old Toronto family that made its fortune here and felt some obligation and responsibility to the city and its people."[35] As a reflection on the Eaton's announcement, Blatchford's column was quite revealing. It signalled, first of all, the way the announcement was the subject of intense debate and discussion. People struggled to find meaning in the news. All the Toronto newspapers printed multiple articles on the announcement, national television stations covered the press conference on evening newscasts, and wire services spread the story across North America. The public was shocked. Metro Chairman Paul Godfrey's office was "swamped with dozens of calls," while the *Toronto Star* received over three thousand messages on the first day of its special Santa Claus parade phone-in line, so many that the system was soon overwhelmed. "This little idea of yours could cut off all sorts of downtown phones – City Hall, the police department," one exasperated technician told *Star* editor Gary Lautens. "The Bell will not be happy."[36] Meanwhile, letters of protest from as far away as Atlanta poured into Eaton's, most of them sent directly to company president Fredrik Eaton. They came from young and old, parents and children, politicians and citizens. Indeed, the scope and scale of the discussion seemed far out of proportion to the real import of the announcement. There had certainly been a much more muted public discussion in Winnipeg and Montreal when Eaton's had cancelled those parades, and some Torontonians wondered about their neighbours' sense of priorities. "The bloodiest massacre of French Jews since World War II took place in Paris on Aug. 9, and *The Star* reported it on Page 11," one letter to the editor complained. "A department store cancelled its annual Santa Claus parade and *The Star* reported it in headlines on the front page."[37] But, in fact, the public discussion in Toronto was probably only the tip of the iceburg, the loudest and most formal expression of a widespread sense of loss. "They will start to cry when they find out," one child, interviewed by the CBC in a Toronto park, commented, no doubt summing up countless small conversations around dinner tables across the city.[38]

These stories, letters, laments, and complaints provide a window onto the social meaning of the parade at its end. Many people shared Blatchford's view that the parade had expressed something special about the Eaton family and their company. "It was a beautiful gift at no cost to the people of North America," Frances Fulton of Scarborough declared.[39] Many letters simply thanked the company for the gift of the parade – "I would like to express my thanks to your company for the years of pleasure ... brought to my family with your wonderful Santa Claus parade," one wrote. Another letter urged Eaton's to ignore the "chronic complainers and greedy whiners"[40] who had violated the paternalist "bargain" at the heart of the parade tradition. "Please don't listen to the horrible criticism which is always given by people who complain about everything," urged one resident of Islington, Ontario. Others, however, took the company's symbolic status in the opposite direction, making it the basis of an ongoing obligation that had to be fulfilled. "One always felt that Eaton's has been a real part of our lives and Eaton's never let us down. Now Eaton's is letting us down and we feel it!" Mrs Edward Phelps complained from Downsview.[41] "As a mother of two and an avid Santa fan I think Eaton's decision to cancel the Santa Claus parade is nothing less than ludicrous," one Toronto parent wrote to the *Sun*. "I fail to see how a big company like this can put out millions of dollars to build that steel and concrete monster [the Eaton Centre in downtown Toronto] and yet cannot support the best advertising gimmick that ever was."[42] The company's symbolic meaning, then, was contested. People could use it to thank Eaton's, excuse it, or hold it to account, but there was always a connection to moral or social principles and a sense of a reciprocal if unequal relationship, a moral economy of corporate paternalism. "Noblesse oblige, after all, is a bargain," wrote Blatchford in her column. "He who can afford it makes the grand gesture, he who receives it is grateful and does not consider it a right. The Eatons kept their share of the deal. We blew it, and all the crocodile tears in the world won't change that."

This moral economy was leavened by the parade's connections to multiple social narratives. Almost everyone wanted to make the parade and its cancellation the symbol of something larger: family, tradition, history, memory, and generational connection. "I think the Santa Claus parade should keep on going because it's really a delight to watch the children's faces when they see Santa coming," one caller told the *Toronto Star*'s Santa Claus phone line.[43] People were specific, highlighting their status as parents, grandparents, siblings, and cousins. "I believe the Santa Claus parade should go on because my little brother hasn't had a chance to see it yet," wrote one little girl.[44] Family narratives were often deployed to point to continuity and connection across genera-tions: "I enjoyed it as a child when my parents took me to see it – my children in turn loved it and looked forward to it – so in turn, did their children." In this sense, too, many of the laments played on memory, connecting past experiences to present complaints. Almost all the let-ters used words like *remember*, *recall*, *recollections*, and *memories*. "I re-member," wrote Lily Coleman, "cold mornings spent snug in snow suit and mittens at the corner of Spadina and Dupont anxiously awaiting the arrival of upside-down clowns, Bo Peep, Pumpkin Head and all the other characters."[45] Similarly, Pamela Smith wrote that "my strongest recollections of my grandfather are of me sitting up on his shoulders, laughing at the clowns and waving frantically at Santa Claus … I was looking forward to taking my nephew to see it this year and sitting him up on my shoulders, like my grandfather did with me."[46]

But personal memory was always connected to some sort of social nar-rative. Even quirky and highly specific memories tended to bleed into the larger connections of family, friendship, and neighbourhood. "One year, our daughter complained about her neck being 'itchy,'" Cynthia Coleman wrote in a five-page letter. "Later, at bedtime, I realized that what I had blamed on a woollen scarf was, in reality, chicken pox. Since we always filled the car with neighbourhood youngsters, the whole street was infected by Christmas." Deeply felt personal memories could also be structured by broader collective experiences. Taking account of the real meaning of the Eaton's announcement often meant placing it within social time, measuring the parade's history and longevity against big historical markers. "After surviving one depression, two world wars, sleet, rain and biting wind, Eaton's Santa Claus parade has succumbed to the current, unprecedented recession," wrote Paul Hellyer in the *Toronto Sun*, a narrative frame echoed in the story by CBC's *The National*.[47] The end of the parade was also connected to broader societal shifts, serving as a barometer of changing times: "Unfortunately, many traditions have of late been relegated to the waste-bin – respect for womanhood, veneration of the elderly and obedience of children, to name a few – and the Santa Claus parade must join its ranks, in the name of 'economy.'"[48] Just as individual memory could take on social context, such broad historical analysis often tied back to individual experience. Generational continuity, in particular, became one way to mark longevity and render history. "As a child of the Depression," wrote Andrea Knox, "they brought sheer magic into our lives, and later on, the memories shared with my own children will always be cherished ones."[49] Personal and social memory, then, were mutually reinforcing. Individual memories were authorized by social categories and collective memory was given potency by personal stories.[50]

Of course, not everyone was sad to see the parade end. Though critics were a distinct minority, some letters argued that the Eaton's announcement presented an opportunity to move Christmas away from corporate identity towards Christian or anti-material meanings. "The decision made by Eaton's to cancel their Santa Claus parade is a step in the right direction to de-commercialize Christmas," Margaret Delemere of Toronto declared.[51] "In keeping with the idea that 'small is beautiful,' I am not at all sad to see the annual extravaganza depart," wrote another correspondent, suggesting everyone go to church instead.[52] Catholic Cardinal Emmett Carter noted that $500,000 a year "would feed a lot of kids somewhere – not only for Christmas. So thanks, Messrs Eaton, and Mr. Godfrey, and Mr. Eggleton, and all of you, but no thanks … I'll be in Calcutta." Others took on the parade's civic image, pointing out that it hadn't kept up with social changes in the city, particularly with its growing ethnic diversity.[53] These counter-laments did not exactly constitute a real debate. Very few correspondents seemed interested in give and take or ongoing dialogue and very few made explicit references to the arguments of others. But the existence of these different positions both punctured the sense of Yuletide consensus around the Eaton's parade and set up a bigger question – could some other group organize a different kind of parade?

"The Good Lord must have put them together"

In the week after the announcement, Torontonians did more than lament. They discussed the future of the parade, suggesting many alternatives to the Eaton's-organized event. Some hoped for an alternative
corporate saviour, like Honest Ed's, Burger King, or the big breweries.
More common were suggestions for a community-focused effort, one
that better represented the diversity of Toronto in 1982, that was less
beholden to powerful circuits of corporate promotion and paternalism,
and that was a creature of civic engagement rather than passive spectatorship. Alderman John Sewell argued for a series of smaller parades
organized in neighbourhoods, while Lorraine Neill of Hamilton suggested a much simpler and smaller parade with just Santa Claus and a
band. "Get volunteers to help," advised Wendy King of Scarborough. "I
bet there are a fair number of older citizens who would love to make
costumes or flowers for floats," while "schools and churches could hold
sales or sell Christmas candy to raise money." Lee Johnson Gillick and
family hoped that the city or some business would provide a space "for
those interested and concerned people to go and donate their time and
talent on a voluntary basis," producing a parade "by the people and for
the people." Leighanne Simpson of Mississauga proposed a whole list
of fundraising ideas, from a Santa Stocking Fund with donation boxes
in stores to "daily interest savings accounts for Santa Claus" and even
lemonade stands. Others suggested that the revived parade ought to
reflect the new realities of Toronto, particularly its diverse population.
"I'd like to see, myself, different ethnic groups involved," declared
William Mole, the founder of Save Our Santa, a group formed in the
wake of the Eaton's announcement. "The Santa Claus parade has always featured just Santa Claus," Carole Ligold of Scarborough argued.
"Each country has its own method and person to celebrate Christmas.
Why not give the residents of our multicultural city a chance to show
how they celebrate Christmas?" All these ideas would have brought the
parade closer to the civic fantastic model that was, by 1982, ubiquitous
across North America. "The important thing to remember," Leighanne
Simspon summed up, "is that everyone has to be involved." A few
Torontonians went beyond suggestions to real action. Several small
businesses volunteered to donate material, and a classic car club offered up antique automobiles. William Mole printed Save Our Santa
buttons, which he sold for $1 to raise money to save the parade. At one

point, he sent a man dressed as Santa to city hall, who only managed to sell a handful of buttons before he was cited for illegal solicitation.[54]

When the revived parade hit the streets in November of that year, the driving force was corporate philanthropy and public relations not community spirit and bottom-up initiative. Its origins began in August with a coincidence of sorts, a chance moment in the office of McDonald's Canada President George Cohon. The chair of Metro Toronto, Paul Godfrey, was called out of a meeting with Cohon to answer a call from his executive assistant, who broke the news of the Eaton's announcement. Godfrey was stunned, but on the way out, he ran into the chair of the Metro Zoo, Ron Barbaro. The three were serious players in Toronto's corporate and government elite, and they soon became the nucleus of a rapid-fire effort to save the parade. "I happened to be in George Cohon's office when I was told about it," Paul Godfrey remembered. "It was a coincidence. As I walked out of the office Ron Barbaro was there. The Good Lord must have put them together there at that time to save the parade."[55] Cohon and Barbaro met that evening in a downtown restaurant to plot strategy, compiling a list of corporations that could afford to put up big money to help sponsor a new parade. The next day, they started to work the phones. Meanwhile, Godfrey met with Fredrik Eaton, who agreed to donate the existing material to the new effort, and the Ontario minister of tourism, who pledged provincial support. Within a week, the team assembled a press conference at the spiffy downtown Sheraton Centre hotel to announce success. Holding Amber Zwegers aloft, they announced a new Metro Santa Claus parade would run, as originally scheduled, on 14 November, but that future scheduling was up in the air.[56]

The new parade had a civic gloss but a corporate structure. On 17 August, Metro Chair Paul Godfrey and Toronto Mayor Art Eggleton jointly announced the creation of a non-profit corporation to finance and organize the revived parade.[57] The new parade was christened the Metro Santa Claus Parade – a name that, alongside Paul Godfrey's active participation, suggested a community effort. (Neither the Metro government nor the City Council contributed actual money to the effort. Indeed, several Metro councillors expressed considerable hostility to that idea.) The *Toronto Star* celebrated the parade's "new civic nature" and Godfrey made a point of announcing that he had appointed Cohon and Barbaro as co-chairs of a "citizens committee to save the parade." As in the civic fantastic, the new organizers embraced plural participation, turning their back on the corporate singularity of the original Eaton's parade, including floats sponsored by several companies and one by the Ontario government. The parade itself ended at Nathan Phillips Square, the site of Toronto's City Hall.[58]

In practice, however, the Toronto parade was more poly-corporate than truly civic, recasting rather than overturning the corporate cultural politics of the Eaton's era. The parade was saved, in the first instance, by small number of prominent businessmen working their corporate Rolodex. Cohon was the president of McDonald's Canada, by then the largest food service company in the country, while Barbaro was an insurance executive who served as chair of the Metro Zoo. Though neither represented the old money behind Eaton's, they were both experienced salesmen, the kind of men who could work the phones to raise a half-million dollars in a few days. In the middle of the effort, Cohon received a sales call from an investment counsellor at Dominion Securities, got the company president on the line, and sold him a float. Barbaro, meanwhile, headed off to lunch at the "spiffy" Wellington restaurant to "chat up someone with bank contacts."[59] Within a few days, they had lined up nineteen companies that could put up $75,000 for a three-year sponsorship commitment. The twentieth float went to the Ontario government, a connection forged by Godfrey, who went to high school with the minister of tourism and culture (see table of sponsors). In this sense, it was hardly chance or the Lord that put Cohon and Barbaro together at that key moment in August – it was the social and business circuits of corporate Toronto.

Sponsors of 1982 Metro Santa Claus Parade:
> Canada's Wonderland
> Canadian Tire
> Consumers Distributing
> Coca Cola
> Dominion Securities Ames Ltd
> Baskin-Robbins (ice cream chain)
> Black's Cameras
> General Mills Canada Ltd
> General Motors
> Greymore Trust Co.
> Imperial Oil
> Irwin Toy Ltd
> Knob Hill Farms

Kodak Canada Ltd
Mattel Canada Ltd
McDonald's Canada
Province of Ontario
Shopper's Drug Mart
Speedy Muffler King
Willy Wonderful Ltd[60]

The "citizens committee" also set up a parade that reflected their thoroughly business-oriented way of thinking. "We will have a director and a board similar to that which operates the Metro Zoo," Barbaro told the *Globe and Mail*. "Operating the parade will be a big business." The actual organizing, moreover, continued to be in the hands of a professional staff. Initially, Peter Labbett, who had chaired the Grey Cup parade organizing committee, took charge of the effort, while long-time Eaton's employees were hired to do the actual design and construction work. The result was slick and professional.[61] As in the Eaton's era, volunteers were recruited to participate, but always on terms set by Santa Claus Parade Inc. Participants were slotted into professionally made costumes and floats and were provided scripted instructions, including a strict ban on going out of place or communicating with spectators. In 1983, the board set up an exclusive club of corporate clowns, who were given the unique right to approach the crowds. The clowns were prominent business people who could put up $1,000 a year and withstand the intense vetting of existing members, joining an elite club complete with cufflinks and lapel pins. Not surprisingly, the group reflected the existing social base of corporate Toronto. Indeed, after two decades, 90 per cent of the corporate clowns were men, despite efforts to attract women. The parade content also reflected the promotional priorities of sponsors. Each float was preceded by a 35-square-foot banner to identify the sponsor, while many floats explicitly referenced the company that sponsored it, like the Canada's Wonderland Roller Coaster Thrills in 1997.[62]

Finally, the new Metro parade actively embraced the existing metropolitan cultural dynamics of the corporate fantastic. On one hand, the Metro parade stepped into the broadcast regime of the Eaton's parade, garnering national and continental coverage. By the 1990s, the parade reached a global audience, including Britain and Russia. Celebrity commentary continued as well. In 1984, the CBS broadcast was hosted by a tag-team of television stars Scott Baio and Celia Weston, while CTV's

Waiting for the parade in Toronto, 2004.
City of Toronto Archives, Fonds 291, Paul Till Fonds, Series 1502, it0010

1990 presentation featured John Dawe and Faye Dance (a coupling paralleled by the francophone coverage with Chantal Roy and Jacques
Aujer), all continuing the long-standing practice of commentary from
prominent television stars and mixed gender teams.[63] At the same time,
the metropolitan dynamics were reinforced by the parade's location in
the most important and powerful city in the country. Hamilton's volunteer organizers complained about the Ontario government's rather
hefty three-year $75,000 contribution to the Metro parade, noting that
they had to *pay* $1,800 in transportation and assembly costs to bring
a provincial float to Hamilton. "If Toronto receives $25,000 [per year]
then in a population proportion, we should receive something," complained Ed Cummings, the former parade chairman. "There's no damn
way we can understand why we should have to pay." Meanwhile, in
the Ontario legislature, local MPP Sheila Copps complained that "as
usual the government has turned its back on Hamilton." It was a hard
argument to refute, despite the heroic efforts of Ministry of Culture
spokesperson Pat Tyrell, who claimed the Toronto money was a grant
to the newly formed non-profit, who would own the float: "It's really
a different situation. The Toronto situation was to save a major event
which had a kind of historical background."[64]

The corporate and metropolitan rather than civic nature of the new
parade is brought into even greater relief when it is compared with
similar events in Winnipeg, where a quite different set of dynamics followed Eaton's cancellation of the parade in February 1967. In that case,

no corporate board of directors moved in to save the parade. Instead, the parade remained in limbo until May, when the Greater Winnipeg Fire Prevention and Education Committee, a body made up of full-time fire departments in the area, stepped up to organize a civic parade as an extension of their long-standing Christmas Toy Drive. The firefighters invited volunteer and community participation. Firms and groups could sponsor an existing float or build their own, but the actual organization was largely volunteer.[65] With no permanent storage space and no large budget to secure one – "we have to scrounge for everything," the parade chairman declared in 1972 – the floats were stored and maintained by Sever Signs (a local sign and printing business) and the costumes were donated to city high schools, where they could be used for amateur theatrical productions until parade time. "It's going to be a self-help operation. Each school is responsible for its costumes and businessmen have financed floats and are responsible for maintenance and storage," noted the parade chair in 1967.[66] The overall result was decidedly unprofessional. In 1972, the *Free Press* noted that the crowd was subdued on a very cold day and confused when a fire truck followed Santa, traditionally the last float and climax to the event.[67] In the long term, moreover, Winnipeg's parade reflected the inherent tensions of the civic fantastic, especially between fragility and resilience. The Fire Prevention Committee continued to coordinate the parade until 1975, when it was taken over by the Jaycees, who later teamed up with Manitoba Hydro. The parade was also local rather than metropolitan, lacking the national reach of the larger Toronto effort. The new parade garnered some local television coverage. In 1981, the Jaycees arranged for CBC coverage of the event, but the network insisted on 6 December to avoid conflicts with the CFL football playoffs. Worried about the weather but desperate for exposure, the Jaycees agreed. The following year, CBC cancelled coverage because of budget cuts.[68] The revived parade was ultimately a success, pulling in many groups and thousands of spectators, but its structure was thoroughly civic and its reach was decidedly local. The after-Eaton's parades in Winnipeg and Toronto, then, are a study in contrasts.

"It's kind of ironic"

It seems perfectly symbolic that George Cohon was at the centre of the revived Toronto parade. Holding Amber Zwegers aloft at the Sheraton Centre in Toronto, the president of McDonald's might have nicely symbolized the changing of the guard in service capitalism. At forty-five, Cohon was still relatively young in corporate terms, and he led a company that was a product of the postwar boom, a second generation of consumer capitalism in Canada. In the middle decades of the century – the golden era of the Eaton's parade – the department store was the exemplar of Canadian and North American consumer capitalism. By the 1980s, however, McDonald's had become the paradigm-setting corporation. Cohon's company was the largest restaurant chain in Canada, a national expression of a global capitalist phenomenon. Sociologist George Ritzer even argued that McDonald's was a symbol of an entire approach to production and marketing, shaping business practice in a whole host of industries, a metaphor for an emerging approach to global commerce. If you wanted to understand consumer capitalism in the 1940s, Eaton's was good place to start; three decades later, the same project would have led you to hamburgers.[69]

The analogy is not perfect – McDonald's Canada was a branch plant of an American company and became only one of many actors in the Metro parade – but Cohon's leading role does help signal the new event's corporate character. The civic content was really only a gloss, with Metro stuck on the title and a few politicians involved. The real core was the social circuits, philanthropic networks, and public relations machines of Toronto's corporate community. Even the exclusive club of corporate clowns reflected such hierarchies, roaming freely through the streets while ordinary volunteers served assigned roles and remained fixed in place. The point is not to criticize the companies and people who put up time, money, and energy to a "free" event, but to make clear the nature and character of the new spectacle. In Winnipeg, a civic and volunteer parade struggled along, with uneven crowds, aging floats, and spotty television coverage. In Toronto, a corporate parade forged ahead, with a board of directors, a professional staff, big money, and eventually a global television broadcast. There may have been a chance, in 1982, for a different tradition to emerge, one more tied to the Toronto that George Moll and John Sewell wanted to see in the parade or (to use Lee Johnson Gillick's words) something more "for the people and by the people." But the poly-corporate result had a certain internal logic. Time was short and (as in Winnipeg) a community effort might have taken weeks to pull together. Once Cohon and Barbaro moved into the short-term vacuum, however, the long-term structure was set. The Toronto parade still brings wonder to spectators, but it is more for the people than by the people.

Conclusion
Enchanted Capitalism

"In the first 80 odd years, Eaton's had it right," Lorraine Fisher of North Vancouver complained in 1999. "But then they started to break away from their worthy traditionals." A week before, the Eaton family had put the firm up for sale, the penultimate act in a long tale of decline that would end, six months later, with the company's bankruptcy. Theories about the company's failure were legion, and the offer of sale became another opportunity for autopsies. Many retail experts complained about Eaton's inability to change, but Fisher argued that the company had been too anxious to depart from its tried-and-true practices. Just in case the point was lost, she offered up a laundry list of Eaton's mistakes: central locations replaced by shopping malls, termination of free delivery, the end of the iconic catalogue in 1976, and finally dropping "their sponsorship of the Santa Claus parade in Toronto, which was renowned internationally." It was departing from such practices – turning its back on its essential *Eatonness* – that led to the company's demise.[1] Fisher's argument was a nice example of what might be called the lament for tradition lost. In the new retail era, Eaton's felt the power but also the burden of its long-standing symbolic status. It was not just any company, and in the list of exhibits meant to prove that point, the Santa Claus parade featured prominently. Indeed, the parade and Eatonness existed in a mutually reinforcing symbolic language. But if the parade lived on in memory, it did so in somewhat tragic terms, invoked as a narrative device to capture the depth of the company's decline.

For a promotional event to take on this kind of meaning and memory, it needs to have longevity, continuity, and depth. For more than seventy years, Eaton's had mounted the most popular annual public event in Canada, spreading processions to five cities and to various forms of mass media. A pageant of the corporate fantastic, the Santa Claus parade dazzled by synthesizing the underlying cultural and emotional impulses of consumer capitalism, and by borrowing visual and auditory strategies from other forms of commercial spectacle. The result played on wonder and abundance and combined both older and newer forms of Christmas, childhood, and popular culture. Over the first half of the twentieth century, when Eaton's was consolidating its hold on Canadian department store retailing, the Santa Claus parade became a modern spectacle that articulated new consumer identities by marshalling what parade makers saw as the traditional fantasy of age-old stories. It was the product of a new metropolitan elite – the big department store – that spoke to consumers through familiar forms of art and fantasy. It set seasonal time, overwhelmed public space, and finally became an agent of mass media. It was at once a parade, a form of Christmas celebration, and an exercise in consumer capitalism.

The most basic appeal was wonder. The parade presented (as *La Presse* put it in 1930) "the most fabulous dreams of childhood."[2] In a modern era of childhood innocence, and at a time when adults sought enchantment through children, this was a language that many Canadians wanted to hear. The Santa Claus parade was certainly a sophisticated form of visual spectacle and public procession for its time, even if the childhood humour was decidedly unsubtle, the sounds quite traditional, and the art based on common forms of commercial design. Eaton's did indeed have it "right," to use Lorraine Fisher's word. There is no way to measure the effect of the parade on sales, or its power as a promotional tool that helped the bottom line, but Fisher's comment makes clear that it was an important aspect of the company's iconic image. Eaton's was an agent of capitalist enchantment and modern Yuletide wonder.[3]

Yet the parade's continued appeal into the second half of the twentieth century remains an analytic puzzle. When the parade began in 1905, the modern culture of the eye was only just in formation. Movies were, at best, a marginal curiosity – short, black and white, and soundless – while commercial radio was yet unknown and television remained a futurist fantasy. Even newspapers were just beginning to fill their pages with a variety of photographs from near and far. At the same time, street processions were mostly well-ordered and respectable articulations of ethnic and civic identity, and while a few stores featured a live Santa around Christmas time, the holiday itself was only emerging from its Victorian commitment to domesticity. As the Santa Claus parade evolved from a simple stunt into a more professional spectacle around the First World War, then, it must have been stunning and wondrous, since urban residents were unused to an annual procession of such visual and narrative richness. But when Eaton's officials in Winnipeg announced the end of their parade a half-century later, they reflected on the social and cultural changes that had undermined Santa's appeal. "Frankly," they wrote, "we feel that the magic of the Winnipeg Santa Claus parade, which prevailed in times past, has been lessened by the exposure the children of today have to so many things not available to their mothers and fathers."[4] Similarly, in the wake of the cancellation in Toronto, one journalist wondered if what was really at stake was the decline of the whole idea of downtown parades, which "like ticker tape receptions, belong to another era, one when 76 trombones did lead the big parade and didn't blare in living color in the rec room every night ... It was a nice idea whose time is past, like the catalogue, seven percent mortgages and nickel cones."[5] Of course, seeing the world as disenchanted was a classic modern tendency, but such observations did contain a grain of truth. Shopping mall Santas, ubiquitous Toylands, and the wonders of screen capitalism surely made the live parade a bit less magical, just as sprawling cities made downtowns more remote and inconvenient. Capitalism had moved on to other enchantments.

Yet in 1967 – and in 1982 – Santa Claus parades continued to draw enormous crowds. The corporate fantastic was no longer the cutting edge of spectacle, but it remained stunningly popular as a live event, even when more convenient mass media experiences were available. The same point might be made about the civic fantastic, which never ranked as the most sophisticated form of fantastic art, but remains a vibrant tradition across North America to this day. Why do Santa Claus parades continue to be so popular? Part of the answer lies in childhood. The parade (as one *Globe and Mail* report put it in 1978) is "really for ... those too young to feel the cold, see the pulleys that make the figures move, and hear the slightly forced quality of Santa's laugh," the kids that construction supervisor Jim Carmichael simply called "the believers."[6] Part of the answer, too, lies in the making of modern adulthood, which sees in children the purest expression of innocence and wonder. Parents found joy less in the spectacle itself than in the reaction of their children. Finally, any explanation of the parade's continued appeal must wrestle with the power of live experience, even in the age of screen capitalism. Liveness itself has a history, but it is hard to deny (and even harder to explain) the continued appeal of joining a crowd as a social moment and of experiencing an event beyond the mechanical sights and sounds of screen and speaker.[7]

The Eaton's parade was not just popular, however, it was hegemonic, an exercise in cultural power. Many institutions worked to marshal Yuletide wonder, but Eaton's deployed its economic and institutional power to press its corporate agenda onto the season to an unmatched degree. Enchantment was built on organization. The company's professional staff kept a close eye on the biggest and best parades on the continent and spent massive amounts of money to produce a professional product. The company's parades far surpassed the quality and art of most street processions in the middle decades of the century, and this fact, as well as the promotional machine behind the parade, ensured large crowds of exceptional enthusiasm. Managers like Jack Brockie and Scott Brewster had the theatrical flair and the organizational smarts to put together a professional parade that played on multiple forms of wonder and enchantment, just as the company's advertising department had the expertise to mobilize mass media to promote the parade and extend its power far beyond the live performance. Over time, the Eaton's processions became powerful local events, reached out to their regions, and (in the case of the Toronto parade) became a national and even international tradition. But they were corporate not civic spectacles, tightly controlled events that marshalled the company's own public relations resources and staff. In building its corporate spectacle into a Canadian institution, the company added a new element to Christmas celebration. Here, the interpretive issue is not the commercialization of some supposedly authentic religious or traditional holiday – the fusion of commerce and culture in Christmas was long-standing and, regardless, somewhat muted in the pageant itself – but Eaton's ability to insert its corporate agenda into Canada's seasonal traditions. Commercialism, after all, could be a diffuse process involving many actors and institutions; the Eaton's parade was much more singular in design.

Of course, Eaton's never controlled the agenda completely. Christmas was too broad and varied to be dominated by a single institution. Indeed, the company couldn't even control the broader meaning of its own spectacle. Bands and performers undermined the company's careful planning; spectators pushed and shoved; fathers and mothers complained; television executives brought their own priorities to the table. The parade was an event in too many places over too many years for any singular meaning or experience to emerge. Even the company recognized the need for some local variation, so central control was never seriously considered, and when the Toronto parade was shipped to Montreal, new material was added, some subtracted, and some rearticulated. If the parade makers aspired to universal Christmas cheer, they faced serious cultural problems, making only half-hearted stabs at reaching "New Canadians" in the Toronto crowd and scrambling for last-minute concessions to French Canadians in the television audience. Many Canadians, from the wives of soldiers to philanthropic organizations, actively took up the parade as a symbol of the promise of universal Christmas cheer; by the 1970s, others made a similar point more negatively, pointing to the parade as an example of how Christmas started too early, had become too commercial, or represented "Anglo-Saxon" culture in a binational country. Spectators themselves were never passive receivers of the company's agenda: along the route, they pushed and shoved, climbed poles, took over the streets, swarmed into offices, and disrupted the rhythms of city life; across the country, they complained that the parade was not shown, that the commentary was uninspiring, or that the translations were poor. Whether watching the parade live or on TV, many adults found more delight in the reactions of children than in the parade itself. But more than the many other institutions creating and reflecting these dynamics, Eaton's moved to the centre of Christmas wonder. This fact did impose obligations on the company but was also the source of tremendous cultural power.

In the end, the corporate fantastic was power with a paradox. The singularity of the corporate fantastic – the source of its initial strength – turned out to be a brittle form of hegemony. The corporate fantastic was ultimately too dependent on a single company at a time when that company was in decline – when, in fact, the entire form of business it represented was facing a structural crisis. Today, both the Eaton's parades and the company itself exist only in memory. There are Santa Claus parades of some kind in almost all of the original five cities, but they are organized by a coalition of interests and do not reflect the promotional priorities of a single institution. In Montreal, a local entrepreneur mounted two parades in the early 1980s, and then the Downtown Business Association brought the parade back for good in 1993. Business groups in both Calgary and Edmonton ran indoor parades (touring through the downtown network of walkways and malls) for many years, while in the latter city an events company brought the spectacle back outside in 2015. These are new traditions, but even in Winnipeg and Toronto, where the parade has run continuously for more than a century, more than a generation has passed since the Eaton's era.

After 1981, Eaton's never again organized a Santa Claus parade, and, of course, the company itself went bankrupt in 1999. Eaton's, and the corporate Santa Claus parade it helped pioneer, is now a historical artefact that lives only in memory.

Oddly, then, the civic fantastic turned out to be less powerful but more resilient, growing from a civic ecology that could hardly compete with Eaton's in economic resources, professional expertise, or promotional might, but made up for it in organizational plurality, volunteer spirit, and community service. The story of the Santa Claus parade turns out to be as much about Henry Gessenbier as Jack Brockie, as much about civic spirit as corporate promotion, as much about Sudbury as Toronto. Today, as a result of such civic efforts, the Santa Claus parade remains one of the most vibrant forms of Christmas celebration across North America. Most are unprofessional, few are organized by department stores, and none by Eaton's, whose trademarks are now owned but unused by its former competitor, Sears. In this sense, the surviving Toronto parade – as one species of big-money Christmas festivals – seems startlingly out of place. Professional in design, corporate in organization, and global in reach, it nonetheless serves as a poor representative of the typical Santa Claus parade. The corporate fantastic was, already by 1982, a tiny island in a vast sea of civic parades, organized by diverse groups across the country, sometimes with artistic panache but more often with spirited volunteerism and unprofessional wonder. Though rarely a full mile of make-believe, they bring their own kind of joy.

Notes

Introduction: Alfreda's Lament

1 Alfreda Hall, letter to editor, *Globe and Mail*, 17 August 1982, 1. On the cancellation, see *Globe and Mail*, 10 August 1982, 5, and 16 August 1982, 6.
2 Mary Ryan, "The American Parade," in Lynn Hunt, *The New Cultural History* (Berkeley: University of California Press, 1989), 133, 138.
3 The literature is vast. Influential works include Mary Ryan, *Civic Wars: Democracy and Public Life in the American City during the Nineteenth Century* (Berkeley: University of California Press, 1997); Susan Davis, *Parades and Power: Street Theater in Nineteenth Century Philadelphia* (Philadelphia: Temple University Press, 1985); H.V. Nelles, *The Art of Nation Building: Pageantry and Spectacle at Quebec's Tercentenary* (Toronto: University of Toronto Press, 1999). For an extended use of linguistic analogies, see Louis Morin, "Establishing a Signification for Social Space: Demonstration, Cortege, Parade, Procession" in his *On Representation* (Stanford: Stanford University Press, 1994), 38–53.
4 Brooks McNamara, *Day of Jubilee: The Great Age of Public Celebrations in New York, 1788–1909* (New Brunswick: Rutgers University Press, 1997).
5 On these themes, see especially Ryan, *Civic Wars*. For Toronto, see Peter Goheen, "The Assertion of Middle-Class Claims to Public Space in Late Victorian Toronto," *Journal of Historical Geography* 29 (2003): 73–92; Goheen, "Negotiating Access to Public Space in Mid-Nineteenth Century Toronto," *Journal of Historical Geography* 20, no. 4 (1994): 430–49; Goheen, "Symbols in the Streets: Parades in Victorian Urban Canada," *Urban History Review* 18, no. 3 (February 1990): 237–43. For an interesting take that foregrounds sensory perceptions, see Nicolas Kenny, *The Feel of the City: Experiences of Urban Transformation* (Toronto: University of Toronto Press, 2014), esp. ch. 5.

6　William Leach, *Land of Desire: Merchants, Power and the Rise of a New American Culture* (New York: Vintage Books, 1993), 331–8; Karal Ann Marling, *Merry Christmas! Celebrating America's Greatest Holiday* (Cambridge: Harvard University Press, 2000), 83–120.

7　Marling, *Merry Christmas*; Leigh Eric Schmidt, *Consumer Rites: The Buying and Selling of American Holidays* (Princeton, NJ: Princeton University Press, 1995); Jean-Phillipe Warren, *Hourra pour Santa Claus! La commercialisation de la saison des fêtes au Québec, 1885–1915* (Montreal: Boreal, 2006).

8　On this theme, see especially Schmidt, *Consumer Rites*.

9　Leach, *Land of Desire*, 15.

10　On Macy's, Wanamaker, and early department stores, see Leach, *Land of Desire*.

11　On Eaton's, see Joy Santink, *Timothy Eaton and the Rise of His Department Store* (Toronto: University of Toronto Press, 1990); David Monod, *Store Wars: Shopkeepers and the Culture of Mass Marketing, 1890–1939* (Toronto: University of Toronto Press, 1996); Donica Belisle, *Retail Nation: Department Stores and the Making of Modern Canada* (Vancouver: University of British Columbia Press, 2011).

12　Leach, *Land of Desire*; Monod, *Store Wars*, 116. For the Nystrom quotation, see Paul Nystrom, *The Economics of Retailing* (New York: Ronald Press, 1919), 259.

13　Belisle, *Retail Nation*, 39.

14　The key work on this organizational revolution is Alfred Chandler, *The Visible Hand: The Managerial Revolution in American Business* (Cambridge, MA: Belknap Press, 1977). Many studies highlighted the department store's organizational approach and the management shifts that accompanied the rise of the mass market. See, for example, Susan Porter Benson, *Counter Cultures: Saleswomen, Managers, and Customers in American Department Stores, 1890–1940* (Urbana: University of Illinois Press, 1986); Susan Strasser, *Satisfaction Guaranteed: The Making of the American Mass Market* (New York: Pantheon, 1989); Richard Tedlow, *New and Improved: The Story of Mass Marketing* (New York: Basic Books, 1990). On Canada, see Belisle, *Retail Nation*; Monod, *Store Wars*; and especially Monod, "Bay Days: The Managerial Revolutions and the Hudson Bay Company Department Stores, 1912–1939," *Historical Papers / Communications historiques* 21, no. 1 (1986): 173–96.

15　On these developments, see Santink, *Timothy Eaton*; Monod, *Store Wars*; Belisle, *Retail Nation*; Samuel Ditchett, *Eaton's of Canada: A Unique Institution of Extraordinary Magnitude* (New York: Dry Goods Economist, 1923); Paul Nystrom, *The Economics of Retailing* (New York: Ronald Press, 1919).

16 Lorraine O'Donnell, "Visualizing the History of Women at Eaton's, 1869 to 1976" (PhD dissertation, McGill University, 2002), and "Le voyage virtuel: Les consommatrices, le monde de l'étranger et Eaton à Montréal, 1880–1980," *Revue d'Histoire d'Amérique Française* 58, 4 (printemps 2005): 535–68.

17 Nystrom, *The Economics of Retailing*, 250. See also William Leach, "Transformations in a Culture of Consumption: Women and Department Stores, 1890–1925," *Journal of American History* 71, no. 2 (September 1984): 319–42.

18 Keith Walden, "Speaking Modern: Language, Culture, and Hegemony in Grocery Window Displays, 1887–1920," *Canadian Historical Review* 70, no. 3 (1989): 285–310; Leach, *Land of Desire*; O'Donnell, "Visualizing."

19 Belisle, *Retail Nation*, makes much of this theme.

20 Ditchett, *Eaton's of Canada*; Santink, *Timothy Eaton*, 181.

21 Santink, *Timothy Eaton*, 156.

22 Cited in Leach, *Land of Desire*, 31.

23 See, for example, the documents in Archives of Ontario, T. Eaton Company Fonds, series F229-116, "Files on a comparative study between Eaton's and Simpson's catalogues." (The T. Eaton Collection will hereafter be cited as TEF). On the broader practice of emulation in mass marketing, see Monod, *Store Wars*.

24 Peter Stearns, *Consumerism in World History* (New York: Routledge, 2001); Sarah Elvins, *Sales and Celebrations: Retailing and Regional Identity in Western New York State, 1920–40* (Athens: Ohio University Press, 2004).

25 Robert Trudel, "Famille, foi et patrie: le credo de Dupuis Frères," *Cap-aux-Diamants: la revue d'histoire du Québec* 40 (1995), 26–9; Mary Catherine Matthews, "Working for Family, Nation and God: Paternalism and the Dupuis Frères Department Store, 1926-52" (MA thesis, McGill University, 1997).

26 Belisle, *Retail Nation*, 30–44

27 Belisle, *Retail Nation*; Monod, *Store Wars*; C.F. Bodsworth, "Simpson's versus Eaton's: The Big Battle of the Stores," *Maclean's*, 1 February 1955, 9–11, 43–4. Richard Longstreth studies modernization of department stores in the middle decades of the twentieth century. See his *The American Department Store, 1920–1960* (New Haven: Yale University Press, 2010). There is little scholarly research on Canadian department stores after the Second World War, though James Opp's recent study of the tensions around expansion and iconography at the Bay raises the bar for consumer history in Canada. See his "Branding 'the Bay/la Baie': Corporate Identity, the Hudson's Bay Company, and the Burden of History in the 1960s," *Canadian Historical Review* 96, no. 2 (June 2015): 223–56.

28 See Belisle, *Retail Nation*; Bella, *The Christmas Imperative*, 147–8; Monod, *Store Wars*, 122–4; Thelma Dennis, "Eaton's Catalogue: Furnishings for Rural Alberta, 1886–1930," *Alberta History* 37, no. 2 (1989): 21–31; Cynthia Wright, "Rewriting the Modern: Reflections on Race, Nation, and the Death of a Department Store," *Histoire Sociale – Social History* 35 (May 2000): 153–68.

29 *Globe and Mail*, 15 November 1956, 40.

30 Here (and throughout the book), Canadian historians will no doubt recognize the metropolitan thesis, which long ago aimed to show the importance of urban elites projecting their ideas and influence outward. See especially the brilliant (almost deconstructionist) discussion by J.M.S. Careless in "The Toronto *Globe* and Agrarian Radicalism, 1850–67," *Canadian Historical Review* 29, no. 1 (1948): 14–39, and his elaborations of the metropolitan thesis in "Frontierism, Metropolitanism, and Canadian History" *Canadian Historical Review* 35, no. 1 (1954): 1–21, and *Frontier and Metropolis: Regions, Cities, and Identities in Canada before 1914* (Toronto: University of Toronto Press, 1989). I draw on the metropolitan framework loosely and with conscious disregard of its full meaning and elaboration. My aim is modest – not to revisit the thesis or the many debates it engendered, but to understand one aspect of cultural production in the twentieth century. Nonetheless, I think elements of the metropolitan thesis do have much to offer recent discussions of "trans-national history," so to a degree my analysis of the Eaton's parade tries to play on these two frameworks.

31 The collection has already been well used by several historians probing diverse subjects. Indeed, my own analysis of the parades owes a great deal to the rich secondary literature on mass retail in Canada, an area well served by historical scholarship, especially Monod, *Store Wars*; Wright, "The Most Prominent Rendezvous"; O'Donnell, "Visualizing"; and Belisle, *Retail Nation*.

32 This survey is indebted to local history rooms at various public libraries as well as recent efforts to digitize local newspapers, occasionally as commercial efforts but often as public projects.

33 Alan Hustak, "Santa Parade Flourished for 44 Years," *Montreal Gazette*, 23 December 1990, D6.

1 The Corporate Fantastic

1 *Edmonton Journal* (hereafter *EJ*), 2 December 1946, 2.

2 *TDS*, 2 December 1905; *WT*, 1 December 1905, 3; *Omaha Daily Bee*, 10 December 1895, 5.

3 TEF, F229-162-0-585, Christmas – Santa Claus Parade – Description file, "History of T. Eaton Company Ltd. Santa Claus Parades"; *Toronto Daily Star* (hereafter *TDS*), 19 November 1949, 2.

4 *Manitoba Free Press* (hereafter *MFP*), 22 November 1915, 3.

5 The practice of climbing a ladder into the store was first used in Winnipeg, 1906.

6 The 1916 floats in Toronto were Cinderella in a Pumpkin Coach, the Old Woman Who Lived in a Shoe, Miss Muffet, Little Boy Blue, Little Bo Beep, Mother Goose, and Little Red Riding Hood. See TEF, "History of T. Eaton Company Ltd. Santa Claus Parades." For the cavalcade quotation, see *TDS,* November 18, 1927, 11.

7 See TEF, Jack Brockie Files (hereafter BF), F229-151, box 4, file 118: Sales Promotion Meeting Minutes, meetings of 2 January 1948, 15 June 1948, 22 June 1948, and 28 September 1948.

8 *MFP*, 21 November 1921, 18. An outline of parade characters in Toronto from 1905 to 1975 is consolidated in "History of T. Eaton Company Ltd. Santa Claus Parades."

9 *Montreal Gazette* (hereafter *MG*), 30 November 1925, 9; *La Presse*, 26 November 1925, 2; *La Presse*, 30 November 1925, 8; *Calgary Herald* (hereafter *CH*), 25 November 1929, 18; *Edmonton Journal*, 25 November 1929, 10.

10 For typical parade content, see Craig Heron and Steve Penfold, *The Workers' Festival: A History of Labour Day in Canada* (Toronto: University of Toronto Press, 2005), chap. 1; Goheen, "Negotiating Access" and "Symbols in the Streets."

11 The classic article on this tradition in Canada is Bryan Palmer, "Discordant Music: Charivari and Whitecapping in North America," *Labour/Le Travail* 1 (1978): 5–62.

12 *Ottawa Citizen*, 14 June 1872, 4.

13 See Nelles, *Art of Nation Building*; Robert Cupido, "Public Commemoration and Ethnocultural Assertion: Winnipeg Celebrates the Diamond Jubilee of Confederation," *Urban History Review* 38, 2 (Spring 2010), 64–74.

14 Heron and Penfold, *Workers' Festival*.

15 *Calgary Herald*, 25 November 1929, 18; *Edmonton Journal*, 26 November 1937.

16 *MG*, 28 November 1938, 13.

17 TEF, BF, box 4, file: Santa Claus Parade, 1954, "Santa Claus Parade" (press release).

18 *Display in Canada* (December-January 1950–1): 23; *TS*, 20 November 1937, 2; "History of T. Eaton Company Ltd. Santa Claus Parades." For a good

introduction to historical soundscapes, see Mark Smith, ed., *Hearing History: A Reader* (Athens: University of Georgia Press, 2004), and Mark Smith, "Producing Sense, Consuming Sense, Making Sense: Perils and Prospects for Sensory History," *Journal of Social History* 40, no. 4 (2007): 841–58.

19 *Edmontonian*, December 1951, 10. The *Edmontonian* is the newsletter of the Eaton's Edmonton store.

20 TEF, F229-162-0-587, file: Christmas S.C. Parade, Edmonton, *Edmontonian* (December 1953).

21 *Canadian Business* (November 1955): 87; *TS*, 19 November 1948, 8; TEF, BF, box 4, file: Christmas – Santa Claus Parade, Line-Ups, 1949–1952, "Santa Claus Parade, 1949."

22 *TDS*, 20 November 1926; *Globe and Mail* (hereafter *GM*), 18 November 1955, 44.

23 Eaton's official, cited in Jack Karr, "Here Comes Santa Claus," *Star Weekly*, 13 November 1954.

24 *Globe*, 16 November 1928, 15; *MG*, 26 November 1928, 6; *La Presse*, 24 November 1930, 17; *Winnipeg Tribune* (hereafter *WT*), 24 November 1924; *CH*, 25 November 1929, 18; *Edmontonian*, December 1956, 9.

25 *TDS*, 16 November 1929, 27.

26 *MG*, 23 November 1942, 11.

27 *TDS*, 14 November 1931, 2. On multi-ethnic images in interwar parades, see Cupido, "Public Commemoration and Ethnocultural Assertion."

28 *Globe*, 19 November 1923, 14; *TDS*, 13 November 1936, 36; 14 November 1936, 11; *MFP*, 21 November 1921, 18; *WFP* 16 November 1935, 9.

29 *Edmontonian*, December 1951, 10.

30 *TS*, 16 November 1928; *MG*, 24 November 1930, 7; *TDS*, 14 November 1931, 2; *WFP*, 26 November 1951.

31 Philip Deloria, *Playing Indian* (New Haven, CT: Yale University Press, 1999). Many insights into First Nations image making can be found in Paige Raibmon, *Authentic Indians: Episodes of Encounter from the Late-Nineteenth-Century Northwest Coast* (Durham, NC: Duke University Press, 2005).

32 *La Presse*, 26 Novembre 1925, 2; *La Presse*, 25 Novembre 1935, 21.

33 *WT*, 24 November 1951, 3. Sometimes, journalists domesticated rather than exoticized indigenous symbols, making them into one part of Canadian history and culture. "The float of totem poles demonstrated that [Santa's] favorite land is Canada," one report noted. "In them as well as the reindeer Canada made a characteristic contribution to this Yuletide color banquet." Exotic language was more common, however. *TDS*, 19 November 1927.

34 *CH*, 23 November 1935, 13; *MFP*, 17 November 1930, 19; *TDS*, 18 November 1933, 2;*Toronto Telegram*, 16 November 1935, 25.

35 Although there is surprisingly little historical literature on blackface in Canada (despite the ubiquity of the form), the international literature is vast. A classic study is Eric Lott, *Love and Theft* (New York: Oxford University Press, 1993). On Orientalist images, see Kay Anderson, *Vancouver's Chinatown: Racial Discourse in Canada, 1875–1980* (Montreal and Kingston: McGill-Queen's University Press, 1995).

36 *Display in Canada* (December-January 1950–1): 10.

37 *TDS*, 18 November 1933, 2; *CH*, 23 November 1935, 13.

38 *Globe*, 23 November 1925, 11; 22 November 1926, 14; *TDS*, 19 November 1938, 13; *Edmontonian*, December 1948; *Chinook Winds*, December 1947. On occasion in Calgary and Edmonton, Santa was greeted by the store manager and walked with great ceremony through the front door.

39 *La Presse*, 24 November 1947, 11.

40 In a few cases, other commercial institutions took the lead, as in Chicago, where the State Street Business Association initiated the first Christmas procession in 1934. See chapter 4.

41 *Hamilton Spectator*, 18 November 1950, 20 November 1950, in Hamilton Public Library, Local History and Archives, Santa Claus Parade Scrapbook, vol. 1, 1947–1953.

42 On other Christmas parades, see William Leach, *Land of Desire: Merchants, Power, and the Rise of a New American Culture* (New York: Vintage Books, 1994); Karal Ann Marling, *Merry Christmas! Celebrating America's Greatest Holiday* (Cambridge, MA: Harvard University Press, 2001). See also the picture books: Ronnie Minor and Laurie Anne Tamborino, *Detroit's Thanksgiving Day Parade* (Chicago: Arcadia Publishing, 2003); Robert Gripo and Christopher Huskins, *Macy's Thanksgiving Day Parade* (Chicago: Arcadia Publishing, 2004).

43 *TDS*, November 13, 1931; *Contacts*, December 1941, 14.

44 *Globe*, 5 June 1923, 14.

45 Report on the arrival of the Hagenbeck-Wallace circus, *Globe*, 17 June 1922, 17.

46 Janet Davis, *The Circus Age: Culture and Society under the American Big Top* (Chapel Hill: University of North Carolina Press, 2002); Tina Loo and Carolyn Strange, "The Travelling Show Menace: Contested Regulation in Turn of the Century Ontario," *Law and Society Review* 29, no. 4 (1995): 639–68.

47 On Coney Island, see John Kasson, *Amusing the Million: Coney Island at the Turn of the Century* (New York: Hill and Wang, 1978); Woody Register,

The Kid of Coney Island: Fred Thompson and the Rise of American Amusements
(New York: Oxford University Press, 2001); Gary Cross and John Walton,
The Playful Crowd: Pleasure Places in the Twentieth Century (New York:
Columbia University Press, 2005). On Toronto amusement parks, see Diane
Beasley, "Walter Dean and Sunnyside: A Study of Waterfront Recreation in
Toronto, 1880–1930" (MA thesis, University of Toronto, 1995); Mike Filey,
I Remember Sunnyside: The Rise and Fall of a Magical Era (Toronto: Dundurn
Press, 1996). On Winnipeg Beach, see Dale Barbour, *Winnipeg Beach:
Leisure and Courtship in a Resort Town, 1900–1967* (Winnipeg: University
of Manitoba Press, 2010). On the Mardi Gras processsion, see Michael
Immerso, *Coney Island: The People's Playground* (New Brunswick, NJ:
Rutgers University Press, 2002), 122–3.

48 Keith Walden, *Becoming Modern in Toronto: The Industrial Exhibition and the
Shaping of Late Victorian Society* (Toronto: University of Toronto Press, 1997),
and "Speaking Modern: Language, Culture, and Hegemony in Grocery
Store Window Displays, 1887–1920," *Canadian Historical Review* 70, no. 3
(1989): 285–310; William Leach, "Strategists of Display and the Production
of Desire" in Simon Bronner, ed., *Consuming Visions: Accumulation and the
Display of Goods in America, 1880–1920* (New York: Norton, 1989), 99–132;
Register, *The Kid of Coney Island*, 274–84, 293–7; O'Donnell, "Visualizing."
On Apted see TEF, F229-162-0-595, Christmas – Parade – Reminiscenes,
Reminisensces of Santa Claus – Mr. J.J. Vaughn, 20 December 1966. These
are notes of an interview of Vaughn by staff at the Eaton's Archives.

49 TEF, BF, Advertising and Display conferences, January and June 1947,
[internal description of Merchandise Display, n.d. but probably ca 1947], 16.

50 Stephen Nissenbaum, *The Battle for Christmas* (New York: Alfred A. Knopf,
1996), 70–9, 93–4.

51 Penny Restad, *Christmas in America* (New York: Oxford University Press,
1995), 150–2

52 *La Presse*, 22 November 1934; *CH*, 16 December 1949, 1. It should be noted
that the ACJC was not, by the 1930s, as central to Catholic nationalism
in Quebec as it had been in earlier periods. See Louise Bienvenue, *Quand
la jeunesse entre en scène: L'Action catholique avant la Révolution tranquille*
(Montreal: Boréal, 2003).

53 See TEF, BF, file 123, file: Santa Claus Broadcasts, 1946, 1947 & 1948,
Kingsley to Don Sims, CJBC radio, and Sims to Brockie, letters of 28
December 1948 and 3 January 1949; *Globe*, 15 November 1920, 9; EC-OA,
F229-162-0-590, "Eaton's Santa Claus Parade, 1964" p. 10. Note that when
quoting letters to Eaton's from private individuals, I have followed current
academic convention by changing names.

54 *TDS*, 16 November 1920, 18 November 1960.
55 Restad, *Christmas in America*; Jean-Phillipe Warren, *Hourra pour Santa Claus! La commercialisation de la saison des fêtes au Québec, 1885–1915* (Montreal: Boréal, 2006), 103–4. See also Nissenbaum, *The Battle for Christmas*; Leigh Eric Schmidt, *Consumer Rites: The Buying and Selling of American Holidays* (Princeton, NJ: Princeton University Press, 1995); Leslie Bella, *The Christmas Imperative: Leisure, Family, and Women's Work* (Halifax: Fernwood, 1992).
56 T.J. Jackson Lears, *Fables of Abundance: A Cultural History of Advertising in America* (New York: Basic Books, 1994).
57 The "Place of Delight" quotation is from an Eaton's advertisement in *Globe*, 15 November 1910, 16. On Eaton's Toyland, see Bella, *The Christmas Imperative*, 155–6. On Toylands and delight, see Register, *The Kid of Coney Island*, 293–7.
58 *La Presse*, 18 November 1927, 16.
59 *CH*, 25 November 1929, 18; *TDS*, 14 November 1931, 2.
60 *Globe*, 21 November 1924, 18; 19 November 1948; *Toronto Telegram*, 19 November 1960, 21.
61 *TDS*, 18 November 1933, 1; 19 November 1941, 9. On consumer identity and political mobilization, see Donica Belisle, "Exploring Postwar Consumption: The Campaign to Unionize Eatons in Toronto, 1948–1952," *Canadian Historical Review* 86, no. 4 (December 2005): 641–72; Magda Fahrni, *Household Politics: Montreal Families and Postwar Reconstruction* (Toronto: University of Toronto Press, 2005).
62 Lisa Jacobson, *Raising Consumers: Children and the American Mass Market in the Early Twentieth Century* (New York: Columbia University Press, 2004), ch. 1; Gray Cross, *The Cute and the Cool: Wondrous Innocence and Modern American Children's Culture* (New York: Oxford University Press, 2004), ch. 3.
63 Cited in Margaret Munnoch, "The Santa Claus Parade," in Mary Burben and Flora McPherson, eds, *Christmas in Canada* (Toronto: Dent, 1959), 116.
64 *WT*, 1 December 1905, 3; TEF, F229-162-0-594, Christmas – Santa Claus Parade – Reminiscences, "Descriptions gleaned from Colonel Louis Keene, May 1959."
65 Brockie, cited in *New Liberty*, December 1953, 89.
66 Jack Zipes, *Fairy Tales and the Art of Subversion* (New York: Routledge, 2006), and *When Dreams Came True: Classical Fairy Tales and Their Tradition* (New York: Routledge, 1989); Lucy Rollin, *Cradle and All: A Cultural and Psychoanalytic Reading of Nursery Rhymes* (Jackson: University Press of Mississippi, 1992); Nicholas Sammond, *Babes in Tomorrowland: Walt Disney and the Making of the American Child* (Durham, NC: Duke University Press, 2005), 25–80.

67 *TDS*, November 15, 1954, 5.

68 TEF, F229-162-0-575, Santa Claus Parade – Clippings file, *Star Weekly*, 13 November 1954. On Eaton's efforts to understand "New Canadians" in the 1950s, see Wright, "The Most Prominent Rendezvous of the Feminine Toronto: Eaton's College Street and the Organization of Shopping in Toronto, 1920–50" (PhD thesis, Ontario Institute for Studies in Education, 1993), 207–17.

69 *TDS*, 17 November 1951, 1.

70 See Lears, *Fables of Abundance*; Leach, *Land of Desire*; Colin Campbell, *The Romantic Ethic and the Spirit of Modern Consumerism* (New York: Blackwell, 1987).

71 "History of T. Eaton Company Ltd. Santa Claus Parades."

72 TEF, BF, file 92, Mothers Council minutes, 1945. Mothers Council was made up of seventy-five women, mostly heads of Home and School Associations, assembled by Eaton's for commercial advice. Over time, the company tried various versions of the idea that went under different names: Mothers Forum, Women's Committee, etc.

73 T. Eaton & Co., *The Story of a Store* (Toronto, 1952), cited in Maria Kalamas and Robert Tamilia, "Eaton's Fall from Grace: Tracing the Rise and Ultimate Demise of a Venerable Canadian Retailer, 1869–1999," *Conference on Historical Analysis and Research in Marketing (CHARM), Proceedings* 11 (2003), 24. On the theme of corporate image, see David Nye, *Image Worlds: Corporate Identities at General Electric, 1890–1930* (Cambridge, MA: MIT Press, 1985).

74 *WFP*, 17 November 1933, 17.

75 In the late 1950s, the Executive Office tried to control costs, but the long-term effect is not clear. See Bella, *Christmas Imperative*.

76 TEF, BF, box 4, Santa Claus Parade, 1937–41, "Comments Re 1939 Santa Claus parade and Suggestions for 1940," 22 November 1939; TEF, BF, box 4, file: Santa Claus Parade, 1937–41, "Minutes of meeting of the 1941 Santa Claus Parade Committee, held Saturday 1 November 1941."

77 The press wrote several accounts of the production process. See, for example, *Display in Canada* (December-January 1950–1): 23; TEF, F229-162-0-575, Santa Claus Parade – Clippings file, *Star Weekly*, 13 November 1954.

78 *Display in Canada* (December-January 1950–1): 23.

79 *Display World*, October 1961, 14.

80 Nelles, *Art of Nation Building*; Robert Cupido, "Appropriating the Past: Pageants, Politics, and the Diamond Jubilee of Confederation," *Journal of the Canadian Historical Association* 9 (1998): 155–86; Heron and Penfold, *Workers' Festival*.

81 TEF, BF, box 4, file: Santa Claus Parade 1956, part I [handwritten notes on 1956 parade, likely by Brockie]. Thumbing noses and falling asleep: TEF, F229-162-0-597 [notes on parade history].

82 TEF, BF, box 4, file: Santa Claus Parade, 1937–41, "Comments Re: 1939 Santa Claus Parade and Suggestions for 1940" dated 22 November 1939.

83 Ibid.; TEF, F229-81, Eatons Santa Claus Parade Files, 1961–75 [hereafter cited as SCP], box 1, file: Minutes and Arrangements, 1967, "Santa Claus Parade 1967, Responsibilities Handled by Public Relations" dated 2 November 1967. Brockie declared the 1963 Santa to be "slightly thin and his projection not strong. New Santa Claus to be considered for 1964." TEF, SCP, box 1, file: Santa Claus Parade, Minutes and Arrangements, 1961–1964, "EATONS SANTA CLAUS PARADE 1963, POST PARADE NOTES."

84 TEF, BF, box 4, file: Santa Claus Parade 1956, Part I, "Instructions to Marshals, Santa Claus Parade – November 17th 1956" (emphasis in original). On strapping performers down to floats, see *TS*, 14 November 1977, A19.

85 TEF, BF, box 4, file: Santa Claus Parade, 1937–41; "Comments Re: 1939 Santa Claus Parade and Suggestions for 1940," dated 22 November 1939, 4; TEF, BF, box 4, file: Santa Claus Parade 1956, part I [handwritten notes on 1956 parade, likely by Brockie]; TEF, BF, box 4, file: Santa Claus Parade 1956, part I; TEF, SCP, box 1, file: Minutes and Arrangements –1967 "Instructions to Marshals, Santa Claus Parade – November 17th 1956"; TEF, SCP, box 1, "Santa Claus Parade 1967, Responsibilities Handled by Public Relations," dated 2 November 1967; TEF, SCP, box 1, file: Santa Claus Parade, Minutes and Arrangements, 1961–1964; "EATONS SANTA CLAUS PARADE 1963, POST PARADE NOTES."

86 On Brockie, see TEF, F229-221-0-6, Eaton's Archives Office People Files, box 1, "Brockie, J. A. – Toronto, Ontario." On art and business, see Register, *The Kid of Coney Island*; David Garland, *Auto Opium: A Social History of American Automobile Design* (New York: Routledge, 1994), 68–97. Unfortunately, information on the day-to-day life of display artists in Eaton's is very thin. For example, it appears from surviving photos that Scott Brewster was a snappy and stylish dresser with some artistic flair, but evidence on how he negotiated the famously stuffy and conservative atmosphere at Eaton's remains elusive. I thank Meaghan Walker for pressing me on this point after my talk on Santa Claus at the University of Alberta in November 2015.

87 *Canadian Business*, November 1955, 86; *TS*, 15 November 1954, 5.

88 TEF, F229-162-0-597 [notes on parade history]; *Gossip*, 30 November 1968, 4–5, 10; "March of Rhymes," *The Pru Echo*, untitled story in *Northern Circuit*, and untitled story from *Gossip Magazine*, all in TEF, F229-162-0-575, file:

Christmas –Santa Claus Parade – Clippings; *Canadian Business*, November 1955, 86; Bella, *The Christmas Imperative*, 162–70. On Clarke, see TEF, F-229-81, SCP, box 1, file: Santa Claus parade, Minutes and Arrangements, 1972, "Parade Personalities" (press release). Clarke started in the Mail Order Office in the 1920s and made his way to the Display Office, where he designed window displays, and moved from there to Public Relations. In the 1960s, he became Public Relations director. TEF, F229-162-0-591, Eaton's Santa Claus Parade Creator, Eaton's Santa Claus parade 1970.

89 *Canadian Business*, November 1955, 89. On psychedelic colours in 1967, see SF, F229-162-0-591, "Eaton's Santa Claus Parade."

90 TEF, BF, box 4, Advertising and Display Conferences, file 2 of 4, "Merchandise Display Sessions," 13, 14, and 15 January 1947; TEF, BF, file 90, Montreal Correspondence 1944, Lemieux to Brockie, 5 April 1944.

91 "Descriptions gleaned from Colonel Louis Keene."

92 *Northern Circuit*, Christmas 1951, 26; TEF, BF, file: Santa Claus Parade, 1937–41, W.J. Kealer to Brockie, 14 October 1941.

93 *Edmontonian*, December 1947.

94 TEF, BF, Advertising and Display Conferences, Toronto and Winnipeg, 1942–3, Advertising and Display Meeting, 17 May 1943, 3.

95 TEF, BF, box 4, Advertising and Display Conferences, file 2 of 4, "Merchandise Display Sessions" 13, 14, and 15 January 1947, 32. (Present were merchandise display managers from Toronto, Winnipeg, Hamilton, Edmonton, and Canadian Department Stores, formerly a chain of stores in small cities, acquired by Eaton's.)

96 *MG*, 24 November 1961; *MG*, 26 November 1938, 4.

97 TEF, BF, file 128, J. Clifford to Brockie, 14 November 1955.

98 TEF, BF, Extracts from Minutes of Merchandise Office Representatives, 21–3 April 1947, 4

99 Paul-André Linteau, *Histoire de Montréal depuis la Confédération* (Montreal: Boréal, 2000), 323–4. See also Michelle Comeau, "Les grands magasins de la rue Sainte-Catherine à Montreal: des lieux de modernisation, d'homogénéisation et de différenciation des modes de consummation" *Material History Review* 41 (Spring 1995), 58–68.

100 O'Donnell, "Le voyage virtuel," 542–3; Andreé Anne de Seve, "Hourra! Le catalogue Eaton est arrivé" *Cap-aux-Diamants* 40 (hiver 1995).

101 Robert Trudel, "Famille, foi et patrie: le credo de Dupuis Frères," *Cap-aux-Diamants: la revue d'histoire du Québec* 40 (1995): 26–9; Mary Catherine Matthews, "Working for Family, Nation and God: Paternalism and the Dupuis Frères Department Store, 1926–52" (MA thesis, McGill University, 1997).

102 See, for example, *La Presse*, 17 November 1925, 26; 19 November 1925, 14; 20 November 1925, 32.

103 *La Presse*, 17 November 1950, 60.

104 *La Presse*, 12 November 1956, 28.

105 O'Donnell, "Le voyage virtuel," 540–3, 549–50, 554–6, 563–4.

106 See *La Presse*, 21 November 1947, 10. For a schematic but useful glimpse at anglophone advertising approaches in Quebec in the early years of the Quiet Revolution, see Frederick Elkin, "Advertising in French Canada: Innovations and Deviations in the Context of a Changing Society," in G.K. Zollschan and W. Hirsch, eds, *Explorations in Social Change* (Boston: Houghton Mifflin, 1963).

107 *MG*, 5 November 1964.

108 Eaton's promotions and press coverage used term "Sarcee." Following current naming practices, I use Tsuu T'ina but retain "Sarcee" in direct quotations.

109 *CH*, 24 November 1930.

110 On this theme, see especially Mary Ellen Kelm, *A Wilder West: Rodeo in Western Canada* (Vancouver: UBC Press, 2011); Susan Joudry, "Hidden Authority, Public Display: Representations of First Nations Peoples at the Calgary Stampede, 1912–1970" (PhD thesis, Carleton University, 2013).

111 *EJ*, 2 December 1946, 2.

112 *Edmontonian*, December 1946, 9. One Spot was a common presence in rodeos around Alberta in this period. See Joudry, "Hidden Authority."

113 *WFP*, 19 November 1934, 6; 15 November 1952, 43; *WT*, 19 November 1949, 1; 22 November 1952, 1.

114 TEF, F229-151, Advertising and Display conference, 2/4 January and June 1947, 4.

115 *WFP*, 16 November 1935, 9.

116 This idea came together in the first half of 1948. See TEF, BF, box 4, file 118: Sales Promotion Meeting Minutes, meetings of 2 January 1948, 15 June 1948, 22 June 1948, and 28 September 1948.

117 Gene Walz, *Cartoon Charlie: The Life and Art of Animation Pioneer Charles Thorson* (Winnipeg, Great Plains Publications, 1998).

118 See, for example, miscellaneous clippings in TEF, BF, box 4, file: Santa Claus Parade, 1956, part I; TEF, F229-308, box B-427, Eaton's Archives Photographic and Documentary Art Subject Files, file: Christmas – USA – New York – Santa Claus Parade – Macy's (Jack Brockie from Ed Hill), miscellaneous photographs.

119 See Santink, *Timothy Eaton*; Monod, *Store Wars*; O'Donnell, "Visualizing"; Wright, "The Most Prominent Rendezvous"; Belisle, *Retail Nation*, 13–44.

On the broader network of department store entrepreneurs, see Leach, *Land of Desire*.

120 TEF, BF, file 84, Merchandise Office 1944, Budget Notes, 6 July 1944.

121 For Canada, see especially David H. Flaherty and Frank E. Manning, eds, *The Beaver Bites Back? American Popular Culture in Canada* (Montreal and Kingston: McGill-Queen's University Press, 1993). The dialogue of American export and local consumption is a standard theme in many studies of American culture abroad. For a general discussion, see Mel van Elteren, "Rethinking Americanization Abroad: Toward a Critical Alternative to Prevailing Paradigms," *Journal of American Culture* 29, no. 3 (September 2006): 345–367.

122 Leach, *Land of Desire*, 334.

123 Collins interview, *Gossip*, 30 November 1968, 4.

124 See, for example, TEF, BF, box 5, file 94 – New York Office, Correspondence, file: Macy Parade, Bamberger's, "Observations by M. Morrison – Three American Parades." See also TEF, BF, box 4, file 116, Sales Promotion Meeting Minutes, meeting of 13 November 1945; TEF, BF, box 4, file 117, Sales Promotion Meeting Minutes, meeting of 4 November 1947; TEF, BF, box 5, file 143, Miscellaneous Reports, Staff Trips, 1944–1945. On a Jack Clarke trip to New York for the CBS Parade of Parades: TEF, F-229-81, box 1, SCP 1973, Clarke to P. Levitan, Director of Special Events, CBS TV Network, 8 November 1968. A 1947 enumeration of "Out of Town Visitors" lists officials from Macy's (New York), Hudson (Detroit), Eaton's-Montreal, and Eaton's-Winnipeg. TEF, BF, file 127 – Santa Claus Parade 1947. Shreds of evidence also indicate Eaton's officials visited Boston, Pittsburgh, Buffalo, and Cleveland at Christmas time. See TEF, F229-151, Budget 1948, handwritten notes.

125 TEF, BF, box 4, Santa Claus Parade 1956 Part I, Edward Hill, Macy's to Brockie, 21 March 1956. Macy's also sent sketches of Bamburger's and Macy's parades and notes that indicate Macy's representatives had travelled to Orange Bowl parade, Rose Bowl parade, and Mardi Gras to investigate floats.

126 Collins in *Gossip*, 30 November 1968; Fernie interview notes in TEF, F229-162-0-594 (1981 file), Christmas – SCP – Production ca 1947.

127 TEF, BF 128 - Christmas – Santa Claus Parade Line-Ups, 1949–52, Macy's Press release, 16 November 1950, Macy's Publicity 1950.

128 *GM*, 14 November 1959; clipping from *Northern Circuit* magazine, 1951, in TEF, F229-162-0-575, file: Christmas – Santa Claus Parade – Clippings. Eaton's did contemplate celebrity participation in the 1960s, but never followed through on the idea.

129 *New York Times*, 29 November 1935, 16; Minor and Tamborino, *Detroit's Thanksgiving Day Parade*.
130 TEF, BF #100, Paris Buying Office, 1949–58, Brockie to Harold King in Paris buying Office, 28 November 1949.

2 Santa in Public

1 *TDS*, 19 November 1929, 2.
2 Peter Goheen, "Symbols in the Streets" and "The Assertion of Middle-Class Claims to Public Space in Late Victorian Toronto," *Journal of Historical Geography* 29 (2003): 73–92.
3 On the relationship of space and public sphere, see David Wittenberg, "Going Out in Public: Visibility and Anonymity in Michael Warner's 'Publics and Counterpublics,'" *Quarterly Journal of Speech* 88, no. 4 (November 2002): 426–33. The literature on the public sphere is vast. For classic starting points with useful historical content, see Craig Calhoun, ed., *Habermas and the Public Sphere* (Cambridge, MA: MIT Press, 1992); Mary Ryan, *Women in Public: Between Banners and Ballots* (Baltimore: Johns Hopkins University Press, 1990); Mary Ryan, *Civic Wars: Democracy and Public Life in the American City during the Nineteenth Century* (Berkeley: University of California Press, 1998).
4 On business and civic festival, see Heron and Penfold, *Workers' Festival*, ch. 1–2; Goheen, "Symbols in the Streets" and "Assertion of Middle-Class Claims."
5 Keith Walden, *Becoming Modern in Toronto: The Industrial Exhibition and the Shaping of a Late Victorian Culture* (Toronto: University of Toronto Press, 1997); Christopher Ernst, "The Transgressive Stage: The Culture of Public Entertainment in Late Victorian Toronto" (PhD thesis, University of Toronto, 2011).
6 Gary Cross and John Walton, *The Playful Crowd: Pleasure Places in the Twentieth Century* (New York: Columbia University Press, 2005); Paul Moore, *Now Playing: Early Movie-Going and the Regulation of Fun, Toronto, 1906–1918* (Albany: SUNY Press, 2008). On the need to rebalance the history of the senses, see Mark Smith et al., "The Senses in American History: A Round Table," *Journal of American History* 95, no. 2 (September 2008): 378–451; Martin Jay et al., "AHR Forum: The Senses in History," *American Historical Review* 116 (April 2011): 307–400.
7 Goheen, "Symbols"; Goheen, "The Ritual of the Street in Mid-Nineteenth-Century Toronto," *Environment and Planning D: Society and Space* 2 (1993): 127–45; Heron and Penfold, *Workers' Festival*, 5.

8 Bettina Bradbury, *Working Families: Age, Gender, and Daily Survival in Industrializing Montreal* (Toronto: University of Toronto Press, 1993), esp. chap. 1; Gilbert Stelter and Alan Artibise, eds, *The Canadian City: Essays in Urban and Social History* (Ottawa: Carleton University Press, 1984).

9 J.M.S. Careless, *Toronto to 1918: An Illustrated History* (Toronto: Lorimer, 1984).

10 Russell Field, "A Night at the Garden(s): A History of Professional Hockey Spectatorship in the 1920s and 1930s" (PhD thesis, University of Toronto, 2008); James Lemon, *Toronto since 1918: An Illustrated History* (Toronto: Lorimer, 1985); Donald Kerr and Jacob Spelt, *The Changing Face of Toronto: A Study in Urban Geography* (Ottawa: Government of Canada, 1966); Paul Moore, "Movie Palaces on Canadian Downtown Main Streets: Montreal, Toronto, and Vancouver," *Urban History Review* 32, no. 2 (Spring 2004): 3–20, Paul-André Linteau, *Sainte-Catherine Street: At the Heart of Montreal Life* (Montreal: Montreal Museum of Archaeology and History, 2010); Alan Artibise, *Winnipeg: An Illustrated History* (Toronto: Lorimer 1977); Jim Blanchard, *Winnipeg, 1912* (Winnipeg: University of Manitoba Press, 2006); Frances Swyripa, "Edmonton's Jasper Avenue: Public Ritual, Heritage, and Memory on Main Street," in James Opp and John C. Walsh, eds, *Placing Memory and Remembering Place in Canada* (Vancouver: University of British Columbia Press, 2010), 81–106. On the broader development of downtowns, see Alison Isenberg, *Downtown: A History of the Place and the People Who Made It* (Chicago: University of Chicago Press, 2004); Robert Fogelson, *Downtown: Its Rise and Fall, 1880–1950* (New Haven, CT: Yale University Press, 2001).

11 *WT*, 17 November 1926, 1.

12 Linteau, *Histoire*, 30–4, 155–6, 306–11; Linteau, *Sainte Catherine Street*. Most of the department stores had moved to Saint Catherine Street during the 1890s.

13 Linteau, *Histoire*, 310; OA, F229-151, box 4, Jack Brockie Files, file 117, Sales Promotion Meeting Minutes, 1947, 9 December 1947 meeting, item 1.

14 Careless, *Toronto*, 136; Russ Gourluck, *A Store Like No Other: Eaton's of Winnipeg* (Winnipeg: Great Plains Publications, 2004); Linteau, *Sainte Catherine Street*.

15 *La Presse*, 24 November. 1930, 17; *CH*, 27 November 1937, 17; *WT*, 24 November 1951, 1.

16 *GM*, 19 November 1956, 25; *TDS*, 17 November 1956, 1 ; *GM*, 14 November 1959, 1. Note that in 1956, the population of Metropolitan Toronto was approximately 1.3 million, which would have made the one million figure especially stunning.

17 See, for example, *GM*, 17 November 1969, 6.

18 *Edmonton Journal*, 2 December 1946, 2; *La Presse*, 27 November 1967, 27.
19 *MG*, 29 November 1930; *WT*, 22 November 1952, 1.
20 *Plattsburgh Press-Republican*, 12 December 1952, 19. See also *Plattsburgh Press-Republican*, 25 November 1953, 19.
21 *TDS*, 16 November 1951.
22 *TDS*, 17 November 1951, 2; 16 November 1946, 2.
23 *La Presse*, 30 November 1925, 8; *TDS*, 14 November 1952, 3.
24 *MG*, 23 November 1931, 5.
25 *TDS*, 15 November 1941, 31; *WFP*, 18 November 1949; *WT*, 20 November 1953, 1.
26 For a brilliant discussion of crowds and congestion at the turn-of-the-century Industrial Exhibition, see Walden, *Becoming Modern in Toronto*, chap. 7.
27 *Winnipeg Evening Tribune*, 18 November 1916.
28 *TDS*, 16 November 1946, 24; 19 November 1927, 28; 19 November 1932, 3; *GM*, 20 November 1950, 5.
29 *Toronto Star* (hereafter *TS*), 9 June 1975, C1; *WT*, 21 November 1949, 30. I discuss the change to Sunday in chapter 5.
30 *MG*, 24 November 1952; *TS*, 15 November 1941, 6. On festivals in modern urban spaces, see Annie Gérin, "Les espaces multiples de la fête: la Saint-Jean-Baptise 1968 à Montréal," *British Journal of Canadian Studies* 27, no. 1 (2014): 1–20.
31 *La Presse*, 24 November 1930, 17; *CH* 27 November 1937, 17; *TDS*, 19 November 1932, 3; 19 November 1938, 13; 15 November 1947, 1; 17 November 1950, 3; 20 November 1937, 1.
32 *MG*, 23 November 1931, 5; *TDS*, 17 November 1950, 3.
33 *MG*, 28 November 1927, 4; *TDS*, 14 November 1953, 19.
34 Peter Norton, *Fighting Traffic: The Dawn of the Motor Age in the American City* (Cambridge, MA: MIT Press, 2011); Peter Baldwin, *Domesticating the Street: The Reform of Public Space in Hartford, 1850–1930* (Columbus: Ohio State University Press, 1999), 201–29; Clay McShane, *Down the Asphalt Path: The Automobile and the American City* (New York: Columbia University Press, 1994); Stephen Davies, "'Reckless Walking Must Be Discouraged': The Automobile Revolution and the Shaping of Modern Urban Canada to 1930," *Urban History Review* 18 (October 1989): 123–38. Ronald Hovarth has evocatively described this new urban geography in terms of "machine space," that part of the city given over to the automobile (streets, highways, bridges, parking lots, and other automobile-oriented features). Ronald Hovarth, "Machine Space," *Geographical Review* 64, no. 2 (April 1974): 167–173. See also John Jakle and Keith Sculle, *Lots of Parking: Land Use in a Car Culture* (Charlottesville: University of Virginia Press, 2004).

35 *TDS*, 15 November 1947, 2; 15 November 1954, 1.
36 City Council Minutes, Appendix A, Board of Control Report No. 28, October 1953, 2207. On modern sound, see Emily Thompson, *The Soundscape of Modernity: Architectural Acoustics and the Culture of Listening in America, 1900–33* (Cambridge, MA: MIT Press, 2002).
37 See especially Register, *The Kid of Coney Island*.
38 On these themes, see Gray Cross and John Walton, *The Playful Crowd* (New York: Columbia University Press, 2005).
39 Field "A Night at the Gardens," p. 29.
40 Richard Butsch, *The Making of American Audiences: From Stage to Television, 1750–1900* (Cambridge: Cambridge University Press, 2000); Moore, "Movie Palaces," 3–20; Robert Seiler and Tamara Seiler, *Reel Time: Movie Exhibitors and Movie Audiences in Prairie Canada* (Edmonton: AU Press, 2013).
41 *Toronto Telegram*, 17 November 1951, 2; *TS*, 17 November 1973, A3; *TS*, 17 November 1973, A3.
42 *Toronto Telegram*, 17 November 1951, 2.
43 *WT*, 18 November 1922, 1; *TDS*, 17 November 1928, 2; *La Presse*, 30 November 1925, 8.
44 *TDS*, 15 November 1947, 2; Poem by Helen Hill Young of 2525 Dufferin Street, *TDS*, 17 November 1951, 6.
45 *GM*, 15 November 1968, 27. On adult yearning for childhood fun as one of the central experiences of twentieth-century masculinity and consumerism, see Register, *The Kid of Coney Island*.
46 Cross, *The Cute and the Cool*, 27; Register, *The Kid of Coney Island*.
47 Gray Cross, "Crowds and Leisure: Thinking Comparatively across the 20th Century," *Journal of Social History* 39, no. 3 (Spring 2006): 637.
48 *MG*, 29 November 1947.
49 *Toronto Daily News*, 16 November 1918.
50 Brockie cited in *TS*, 12 November 1954, 10.
51 *WT*, 19 November 1949, 3; *Globe*, 20 November 1933, 12; *WFP*, 20 November 1965, 1; *GM*, 18 November 1968, 5.
52 *TS*, 6 November 1980, D21; *TS*, 23 December 1980, A14. Diddy did not confine himself to debunking Santa Claus: in July 1980, he walked onto stage at a world convention of the Baptist church with a sign reading, "Jesus is not coming back." *TS*, 6 November 1980, D21.
53 *TS*, 6 November 1978, A12.
54 *WT*, 1 December 1906, 15.
55 *TS*, 15 November 1976, C1.
56 *TDS*, 15 November 1969, 1; *TS*, 17 November 1928, 2; *Globe*, 19 November 1934, 4–5; *TS*, 16 November 1938, 32; *WT*, 1 December 1906, 15; *La Presse*, 28 November 1927, 4; *WT*, 28 November 1942, 15.

57 *TS*, 8 November 1980, B3, Majorie Babcock, letter to editor; *Globe*, 19 November 1934, 4–5.
58 *TDS*, 18 November 1966, 34.
59 *TDS*, 15 November 1971, 3.
60 *TDS*, 17 November 1945, 22.
61 *TS*, 3 November 1981.
62 Indeed, the watching crowd at the Eaton's parade was even less "participatory" than the "playful crowd" at amusement parks. See Cross and Walton, *Playful Crowd*. Paul Moore stresses the way watching and spectatorship (for his case, at movies) was transforming urban crowds into "attentive mass audiences." See his "Movie Palaces." Richard Butsch, *The Making of American Audiences: From Stage to Television* (New York: Cambridge University Press, 2008), examines the distinction between active and passive audience at length. For an excellent discussion of the meaning of watching in modern urban spaces, see Walden, *Becoming Modern in Toronto*, chap. 3.
63 *GM*, 21 November 1955, 19. Thanks to Craig Heron for pointing out this aspect of West's column.
64 Joyce C. Lewis, *The Celebration and the New Year in Mid-Nineteenth Century Ontario: A Survey of Changes in Attitudes and Practices* (Toronto: Joyce C. Lewis, 2014).
65 For an interesting temperance speech highlighting the dangers of exposing young people to normalized drinking at Christmas, see "Grant Temperance Demonstration," *Globe* (Toronto), 9 December 1853.
66 On these themes, see Nissenbaum, *The Battle for Christmas*; Susan Davis, *Parades and Power: Street Theatre in Nineteenth Century Philadelphia* (Berkeley: University of California Press, 1985);
67 Restad, *Christmas in America*; Warren, *Hourra pour Santa Claus!*; Schmidt, *Consumer Rites*.
68 *La Presse*, 13 December 1930, 2; Toronto City Council Minutes, 1931, Appendix A, pp. 2559–30; Toronto City Council Minutes, 1930, Appendix A, 2474, Toronto Reference Library; *MFP*, 12 December 1929, 26.
69 On the official and social nature of time, see Vanessa Ogle, "Whose Time Is It? The Pluralization of Time and the Global Condition, 1870s–1940s," *American Historical Review* (December 2013): 1376–1402; Jarrett Rudy, "'Do You Have the Time?' Modernity, Democracy, and the Beginnings of Daylight Saving Time in Montreal, 1907–1928," *Canadian Historical Review* 93, no. 4 (December 2012): 531–54.
70 Warren, *Houra pour Santa Claus!*; Schmidt, *Consumer Rites*.
71 Restad, *Christmas in America*, 161–2. According to Restad, American retailers soon pressed the federal government to fix Thanksgiving one week

earlier in order to extend the shopping season, finally succeeding in 1939. On Canadian Thanksgiving, see Peter Stevens, "A Wealth of Meanings: Thanksgiving in Ontario, 1859–1914" (unpublished major research paper, York University, 1999).

72 "History of T. Eaton Company Ltd. Santa Claus Parade."
73 *TDS*, 5 December 1906; 10 December 1906; 12 December 1906; 13 December 1906; 15 December 1906; 20 December 1906; 21 December 1906; 22 December 1906; 20 November 1928; 21 November 1935.
74 On Gibson's, see Warren, *Santa Claus.*
75 *Financial Post*, 26 November 1955, 7.
76 Clipping from *Home Goods Retailing*, 16 October 1957, in file: Santa Claus Parade 1958, part I, F229-151, Brockie Files, box 4; *WFP*, 12 November 1964, 12; *TS*, 15 November 1974.
77 *TDS*, 14 November 1935, 2; 19 November 1937; *TDS*, 20 November 1946, 24.
78 *WT*, 17 November 1966; *New York Times*, 19 December 1964, 37; William Stephenson, *The Store that Timothy Built* (Toronto: McClelland and Stewart, 1969), 233. In 1974, a *Toronto Star* reporter claimed that the Eaton's Santa was "the Canadian Claus." *TS*, 10 November 1976, F14.
79 *TDS*, 15 November 1956, 20; 22 November 1956, 13; *WT*, 13 November 1964, 8; *WT*, 14 November 1968, 8. On the suburban trend to early Christmas promotions, see *GM*, 13 November 1964, B5.
80 See chapter 4.
81 *GM*, 9 November 1978, 7, letter to the editor.

3 The Mediated Santa

1 *WFP*, 19 November 1954, 14; *Contacts* (December 1954), TEF, F229-162-0-587.
2 Daniel Dayan and Elihu Katzis, *Media Events: The Live Broadcasting of History* (Cambridge, MA: Harvard University Press, 1992).
3 Nick Couldry, *Media Rituals: A Critical Approach* (New York: Routledge, 2003), and Paddy Scannell, "Broadcast Events," *Media, Culture and Society* 17, no. 1 (1995): 151–7.
4 James Baughman, *The Republic of Mass Culture: Journalism, Filmmaking, and Broadcasting in America since 1941* (Baltimore: Johns Hopkins University Press, 2006); Anthony Smith with Richard Paterson, eds, *Television: An International History* (New York: Oxford University Press, 1998).
5 Mary Vipond, *Mass Media in Canada* (Toronto: Lorimer, 1989), 45–6; Paul Rutherford, *When Television Was Young: Primetime Canada* (Toronto: University of Toronto Press, 1990), 104–13.
6 Vipond, *Mass Media*; Rutherford, *Primetime Canada*.

7 *WT*, 6 November 1954, 6; Knight's letter is in TEF, BF, box 5, file: Santa Claus Parade, 1957, part III. Note that when quoting letters to Eaton's from private individuals, I have followed current academic convention by changing names.

8 *New York Times*, 21 November 1949, 44; Mary Vipond, *Mass Media*, 44.

9 At this time, Radio-Canada had stations in Montreal, Quebec City, Rimouski, Sherbrooke, Jonquière, and Hull.

10 "Hockey Night in Canada – The Television Years," Canadian Communications Foundation, "History of Canadian Broadcasting," http://www.broadcasting-history.ca; Richard Gruneau and David Whitson, *Hockey Night in Canada: Sport, Identities and Cultural Politics* (Toronto: Garamond Press, 1994).

11 *MG*, 20 November 1931, 5.

12 *TDS*, 16 November 1929, 1; *TDS*, 14 November 1936, 11.

13 TEF, BF #107, Public Relations and Display, Vancouver, 1949–58, D. Sutherland, Vancouver Merchandise Display, to Brockie, 11 December 1953 [*sic*]; *WFP*, 7 December 1955, 16.

14 *TDS*, 21 November 1950. In the first radio broadcast of the parade in Montreal, microphones were used to pick up crowd applause. *MG*, 20 November 1931, 5.

15 TEF, BF#123, Santa Claus Broadcasts, 1946, 1947 & 1948, Buckner to Brockie, Brockie to Buckner, 15 November 1948.

16 *La Presse*, 22 November 1935, 3.

17 This film is available on the Toronto Santa Claus Parade YouTube channel.

18 Kinescopes were the most common way to copy a television broadcast in the early years; a film camera was pointed at a TV screen to capture the image.

19 *TDS*, 18 November 1955, 34; TEF, F-229-162-0-595, clippings *Starweek* (1972).

20 TEF, BF, box 4, Santa Claus Parade – 1956, part I, Instructions to Marshalls.

21 TEF, F229-81, box 1, Santa Claus Parade Files, 1961–75, file: Minutes and Arrangements, 1968, memo from Foster to Clarke, 13 November 1968, item 3.2.

22 The letters are collected in TEF, BF, box 5, file: Santa Claus Parade, 1957, part III. Parade planners made a point of not repeating the mistake the following year. See TEF, BF, box 5, Jack Brockie Files, Santa Claus Parade, 1958, part II, Brockie to J.R. Mitchell, City Advertising, 26 September 1958.

23 TEF, BF, box 5, file: Santa Claus Parade, 1957, Part III. On television as social event, see Ron Lembo, *Thinking through Television* (Cambridge: Cambridge University Press, 2000).

24 Dayan and Katzis, *Media Events*, 2. For perceptive thoughts on the relationship between communication and experience, see Gerald Friesen, *Citizens and Nation: An Essay on History, Communication, and Canada* (Toronto: University of Toronto Press, 2000).

25 TEF, BF, box 5, file: Santa Claus Parade, 1957, Part III, emphasis in original.

26 On this theme, see Dayan and Katzis, *Media Events*; Joshua Meyrowitz, *No Sense of Place: The Impact of Electronic Media on Social Behavior* (New York: Oxford University Press, 1985); Mike Huggins, "Projecting the Visual: British Newsreels, Soccer, and Popular Culture, 1918–1939," *International Journal of the History of Sport* 24, no. 1 (2007), 80–102; David Morley, *Television, Audiences, and Cultural Studies* (New York: Routledge, 1992); Richard Butsch, *The Making of American Audiences: From Stage to Television, 1750–1990* (New York: Cambridge University Press, 2000).

27 Colour television, introduced in Canada in 1966, remained a minority experience until the late 1970s. See Dominion Bureau of Statistics, Bulletin 62-202, *Household Facilities and Equipment*, 1977.

28 *WFP*, 18 October 1967, 3.

29 Reminiscence of M.D., OA Santa Claus Turns 100 online exhibit, www.archives.gov.on.ca/english/exhibits/parade/index.html (accessed 23 March 2006). The exhibit has since been significantly shortened.

30 Dayan and Katzis, *Media Events*.

31 TEF, SCP, box 1, file: Santa Claus Parade, Minutes and Arrangements, 1966; TEF, SCP, box 1, file: Santa Claus Parade, Minutes and Arrangements, 1969, letter to Mr J. Bruce, Advertising Manager, Toronto & Central Division, T Eaton Co from J.H. Gibaut, dated 30 September 1969.

32 *TDS*, 17 November 1955, 34. On *Tabloid*, see http://www.film.queensu.ca/CBC/T.htmlQ1.

33 *TDS*, 18 November 1957, 26. In 1979, the International Year of the Child, CBC used Kate Parr (an experienced child actor) as a special commentator. See TEF, F229-162-0-593, Santa Claus Parade Files, 1979, "CBC Santa Claus Parade Commentators."

34 *TDS*, 15 November 1968, 27. The list of hosts is compiled from various files in TEF, Santa Claus Parade Files.

35 Many biographies of early television personalities can be found at the online History of Canadian Broadcasting (http://www.broadcasting-history.ca/index.html).

36 *TDS*, 18 November 1954, 6.

37 *TDS*, 18 November 1954, 6, letter to editor; Radio and Television Column, *TDS*, 16 November 1953, 7.

38 *TDS*, 14 November 1953, 9; 16 November 1957, 1; TEF, BF, box 4, file: Santa Claus Parade, 1956, "Santa Claus parade – 1956."

39 TEF, BF, box 4, file: Santa Claus Parade, 1956, "Santa Claus parade – 1956; TEF, SCP, file: Santa Claus Parade, Minutes and Arrangements, 1969.
40 *New York Times*, 25 November 1959, 59.
41 *GM*, 22 November 1986, E1.
42 Rutherford, *Primetime Canada*.
43 These policies were quoted in a 1970 review. See Library and Archives Canada, CBC collection, file: Santa Claus Parade, Internal Memo by Marcel Ouimet, "Santa Claus Parade – 1970" dated 6 October 1970 and "Santa Claus Parade 1970 – CBC English Television Network."
44 TEF, SCP, box 1, Santa Claus Parade –1972, "Format (Commercial) for CTV Toronto" and "Format (Commercial) for CBC."
45 *TDS*, 19 November 1966, 1; *MG*, 24 November 1956, 37.
46 TEF, SCP, file: Santa Claus Parade – 1968, MacRae to Clarke, 5 March 1973; TEF, SCP, file: Santa Claus Parade, Arrangements, 1973.
47 *Canadian Business*, November 1955, 90.
48 *TS*, 12 November 1979, A9.
49 TEF, SCP, box 1, Santa Claus Parade – 1974, Comments from Marshalls.
50 *TDS*, 19 November 1962, 26; TEF, SCP, box 1, Santa Claus Parade Arrangements, 1974, Irvine to Eaton's and McEachern to Laphen, 18 November 1974. CFTO is the Toronto station of CTV.
51 *TS*, 15 November 1976, C1.
52 TEF, BF, box 5, Santa Claus Parade, 1957, CBC-TV Sales to Eaton's, "Estimate"; TEF, SCP, box 1, file: Santa Claus Parade, Minutes and Arrangements, 1966.
53 *WFP*, 24 February 1967, 3.
54 On the city ban, see *La Presse*, 10 November 1969, 6; *La Presse*, 13 November 1969, 1, 6. On the Eaton's decision, which the company claimed was made "par respect pour l'esprit du règlement voté cette semaine," see *La Presse*, 15 November 1969, 1, 2.
55 Cited in Patricia Phenix, *Eatonians: The Story of the Family behind the Family* (Toronto: McClelland and Stewart, 2002), 61–2.
56 *La Presse*, 22 November 1968; 23 November 1968; 13 November 1969, 1, 6; 15 November 1969, 1, 2. On linguistic politics in 1960s Montreal, see Marc Levine, *The Reconquest of Montreal: Language Policy and Social Change in a Bilingual City* (Philadelphia: Temple University Press, 1991), and Sean Mills, *The Empire Within: Postcolonial Thought and Political Activism in Sixties Montreal* (Montreal and Kingston: McGill-Queen's University Press, 2010).
57 In 1972, CTV (the national private broadcaster) attracted 1,287,000 viewers on twenty-three stations and the CBC (the national public broadcaster) 1,624,000 on forty-five stations. See TEF, SCP, box 1, file: Arrangements, 1973, "Phone Message for Clarke from Rick Lee of CTV." Note that in the

week of its 1976 broadcast, the Eaton's parade was more popular on CBC than *Hockey Night in Canada* but less watched than *Chico and the Man*. The CTV broadcast was not in that network's top ten. *TS*, 10 December 1976, A01.

58 *Starweek* (11–18 November 1972), n.p; *New York Times*, 17 November 1963, X17.

59 Linteau, *Histoire*, 223–4; Lemon, *Toronto since 1918*, 183–6.

60 *New York Times*, 17 November 1963, X17; Linda Young, cited in James Baker, *Thanksgiving: The Biography of an America Holiday* (Durham: University of New Hampshire Press, 2009), 145.

61 Ryan Edwardson, *Canadian Content: Culture and the Quest for Nationhood* (Toronto: University of Toronto Press, 2008); José Igartua, *The Other Quiet Revolution: National Identities in English Canada, 1945–1971* (Vancouver: UBC Press, 2006).

62 TEF, SCP, box 1, file: Minutes and Arrangements, 1969, Barbara Mackay at Toronto Public Library to Mrs. M. Morrison, dated 14 February 1969; TEF, SCP, box 1, file: Minutes and Arrangements, 1966, Don Morrison to J.W. Clarke, Display Department, dated 25 May 1966.

63 TEF, SCP, F229-162-0-591, file: Santa Claus Parade, 1967.

64 Letter to editor, *Winnipeg Free Press*, 9 December 1967, 10.

65 TEF, SCP, box 1, file: Minutes and Arrangements, 1973, Fernand Lachance, Sales Representative, *Radio Canada* to Shirley Hume, T. Eaton Company, dated 24 September 1973; TEF, SCP, box 1, file: Minutes and Arrangements, 1973, "Meeting Report [Eaton's staff and *Radio Canada* staff]" dated 12 & 13 September 1973; TEF, SCP, box 1, file: Minutes and Arrangements, 1973, "Meeting Report [Eaton's staff and *Radio Canada* staff]" dated 5 October 1973; TEF, SCP, box 1, file: Minutes and Arrangements, 1974, "Contact Report, Meeting of 12 August 1974 [Eaton's staff and *Radio Canada* staff]."

66 Denis Bachand and Pierre Bélanger, "Un champ culturel: La télévision canadienne," in Caroline Andrew, ed., *Dislocation et permanence: L'invention du Canada au quotidien* (Ottawa: University of Ottawa Press, 1999), 331.

67 Rutherford, *When Television Was Young*, 134–45; Jean-François Beauchemin, *Ici Radio Canada* (Montreal: Éditions de l'Homme, 2002); Aurélie Luneau, "Radio-Canada et la promotion de la culture francophone (1936–1997)," *Vingtième Siècle* 55 (Jul.-Sep. 1997): 112–23; Michael Behiels, *Canada's Francophone Minority Communities: Constitutional Renewal and the Winning of School Governance* (Montreal and Kingston: McGill-Queen's University Press, 2004), 3–52. On television, nation, and difference more generally, see especially David Morley, "Broadcasting and the Construction of the National Family" in Robert C. Allen and Annette Hill, eds, *The Television Studies Reader* (New York: Routledge, 2004), 418–39.

68 TEF, SCP, box 1, file: Minutes and Arrangements, 1973, "Meeting Report [Eaton's staff and *Radio Canada* staff]" dated 5 October 1973; TEF, SCP, box 1, file: Minutes and Arrangements, 1974, "Contact Report, Meeting of 12 August 1974 [Eaton's staff and *Radio Canada* staff]." In 1974, TVA showed the Eaton's parade on five of its Quebec stations (unlike Radio-Canada, it had no stations outside Quebec). TEF, SCP, box 1, file: Minutes and Arrangements, 1974, Shirley Hume to Area Sales Promotion Managers and Area Advertising Managers, dated 6 November 1974. Unfortunately, the evidentiary trail in the Eaton's collection on this issue ends in 1974.

4 The Civic Fantastic

1 *Sudbury Star*, 4 December 1965, 15
2 *Sudbury Star*, 19 November 1965, 3; 20 November 1965, 1, 3. Mine Mill is the colloquial name for the International Union of Mine, Mill, and Smelter Workers.
3 This paragraph is based on an extensive survey of community newspapers.
4 *Canadian Champion* (Milton), 8 December 1971, 25. The towns were Oakville, Milton, Georgetown, and Burlington.
5 This enumeration is from a survey of reports in the *Windsor Star*, 1 November – 20 December 1977.
6 *Sudbury Star*, 22 November 1968, Scene Today, 1; *Sudbury Star*, 23 November 1968, 3.
7 *Wilmington* (NC) *Star-News*, 2 December 1977, 22.
8 *Windsor Daily Star*, 23 November 1939, 14.
9 *Youngstown Daily Vindicator*, 10 December 1926, 3; *London Free Press*, 25 November 1961, 1, 2; *La Presse* 1961 clipping, in TEF, F229-162-0-575, file: Christmas – Santa Claus Parade – Clippings.
10 *San Jose News*, 14 November 1931, 16; 23 November 1931, 6.
11 *Reading* (PA) *Eagle*, 2 December 1925, 22.
12 *St Joseph* (MO) *Gazette*, 25 November 1931, 1, 2; *Toledo News-Bee*, 14 November 1934, 7; *L'Écho du St. Maurice* (Shawinigan Falls, QC), 30 November 1955, 1; *Sudbury Star*, 20 November 1959, 17.
13 *Sudbury Star*, 27 November 1961, 17.
14 *Sudbury Star*, 20 November 1959, 17; 24 September 1961, 17.
15 John W. Clark, *A Legacy of Leadership: The U.S. Junior Chamber of Commerce Celebrates 75 Years* (Tulsa: U.S. Junior Chamber of Commerce, 1995).
16 Ibid., 34, 46.

17 Ibid., 33. The Jaycees in Windsor clearly demonstrate the cross-border nature of growth. In 1941, the Jaycees arrived in Windsor when Frank Walton read an article on the organization in an American magazine. He gathered fifteen friends to form the core of a local chapter and quickly enrolled over 150 members. With the help of the Detroit chapter, the Windsor group obtained a charter from the Jaycee headquarters and began to function in earnest in June 1941. *Windsor Daily Star*, 22 April 1950, 48.

18 *Globe and Mail*, 20 February 1958, 5.

19 Jeffrey Charles, *Service Clubs in American Society: Rotary, Kiwanis, and Lions* (Urbana: University of Illinois Press, 1993).

20 *Globe*, 20 July 1929, 23; *Globe*, 7 July 1933, 3; *GM*, 21 February 1945, 4; *GM*, 27 September 1965, 10; Ken Coates and Fred McGuiness, *Only in Canada: Kinsmen and Kinettes* (Winnipeg: Peguis Publishers, 1987).

21 Charles, *Service Clubs*; Craig Heron, *Lunch-Bucket Lives: Remaking the Workers' City* (Toronto: Between the Lines, 2015), chap. 18; Shirley Tillotson, *Contributing Citizens: Modern Charitable Fundraising and the Making of the Welfare State, 1920–66* (Vancouver: UBC Press, 2008); Leach, *Land of Desire*.

22 Cited in Charles, *Service Clubs*, 39.

23 Paul Harris, *This Rotarian Age* (Chicago: Rotary International, 1935), 23.

24 Giessenbier, cited in Clark, *A Legacy in Leadership*, 19. For Harris on the eloquence of deeds, see his *This Rotarian Age*, 27. For Young Men of Action, see recruitment poster reprinted in *Kingston Whig Standard*, 27 January 1971, in Kingston Public Library, Subject Files, Associations and Clubs, Junior Chamber of Commerce.

25 *Oakville Beaver*, 2 December 1971.

26 On the folklore of retailing, see Monod, *Store Wars*; McQuarrie is cited on page 79.

27 *Hamilton Spectator*, 3 February 1920, 16, cited in Craig Heron, *Lunch Bucket Lives*, chap. 18; *Nation's Business*, December 1953, 91

28 Charles, *Service Clubs*; Clark, *A Legacy of Leadership*; Paul Martin, *We Serve: A History of the Lions Clubs* (Washington, DC: Regnery Gateway, 1991), 43.

29 TEF, BF, box 4, file 130, Santa Claus Parade, Jean Gros, 1947, copy of letter from Jas. T. Bennett, Chairman, Retail Section, Board of Trade to Retail Section of the Board of Trade, dated 20 October 1947.

30 *Eugene Register-Guard*, 24 November 1948, 1.

31 For one example of vociferous complaints about the negative commercial effects of the crowds on parade day, see *Hamilton Spectator*, 3 December 1986 and 24 April 1987, in Hamilton Public Library, Local History and Archives, Santa Claus Parade Scrapbook, Volume II.

32 *Windsor Daily Star*, 17 November 1936, 5.

33 *Clinton Country Times*, 25 November 1938, 4; *St Petersburg Times*, 16 December 1933, 1, 7; *Gettysburg Times*, 28 November 1936, 1.

34 *The Star Journal* (Sandusky, OH), 21 November 1930, 1, 14; *Kitchener-Waterloo Record*, 17 November 1962.

35 *Regina Leader-Post*, 16 December 1954, 19.

36 *Kingston Whig-Standard*, 22 November 1960, 1; *Regina Leader-Post*, 10 August 1966, 3.

37 *Windsor Daily Star*, 11 November 1952, 31.

38 *Sudbury Star*, 21 November 1978, 2.

39 *Regina Leader-Post*, 16 December 1954, 19.

40 *Regina Leader-Post*, 28 December 1950, 11 [editorial].

41 *Regina Leader-Post*, 27 October 1952, 5.

42 *Winnipeg Free Press*, 3 December 1951, 7; *London Free Press*, 27 November 1961, 1.

43 *Sudbury Star*, 25 November 1961, 1. Regina had the same problem in 1959: *Regina Leader-Post*, 12 November 1959, 3.

44 *Lawrence* (KS) *Daily Journal*, 28 November 1936, 1; 8 December 1936, 1.

45 Canadian Press wire story, reprinted in *Simcoe Reformer*, 4 December 1961, 2; *Owosso Argus-Press*, 22 November 1947, 1.

46 *Lewiston* (ID) *Morning Tribune*, 7 December 1952, 16.

47 *Winnipeg Free Press*, 1 December 1969, 1.

48 *Post* (Buckingham, QC), 22 December 1950, 1.

49 *Canadian Champion* (Milton, ON), 3 December 1975, 36.

50 *Youngstown Daily Vindicator*, 25 November 1927, 1, 37; *Hamilton Spectator*, 18 November 1961, in Hamilton Public Library, Archives and Local History, Santa Claus Parade Scrapbook, Volume I.

51 *Winnipeg Free Press*, 27 November 1952, 14; *La Presse*, 16 November 1953, 23; *St Joseph Gazette*, 25 November 1931, 1, 2.

52 *L'Oeil Régional*, 9 December 1970, 1; *Canadian Champion* (Milton, Ontario), 17 December 1953, 1.

53 See "Wilf Salo: Mr. Santa Claus," in Oiva Saarinen, *Between a Rock and a Hard Place: A Historical Geography of the Finns in the Sudbury Area* (Waterloo, ON: Wilfrid Laurier University Press, 1999), 246–7.

54 *La Gazette de Valleyfield*, 20 December 1951, 9.

55 *Winnipeg Free Press*, 27 November 1952, 14.

56 Charles, *Service Clubs*, 51.

57 Charles, *Service Clubs*, 41, 48; Harris, *This Rotarian Age*, 40; *La Presse*, 19 November 1947, 16.

58 Kitchener Public Library, Clippings Files: Santa Claus Parade, Cambridge.

59 *Pittsburgh Press*, 23 November 1928, 49.

60 *Windsor Star*, 29 November 1969, 3.

61 *Picton Gazette*, 1 December 1954.

62 *Regina Leader-Post*, 12 November 1959, 3; *Ludington Daily News*, 3 December 1952, 1.

63 *Washington* (PA) *Observer*, 24 November 1959, 8.

64 *Winnipeg Free Press*, 8 December 1953, 10.

65 *Eugene Register-Guard*, 6 December 1959, 12.

66 *Pittsburgh Press*, 24 November 1934, 1.

67 On modern liberal ideas of governance, many insights can be found in Tillotson, *Contributing Citizens*.

68 *Kiwanis Magazine* (1952), cited in Charles, *Service Clubs*, 143. I borrow the term social imaginaries from Charles Taylor, *Modern Social Imaginaries* (Durham, NC: Duke University Press, 2004), esp. 23–30.

69 The national Jaycees in Canada allowed local chapters to admit women as early as 1971, but many didn't do so until much later (in Kingston, Ontario, for example, no women were allowed until 1985, and by then the organization was small and perhaps desperate for members). In the United States, court orders forced the Jaycees to open the doors to women in the 1980s. See Clark, *Legacy of Leadership*.

70 See, for example, *Kitchener-Waterloo Record*, 17 November 1961. The *Record* noted that the Jaycettes rounded up the clowns and characters and made about a quarter of the costumes.

71 *Temiskaming Speaker*, 16 November 1950, 6. I have found only two examples of parades where a woman took the main organizing role.

72 Charles, *Service Clubs*, 28; Leslie Bella, *The Christmas Imperative: Leisure, Family, and Women's Work* (Halifax: Fernwood Publishers, 1992).

73 *Newmarket Era and Express*, 13 December 1951, 1; *Canadian Champion* (Milton, ON), 18 December 1952, 1

74 *London Free Press*, 24 November 1989, B3.

75 Gordon Jardene, letter to editor, *London Free Press*, 9 December 1989, F3.

76 David Price, letter to the editor, *London Free Press*, 2 December 1989, F3.

77 Ida De Busschere, letter to the editor, *London Free Press*, 13 December 1989, A15.

78 *Hamilton Spectator*, 14 November 1964, in Hamilton Public Library, Archives and Local History, Santa Claus Parade Scrapbook, Volume I.

79 *Spokane Daily Chronicle*, 24 November 1933, 23.

80 *Chicago Daily Defender*, 9 December 1968, 3.

81 *Chicago Daily Defender*, 12 December 1968, 23.

82 *Chicago Daily Defender*, 30 November 1970, 3. See also *Milwaukee Journal*, 19 November 1966, 1. Watts, in Los Angeles, also had a "black Santa" parade for many years in this period.

83 *New York Times*, 7 December 1969, 78.

84 T.M. Brown, letter to editor, *TS*, 24 August 1982, A15.

85 *Sudbury Star*, 29 September 1955, 13.

86 TEF, BF, file 128 – Santa Claus Parade 1955 Part II, W.E. Gooderelle to Armstrong, copied to Brockie, 7 October 1955.

87 TEF, F229-81, SCP, Santa Claus Parade – Minutes and Arrangements 1966; TEF, BF, Santa Claus Parade 1955, Part II, telegram from Cornwall Jaycees dated 9 November 1955.

88 TEF, BF, box 5, Santa Claus Parade, 1958, Part II, Barry Cheeseman, Chairman, Programme Committee, Sudbury Junior Chamber of Commerce to Brockie, dated 11 September 1958; Brockie to Cheeseman, 15 September 1958.

89 Santa in single car: see Chatham story in TEF, F229-162-0-575, Santa Claus Parade – Clippings file, *Eatonian*; *Manitoba Leader* (Portage la Prairie), 11 December 1947, 1 and 15 January 1948, 7. In Portage la Prairie, local organizers also visited "the Big City [Winnipeg] last Saturday to study the parade. They then talked to the parade designers to find out what really made it tick." *Manitoba Leader* (Portage la Prairie), 27 November 1947, 3.

90 *Toledo News-Bee*, 14 November 1934, 7; *St Petersburg Times*, 16 November 1959, 14.

91 *Kitchener-Waterloo Record*, 13 October 1988.

92 For Punkinhead in a civic parade, see *Canadian Champion* (Milton, ON), 8 December 1960, 1. For balloons in Sudbury, see *Sudbury Star*, 20 November 1964, Scene Today.

93 *Youngstown Daily Vindicator*, 17 November 1926, 5; *Palm Beach Post*, 25 November 1934, 1, 3; Janet Davis, *The Circus Age: Culture and Society under the American Big Top* (Chapel Hill: University of North Carolina Press, 2002).

94 *Windsor Daily Star*, 10 July 1948, 14; "Santa Claus COD," *Saturday Night*, 27 December 1949, 9.

95 *Calgary Herald*, 30 December 1961, 24. Dalke was born in Enid, Oklahoma, in 1885, came to Canada 1912, and settled in the Swift Current district; in 1922, he moved north to Tisdale to farm.

96 Company bulletins appear in TEF, BF, box 4, file 130, Santa Claus Parade, Jean Gros, 1947. The background material on Jean Gros is from *Milwaukee Sentinal*, 2 November 1949, Women's and Society Pages, 1; 17 November 1949, sect. 3, 5.

97 Before Thatcher arrived in Palm Beach, the company sent an advance agent to arrange for local kids to fill out the parade. Local organizers had mass meeting in a local high school gym so that children could be picked from local recreation clubs. *Palm Beach Post*, 25 November 1934, 1; 15 December 1934, 1.

98 *Newmarket Era and Express*, 13 December 1951, 1.
99 *Sudbury Star*, 18 November 1966, 3; 21 November 1966, 15; *Anson Record*, 21 June 1977, 1.
100 *Windsor Daily Star*, 23 November 1937, 3.
101 *Winnipeg Free Press*, 19 October 1962, 15.
102 *Sudbury Star*, 15 November 1982, 3.
103 *Windsor Daily Star*, 18 November 1950, 54: News and Views about Lambton County.
104 *Windsor Star*, 28 November 1977, 52.
105 This summary is based on a survey of the annual Windsor parades in the *Windsor Daily Star/Windsor Star*, 1950–1975.

5 Casualty of the Times

1 *TS*, 20 August 1982, A6.
2 *TS*, 2 January 1969, A7.
3 Statistics Canada, *Department Stores in Canada, 1923–1976* (Ottawa: Statistics Canada, 1979), 53; Gary Cross, *Kids' Stuff: Toys and the Changing World of American Childhood* (Cambridge, MA: Harvard University Press, 1999); Braden Hutchinson, "Objects of Affection: Producing and Consuming Toys and Childhood in Canada, 1840–1989" (PhD thesis, Queen's University, 2013).
4 Statistics Canada, *Department Stores in Canada*, 53; Richard Harris, *Building a Market: The Rise of the Home Improvement Industry* (Chicago: University of Chicago Press, 2012).
5 Ed Mirvish, *How to Build an Empire on an Orange Crate* (Toronto: Key Porter, 1993), 56.
6 Statistics Canada, *Department Stores in Canada*.
7 Cited in *Financial Post*, 12 March 1966.
8 Cited in Barbara Ameil, "Trouble in Eatonia," *Maclean's*, 31 May 1975, 27–8.
9 Douglas Harker, *The Woodward's: The Story of a Distinguished British Columbia Family, 1850–1975* (Vancouver: Mitchell Press, 1975).
10 Ross Gourluck, *A Store Like No Other: Eaton's of Winnipeg* (Winnipeg: Great Plains Publications, 2005), 182–3.
11 Statistics Canada, *Department Stores in Canada*.
12 Harvey Sector in *GM*, 13 May 1978, B14, cited in Statistics Canada, *Department Stores in Canada*, 58.
13 According to Statistics Canada, ten companies comprised the same share of the market in 1976 that had been occupied by three companies in 1930. The big three of the 1930s – Eaton's, Simpson's, and the Hudson's Bay

Company – had by the 1970s been joined by Simpsons-Sears, Kmart, Woolco, Zellers, a much larger Woodward's, and many others, each with several stores. Statistics Canada, *Department Stores in Canada*, 9. Researchers at Ryerson University counted five department stores (under three corporate banners) in the Greater Toronto Area in 1955 and eighty-nine by 1975 (under sixteen different corporate banners). See Michael Doucet, *The Department Store Shuffle: Rationalization and Change in the Greater Toronto Area* (Toronto: Centre for the Study of Commercial Activity, Ryerson University, 2001), 8–9.

14 In this acquisition, Simpson's was divided from Sears, which continued to operate as a rival to the Bay.

15 *TS*, 10 August 1982, E1.

16 Statistics Canada, *Department Stores in Canada*, 36.

17 *Washington Post*, 24 August 1999, E01.

18 Rod McQueen, *The Eatons*, covers the company's internal problems in great detail.

19 See ibid. for a thorough discussion of Eaton's internal problems and the role of the family in management.

20 Cited in *Washington Post*, 24 August 1999, E01.

21 Belisle, *Retail Nation*.

22 Rod McQueen, *The Eatons*; Phenix, *Eatonians*; Belisle, *Retail Nation*.

23 *TS*, 10 August 1982, E01 and A14

24 Sue Harrison, letter to editor, *TS*, 18 June 1975, B5; Willison Pedlar, letter to editor, *TS*, 18 June 1975, B5; Jane Long, letter to editor, *TS* 11 July 1975, B5.

25 TEF, F229-207, F.S. Eaton's Parade and Personal Files, file: Christmas Parade, 1978–80, letter to Fredrik Eaton.

26 TEF, F229-207, F.S. Eaton's Parade and Personal Files, file: Christmas Parade, 1978–80, letter to Fredrik Eaton.

27 *GM*, 9 November 1978, 7

28 *TS*, 24 December 1980, A9. There is much more literature in the United States than in Canada on the rise of this new consumer consciousness. A good starting point is Lizabeth Cohen, *A Consumers' Republic: The Politics of Mass Consumption in Postwar America* (New York: Vintage Books, 2004). On Canada, see C. Tower, "Who Needs Ralph Nader?" *Maclean's* (April 1970), 1, 3; W. Neilson, "Protecting the Consumer," *Canadian Forum*, June 1968, 57–9; "Canada's Ralph Naders Keep a Much Lower Profile," *Financial Post*, 24 February 1973, 13.

29 Cross, *The Cute and the Cool*, 190–2.

30 On general worries about children and commercialism in Canada, see Braden Hutchinson, "Objects of Affection: Producing and Consuming Toys and Childhood in Canada, 1840–1989" (PhD thesis, Queen's University,

2013); D. Marshall, "Modest Proposal: Ban Commercials from the CBC," *Saturday Night*, March 1973, 28–31; "CBC to End Advertising on Programs for Kids under 12," *Marketing*, 23/30 December 1974, 19; "CBC Will Drop Ads in Fall Kids' TV," *Marketing*, 20 January 1975, 1

31 *TS*, 11 November 1980, A9.
32 *TS*, 7 November 1981, A3.
33 *GM*, 7 November 1981, 4; TEF, F229-207, F.S. Eaton's Parade and Personal Files, letter to Fred Eaton, 13 November 1978.
34 Fredrik Eaton, cited in *Financial Post*, 21 August 1982.
35 *Toronto Sun* (hereafter *Sun*), 11 August 1982, 51.
36 *GM*, 11 August 1982, 2; *TS*, 11 August 1982, A3.
37 Aviva Layton, letter to editor, *TS*, 14 August 1982, B3.
38 "Eaton's Axes the Santa Claus Parade," *The National*, originally aired 9 August 1982, accessed on CBC Digital Archives.
39 Letter to editor, *TS*, 17 August 1982, A13.
40 TEF, F229-207, F.S. Eaton's Parade and Personal Files, file: Christmas Parade, Cancellation, letter to Fredrik Eaton.
41 TEF, F229-207, F.S. Eaton's Parade and Personal Files, file: Christmas Parade, Cancellation, letters to Fredrik Eaton.
42 Joan, Bill, Jacqueline and Kimberly McKeig, letter to editor, *Sun*, 13 August 1982, 10.
43 *TS*, 11 August 1982, A1.
44 *TS*, 11 August 1982, A1.
45 TEF, F229-207, F.S. Eaton's Parade and Personal Files, file: Christmas Parade, Cancellation, letter to Fredrik Eaton.
46 Pamela Smith, letter to editor, *TS*, 14 August 1982, B3.
47 *Sun*, 15 August 1982, 11.
48 Mrs M. Aitken, Toronto, letter to editor, *TS*, 17 August 1982, A13.
49 TEF, F229-207, F.S. Eaton's Parade and Personal Files, file: Christmas Parade, Cancellation, letters to Fredrik Eaton.
50 The literature on historical memory is now vast. A good introduction can be found in Anne Whitehead, *Memory* (New York: Routledge, 2009), chap. 4.
51 Margaret Delemere, letter to editor, *Sun*, 17 August 1982, 10.
52 *GM*, letter to editor, 14 August 1982, 7.
53 *TS*, 14 August 1982, A3.
54 GM, 17 August 1982, 5; *TS*, 17 August 1982, A7.
55 *TS*, 15 November 1982, A6.
56 *TS*, 20 August 1982, A6.
57 *GM*, 17 August 1982, 1.
58 *TS*, 15 November 1982, A6.
59 *TS*, 18 August 1982, A4.

60 *TS*, 20 August 1982, A6.

61 *GM*, 17 August 1982, 2.

62 *GM*, 15 November 1997, C30.

63 Both telecasts are available on the Santa Claus Parade Inc. YouTube channel.

64 *HS*, 19 November 1982, in HPL Local History and Archives, Santa Claus Parade Scrapbook, Volume 1, 1947–93.

65 *WFP*, 6 May 1967, 59, 17 May 1967, 21.

66 *WFP*, 16 November 1972, 1; *WFP*, 3 November 1967, 11.

67 *WFP*, 20 November 1972, 3.

68 *WFP*, 3 November 1981, 3; *WFP*, 1 December 1982, 47.

69 George Ritzer, *The McDonaldization of Society* (Thousand Oaks, CA: Pine Forge Press, 1993); Steve Penfold, "Selling by the Carload: The Early Years of Fast Food in Canada," in Magda Fahrni and Robert Rutherdale, eds, *Creating Postwar Canada, 1945–75* (Vancouver: University of British Columbia Press, 2008).

Conclusion: Enchanted Capitalism

1 *Vancouver Sun*, 29 May 1999, A22, letter to the editor.

2 *La Presse*, 24 November 1930, 17.

3 On enchantment as an aspect of modernity, see Michael Saler, "Modernity and Enchantment: A Historiographic Review," *American Historical Review* (June 2006): 692–716; Saler, ed., *Re-Enchantment of the World: Secular Magic in a Rational Age* (Stanford, CA: Stanford University Press, 2009); Susan Buck-Morss, *The Dialectics of Seeing: Walter Benjamin and the Arcades Project* (Boston: MIT Press, 1991); Colin Campbell, *The Romantic Ethic and the Spirit of Modern Consumerism* (New York: Blackwell, 1987); Walter Benjamin, *The Arcades Project*, trans. Howard Eiland and Kevin McLaughlin (Cambridge, MA: Belknap Press, 1999)

4 *WFP*, 24 February 1967, 3.

5 *Sun*, 12 August 1982, 4.

6 *GM*, 4 November 1978, 33.

7 "Prior to the advent of these technologies (e.g., sound recording and motion pictures)," writes Philip Auslander, "there was no need for a category of 'live' performance, for that category has meaning only in relation to an opposing possibility." See his "Digital Liveness: A Historical Philosophical Perspective," *PAJ: A Journal of Performance and Art* 34, no. 3 (September 2012): 3–11 (quotation on page 3), and his *Liveness: Performance in a Mediatized Culture*, 2nd ed. (New York: Routledge, 2008). I thank the audience for my talk at the University of Manitoba in the fall of 2011 for pressing me on this question. I am sure the conversation at that event came much closer to answering the question than I have here.

Bibliography

Archival Collections

T. Eaton Company Collection, Archives of Ontario

Series F229-81, Eaton's Santa Claus Parade Files, 1961–75
Series F229-82, Eaton's Merchandise Display Office Christmas and miscellaneous records
Series F229-90, Eaton's Merchandise Display Office Christmas and miscellaneous records
Series F229-141, Eaton's employee magazines
Series F229-146, D.H. Morrison's Public Relations Office files
Series F229-151, J.A. Brockie's Files
Series F229-162, Eaton's Archives Office subject files
Series F229-193, T. Eaton Company of Winnipeg correspondence files
Series F229-207, F.S. Eaton's parade and personal files
Series F229-221, Eaton's Archives Office people files
Series F229-237, Minutes of the Directors of the T. Eaton Company Limited
Series F229-271, Records of Eaton's Executive Office
Series F 229–304, Eaton's Toronto Queen Street store merchandise display photographs
Series F229-308, Eaton's Archives Photographic and Documentary Art Subject Files
Series F229-400, Moving image records of the Santa Claus Parade
Series F229-401, Sound and moving images documenting Eaton's history

City of Vancouver Archives

Fonds AM605 – Vancouver Junior Chamber of Commerce (Jaycees) fonds

Toronto Reference Library

City of Toronto Council Minutes
Metropolitan Toronto Council Minutes

Newspapers and Periodicals

Anson Record
Buckingham (Quebec) *Post*
Le Bulletin de Buckingham
Canadian Business
Calgary Herald
Canadian Champion (Milton, ON)
Chicago Daily Defender
Clinton Country Times
Le Devoir
Display in Canada
Display World
Edmonton Journal
Eugene Register-Guard
L'Écho du St Maurice
Financial Post
La Gazette de Valleyfield
Gettysburg Times
Globe and Mail
Gossip
Halifax Chronicle-Herald
Hamilton Spectator
Kitchener-Waterloo Record
Lawrence (Kansas) *Daily Journal*
Lewiston (Idaho) *Morning Tribune*
London Free Press
Ludington Daily News
Manitoba Leader (Portage la Prairie)
Milwaukee Journal
Milwaukee Sentinal
Montreal Gazette
Newmarket Era and Express
New Liberty

New York Times
Northern Circuit
L'Oeil Régional
Omaha Daily Bee
Ottawa Citizen
Owosso Argus-Press
Palm Beach Post
Picton Gazette
Pittsburgh Press
Plattsburgh Press-Republican
La Presse (Montreal)
Prince George (BC) *Citizen*
Le Progrès du Golfe
Reading (Pennsylvania) *Eagle*
Regina Leader Post
St Joseph (Missouri) *Gazette*
San Jose News
Sandusky (Ohio) *Star Journal*
St Petersburg Times
Spokane Daily Chronicle
Sudbury Star
Toledo News-Bee
Toronto Star
Toronto Telegram
Toronto Sun
Vancouver Sun
Windsor Star
Washington (PA) *Observer*
Wilmington (NC) *Star-News*
Winnipeg Free Press
Winnipeg Tribune
Youngstown Daily Vindicator

Selected Secondary Sources

Anderson, Kay. *Vancouver's Chinatown: Racial Discourse in Canada, 1875–1980*. Montreal and Kingston: McGill-Queen's University Press, 1995.

Alan Artibise. *Winnipeg: An Illustrated History*. Toronto: Lorimer, 1977.

Ausladner, Philip. "Digital Liveness: A Historical Philosophical Perspective." *PAJ: A Journal of Performance and Art* 34, no. 3 (September 2012): 3–11.

Ausladner, Philip. *Liveness: Performance in a Mediatized Culture*. 2nd ed. NewYork: Routledge, 2008.

Bachand, Denis, and Pierre Bélanger. "Un champ culturel: la télévision canadienne." In Caroline Andrew, ed., *Dislocation et permanence: L'invention du Canada au quotidien*, 317–46. Ottawa: University of Ottawa Press, 1999.

Baldwin, Peter. *Domesticating the Street: The Reform of Public Space in Hartford, 1850–1930*. Columbus: Ohio State University Press, 1999.

Baker, James. *Thanksgiving: The Biography of an America Holiday*. Durham: University of New Hampshire Press, 2009.

Barbour, Dale. *Winnipeg Beach: Leisure and Courtship in a Resort Town, 1900–1967*. University of Manitoba Press, 2001.

Baughman, James. *The Republic of Mass Culture: Journalism, Filmmaking, and Broadcasting in America since 1941*. Baltimore: Johns Hopkins University Press, 2006.

Beasley, Diane, "Walter Dean and Sunnyside: A Study of Waterfront Recreation in Toronto, 1880-1930." MA thesis, University of Toronto, 1995.

Behiels, Michael. *Canada's Francophone Minority Communities: Constitutional Renewal and the Winning of School Governance*. Montreal and Kingston: McGill-Queen's University Press, 2004.

Beauchemin, Jean-Francois. *Ici Radio-Canada: 50 ans de télévision française*. Montreal: Messageries ADP, 2002.

Belisle, Donica. "Exploring Postwar Consumption: The Campaign to Unionize Eatons in Toronto, 1948–1952." *Canadian Historical Review* 86, no. 4 (December 2005): 641–72.

– *Retail Nation: Department Stores and the Making of Modern Canada*. Vancouver: University of British Columbia Press, 2011.

Bella, Leslie. *The Christmas Imperative: Leisure, Family, and Women's Work*. Halifax: Fernwood, 1992.

Benjamin, Walter. *The Arcades Project*. Translated by Howard Eiland and Kevin McLaughlin. Cambridge, MA: Belknap, 1999.

Benson, Susan Porter. *Counter Cultures: Saleswomen, Managers, and Customers in American Department Stores, 1890–1940*. Urbana: University of Illinois Press, 1986.

Bienvenue, Louise. *Quand la jeunesse entre en scène: L'Action catholique avant la Révolution tranquille*. Montreal: Boréal, 2003.

Blanchard, Jim. *Winnipeg, 1912*. Winnipeg: University of Manitoba Press, 2006.

Bradbury, Bettina. *Working Families: Age, Gender, and Daily Survival in Industrializing Montreal*. Toronto: University of Toronto Press, 1993.

Buck-Morss, Susan. *The Dialectics of Seeing: Walter Benjamin and the Arcades Project*. Cambridge, MA: MIT Press, 1991.

Burben, Mary, and Flora McPherson. *Christmas in Canada*. Toronto: Dent, 1959.

Butsch, Richard. *The Making of American Audiences: From Stage to Television, 1750–1900*. New York: Cambridge University Press, 2000.

Calhoun, Craig, ed. *Habermas and the Public Sphere*. Cambridge, MA: MIT Press, 1992.

Campbell, Colin. *The Romantic Ethic and the Spirit of Modern Consumerism*. New York: Oxford University Press, 1987.

Careless, J.M.S. *Toronto to 1918: An Illustrated History*. Toronto: Lorimer, 1984.

Chandler, Alfred. *The Visible Hand: The Managerial Revolution in American Business*. Cambridge: Belknap Press, 1977.

Charles, Jeffrey. *Service Clubs in American Society: Rotary, Kiwanis, and Lions*. Urbana: University of Illinois Press, 1993.

Clark, John W. *A Legacy of Leadership: The U.S. Junior Chamber of Commerce Celebrates 75 Years*. Tulsa: U.S. Junior Chamber of Commerce, 1995.

Coates, Ken, and Fred McGuiness. *Only in Canada: Kinsmen and Kinettes*. Winnipeg: Peguis Publishers, 1987.

Couldry, Nick. *Media Rituals: A Critical Approach*. New York: Routledge, 2003.

Comeau, Michelle. "Les grands magasins de la rue Sainte-Catherine à Montréal: Des lieux de modernisation, d'homogénéisation et de différenciation des modes de consummation." *Material History Review* 41 (Spring 1995): 58–68.

Cross, Gary. *Kids' Stuff: Toys and the Changing World of American Childhood*. Cambridge, MA: Harvard University Press, 1999.

– *The Cute and The Cool: Wondrous Innocence and Modern American Children's Culture*. New York: Oxford University Press, 2004.

– "Crowds and Leisure: Thinking Comparatively across the 20th Century." *Journal of Social History* 39, no. 3 (Spring 2006): 631–50.

Cross, Gary, and John Walton. *The Playful Crowd: Pleasure Places in the Twentieth Century*. New York: Columbia University Press, 2005.

Cupido, Robert, "Appropriating the Past: Pageants, Politics, and the Diamond Jubilee of Confederation." *Journal of the Canadian Historical Association* 9 (1998): 155–86.

- "Public Commemoration and Ethnocultural Assertion: Winnipeg Celebrates the Diamond Jubilee of Confederation." *Urban History Review* 38, no. 2 (Spring 2010): 64–74.

Davies, Stephen, "'Reckless Walking Must Be Discouraged': The Automobile Revolution and the Shaping of Modern Urban Canada to 1930." *Urban History Review* 18 (October 1989): 123–38.

Davis, Janet. *The Circus Age: Culture and Society under the American Big Top.* Chapel Hill: University of North Carolina Press, 2002.

Davis, Susan. *Parades and Power: Street Theater in Nineteenth Century Philadelphia.* Philadelphia: Temple University Press, 1985.

Dayan, Daniel, and Elihu Katzis. *Media Events: The Live Broadcasting of History.* Cambridge, MA: Harvard University Press, 1992.

Deloria, Philip. *Playing Indian.* New Haven, CT: Yale University Press, 1999.

Dennis, Thelma. "Eaton's Catalogue: Furnishings for Rural Alberta, 1886–1930." *Alberta History* 37, no. 2 (1989): 21–31.

de Seve, Andreé Anne. "Hourra! Le catalogue Eaton est arrive." *Cap-aux-Diamants* 40 (hiver 1995): 18–21.

Ditchett, Samuel. *Eaton's of Canada: A Unique Institution of Extraordinary Magnitude.* New York: Dry Goods Economist, 1923.

Doucet, Michael. *The Department Store Shuffle: Rationalization and Change in the Greater Toronto Area* (Toronto: Centre for the Study of Commercial Activity, Ryerson University, 2001).

Edwardson, Ryan. *Canadian Content: Culture and the Quest for Nationhood.* Toronto: University of Toronto Press, 2008.

Elkin, Frederick. "Advertising in French Canada: Innovations and Deviations in the Context of a Changing Society." In G.K. Zollschan and W. Hirsch, eds, *Explorations in Social Change*, 522–46. Boston: Houghton Mifflin, 1963.

Elvins, Sarah. *Sales and Celebrations: Retailing and Regional Identity in Western New York State, 1920–40.* Athens: Ohio University Press, 2004.

Ernst, Christopher. "The Transgressive Stage: The Culture of Public Entertainment in Late Victorian Toronto." PhD thesis, University of Toronto, 2011.

Fahrni, Magda. *Household Politics: Montreal Families and Postwar Reconstruction.* Toronto: University of Toronto Press, 2005.

Field, Russell. "A Night at the Garden(s): A History of Professional Hockey Spectatorship in the 1920s and 1930s." PhD thesis, University of Toronto, 2008.

Fogelson, Robert. *Downtown: Its Rise and Fall, 1880–1950.* New Haven, CT: Yale University Press, 2001.

Filey, Mike. *I Remember Sunnyside: The Rise and Fall of a Magical Era.* Toronto: Dundurn Press, 1996.

Flaherty, David, and Frank Manning, eds. *The Beaver Bites Back? American Popular Culture in Canada.* Montreal and Kingston: McGill-Queen's University Press, 1993.

Friesen, Gerald. *Citizens and Nation: An Essay on History, Communication, and Canada.* Toronto: University of Toronto Press, 2000.

Garland, David. *Auto Opium: A Social History of American Automobile Design.* New York: Routledge, 1994.

Gérin, Annie. "Les espaces multiples de la fête: La Saint-Jean-Baptise 1968 à Montréal." *British Journal of Canadian Studies* 27, no. 1 (2014): 1–20.

Goheen, Peter. "Symbols in the Streets: Parades in Victorian Urban Canada." *Urban History Review* 18, no. 3 (February 1990): 237–43.

– "The Ritual of the Street in Mid-Nineteenth-Century Toronto." *Environment and Planning D: Society and Space* 2 (1993): 127–45.

– "Negotiating Access to Public Space in Mid-Nineteenth Century Toronto." *Journal of Historical Geography* 20, no. 4 (1994): 430–49.

– "The Assertion of Middle-Class Claims to Public Space in Late Victorian Toronto." *Journal of Historical Geography* 29 (2003): 73–92.

Gourluck, Russ. *A Store Like No Other: Eaton's of Winnipeg.* Winnipeg: Great Plains Publications, 2004.

Gripo, Robert, and Christopher Huskins. *Macy's Thanksgiving Day Parade.* Chicago: Arcadia Publishing, 2004.

Gruneau, Richard, and David Whitson. *Hockey Night in Canada: Sport, Identities and Cultural Politics.* Toronto: Garamond Press, 1994.

Harker, Douglas. *The Woodward's: The Story of a Distinguished British Columbia Family, 1850–1975.* Vancouver: Mitchell Press, 1975.

Harris, Paul. *This Rotarian Age.* Chicago: Rotary International, 1935.

Heron, Craig. *Lunch-Bucket Lives: Remaking the Workers' City.* Toronto: Between the Lines, 2015.

Heron, Craig, and Steve Penfold. *The Workers' Festival: A History of Labour Day in Canada.* Toronto: University of Toronto Press, 2005.

Hovarth, Ronald. "Machine Space." *Geographical Review* 64, no. 2 (April 1974): 167–73.

Huggins, Mike. "Projecting the Visual: British Newsreels, Soccer, and Popular Culture, 1918–1939." *International Journal of the History of Sport* 24, no. 1 (2007): 80–102.

Hutchinson, Braden. "Objects of Affection: Producing and Consuming Toys and Childhood in Canada, 1840–1989." PhD thesis, Queen's University, 2013.

Igartua, José. *The Other Quiet Revolution: National Identities in English Canada, 1945–1971*. Vancouver: UBC Press, 2006.

Immerso, Michael. *Coney Island: The People's Playground*. New Brunswick, NJ: Rutgers University Press, 2002.

Isenberg, Alison. *Downtown: A History of the Place and the People Who Made It*. Chicago: University of Chicago Press, 2004.

Jacobson, Lisa. *Raising Consumers: Children and the American Mass Market in the Early Twentieth Century*. New York: Columbia University Press, 2004.

Jakle, John, and Keith Sculle. *Lots of Parking: Land Use in a Car Culture*. Charlottesville: University of Virginia Press, 2004.

Jay, Martin, et al. "AHR Forum: The Senses in History." *American Historical Review* 116 (April 2011): 307–400.

Kalamas, Maria, and Robert Tamilia. "Eaton's Fall from Grace: Tracing the Rise and Ultimate Demise of a Venerable Canadian Retailer, 1869–1999" *CHARM Proceedings*. 2003.

Kasson, John. *Amusing the Million: Coney Island at the Turn of the Century*. New York: Hill and Wang, 1978.

Kelm, Mary Ellen. *A Wilder West: Rodeo in Western Canada*. Vancouver: UBC Press, 2011.

Kerr, Donald, and Jacob Spelt. *The Changing Face of Toronto: A Study in Urban Geography*. Ottawa: Queen's Printer, 1966.

Landy, Joshua, and Michael Saler, eds. *Re-Enchantment of the World: Secular Magic in a Rational Age*. Stanford, CA: Stanford University Press, 2009.

Leach, William, "Transformations in a Culture of Consumption: Women and Department Stores, 1890–1925." *Journal of American History* 71, no. 2 (September 1984): 319–42.

– *Land of Desire: Merchants, Power and the Rise of a New American Culture*. New York: Vintage Books, 1993.

Lears, T. Jackson. *Fables of Abundance: A Cultural History of Advertising in America*. New York: Basic Books, 1994.

Lembo, Ron. *Thinking through Television*. New York: Cambridge University Press, 2000.

Lemon, James. *Toronto since 1918: An Illustrated History*. Toronto: Lorimer, 1985.

Linteau, Paul-André. *Histoire de Montreal depuis la Confédération*. Montreal: Boréal, 1992.

Linteau, Paul-André. *Sainte-Catherine Street: At the Heart of Montréal Life*. Montreal: Montreal Museum of Archaeology and History, 2010.

Loo, Tina, and Carolyn Strange. "The Travelling Show Menace: Contested Regulation in Turn of the Century Ontario." *Law and Society Review* 29, no. 4 (1995): 639–68.

Lott, Eric. *Love and Theft*. New York: Oxford University Press, 1993.

Luneau, Aurélie. "Radio-Canada et la promotion de la culture francophone, 1936–1997." *Vingtième Siècle* 55 (July-September 1997): 112–23.

Marling, Karal Ann. *Merry Christmas! Celebrating America's Greatest Holiday*. Cambridge, MA: Harvard University Press, 2000.

Marriott, Stephanie. *Live Television: Time, Space, and the Broadcast Event*. Thousand Oaks, CA: Sage, 2007.

Martin, Paul. *We Serve: A History of the Lions Clubs*. Washington, DC: Regnery Gateway, 1991.

Matthews, Mary Catherine. "Working for Family, Nation and God: Paternalism and the Dupuis Frères Department Store, 1926–52." MA thesis, McGill University, 1997.

McNamara, Brooks. *Day of Jubilee: The Great Age of Public Celebrations in New York, 1788–1909*. New Brunswick, NJ: Rutgers University Press, 1997.

McShane, Clay. *Down the Asphalt Path: The Automobile and the American City*. New York: Columbia University Press, 1994.

Meyrowitz, Joshua. *No Sense of Place: The Impact of Electronic Media on Social Behavior*. New York: Oxford University Press, 1985.

Minor, Ronnie, and Laurie Anne Tamborino. *Detroit's Thanksgiving Day Parade*. Chicago: Arcadia Publishing, 2003.

Monod, David. *Store Wars: Shopkeepers and the Culture of Mass Marketing, 1890–1939*. Toronto: University of Toronto Press, 1996.

Monod, David. "Bay Days: The Managerial Revolutions and the Hudson Bay Company Department Stores, 1912–1939." *Historical Papers/Communications Historiques* 21, no. 1 (1986): 173–96.

Moore, Paul. "Movie Palaces on Canadian Downtown Main Streets: Montreal, Toronto, and Vancouver." *Urban History Review* 32, no. 2 (Spring 2004): 3–20.

– *Now Playing: Early Moviegoing and the Regulation of Fun*. Albany: SUNY Press, 2008.

Morin, Louis. "Establishing a Signification for Social Space: Demonstration, Cortege, Parade, Procession." In *On Representation*, 38–53. Stanford, CA: Stanford University Press, 1994.

Morley, David. *Television, Audiences, and Cultural Studies*. New York: Routledge, 1992.

Morley, David. "Broadcasting and the Construction of the National Family." In Robert C. Allen and Annette Hill, eds, *The Television Studies Reader*, 418–41. New York: Routledge, 2004.

Nelles, H.V. *The Art of Nation Building: Pageantry and Spectacle at Quebec's Tercentenary*. Toronto: University of Toronto Press, 1999.

Nissenbaum, Stephen. *The Battle for Christmas*. New York: Alfred A. Knopf, 1996.

Norton, Peter. *Fighting Traffic: The Dawn of the Motor Age in the American City*. Cambridge, MA: MIT Press, 2011.

Nystrom, Paul. *The Economics of Retailing*. New York: Ronald Press, 1919.

O'Donnell, Lorraine. "Visualizing the History of Women at Eaton's, 1869 to 1976." PhD dissertation, McGill University, 2002.

O'Donnell, Lorraine. "Le voyage virtuel: Les consommatrices, le monde de l'étranger et Eaton à Montréal, 1880–1980." *Revue d'histoire d'Amérique française* 58, no. 4 (printemps 2005): 535–68.

Palmer, Bryan. "Discordant Music: Charivari and Whitecapping in North America." *Labour/Le Travail* 1 (1978): 5–62.

Raibmon, Paige. *Authentic Indians: Episodes of Encounter from the Late-Nineteenth-Century Northwest Coast*. Durham, NC: Duke University Press, 2005.

Register, Woody. *The Kid of Coney Island: Fred Thompson and the Rise of American Amusements*. NewYork: Oxford University Press, 2001.

Restad, Penny. *Christmas in America*. New York: Oxford University Press, 1995.

Rollin, Lucy. *Cradle and All: A Cultural and Psychoanalytic Reading of Nursery Rhymes*. Jackson: University Press of Mississippi, 1992.

Rutherford, Paul. *When Television Was Young: Primetime Canada*. Toronto: University of Toronto Press, 1990.

Ryan, Mary. "The American Parade." In Lynn Hunt, ed., *The New Cultural History*, 131–53. Berkeley: University of California Press, 1989.

– *Women in Public: Between Banners and Ballots*. Baltimore: Johns Hopkins University Press, 1990.

– *Civic Wars: Democracy and Public Life in the American City during the Nineteenth Century*. Berkeley: University of California Press, 1997.

Saarinen, Oiva. *Between a Rock and a Hard Place: A Historical Geography of the Finns in the Sudbury Area*. Waterloo, ON: Wilfrid Laurier University Press, 1999.

Saler, Michael. "Modernity and Enchantment: A Historiographic Review." *American Historical Review* (June 2006): 692–716.

Sammond, Nicholas. *Babes in Tomorrowland: Walt Disney and the Making of the American Child*. Durham, NC: Duke University Press, 2005.

Santink, Joy. *Timothy Eaton and the Rise of his Department Store*. Toronto: University of Toronto Press, 1990.

Scannell, Paddy. "Broadcast Events." *Media, Culture and Society* 17, no. 1 (1995): 151–7

Schmidt, Leigh Eric. *Consumer Rites: The Buying and Selling of American Holidays*. Princeton, NJ: Princeton University Press, 1995.

Seiler, Robert, and Tamara Seiler. *Reel Time: Movie Exhibitors and Movie Audiences in Prairie Canada*. Edmonton: AU Press, 2013.

Smith, Anthony, with Richard Paterson, eds. *Television: An International History*. New York: Oxford University Press, 1998.

Smith, Mark, ed. *Hearing History: A Reader*. Athens: University of Georgia Press, 2004.

– "Producing Sense, Consuming Sense, Making Sense: Perils and Prospects for Sensory History." *Journal of Social History* 40, no. 4 (2007): 841–58.

Smith, Mark, et al. "The Senses in American History: A Round Table" *Journal of American History* 95, no. 2 (September 2008): 378–451.

Statistics Canada. *Department Stores in Canada, 1923–1976*. Ottawa: Queen's Printer, 1979.

Stelter, Gilbert, and Alan Artibise, eds. *The Canadian City: Essays in Urban and Social History*. Ottawa: Carleton University Press, 1984.

Strasser, Susan. *Satisfaction Guaranteed: The Making of the American Mass Market*. New York: Pantheon, 1989.

Taylor, Charles. *Modern Social Imaginaries*. Durham, NC: Duke University Press, 2004.

Tedlow, Richard. *New and Improved: The Story of Mass Marketing*. New York: Basic Books, 1990.

Thompson, Emily. *The Soundscape of Modernity: Architectural Acoustics and the Culture of Listening in America, 1900–33*. Cambridge, MA: MIT Press, 2002.

Tillotson, Shirley. *Contributing Citizens: Modern Charitable Fundraising and the Making of the Welfare State, 1920–66*. Vancouver: UBC Press, 2008.

Trudel, Robert. "Famille, foi et patrie: Le crédo de Dupuis Frères." *Cap-aux-Diamants: La revue d'histoire du Québec* 40 (1995): 26–9.

van Elteren, Mel. "Rethinking Americanization Abroad: Toward a Critical Alternative to Prevailing Paradigms." *Journal of American Culture* 29, no. 3 (September 2006): 345–67.

Vipond, Mary. *Mass Media in Canada*. Toronto: Lorimer, 1989.

Walden, Keith. "Speaking Modern: Language, Culture, and Hegemony in Grocery Window Displays, 1887–1920." *Canadian Historical Review* 70, no. 3 (1989): 285–310.

– *Becoming Modern in Toronto: The Industrial Exhibition and the Shaping of a Late Victorian Culture*. Toronto: University of Toronto Press, 1997.

Walz, Gene. *Cartoon Charlie: The Life and Art of Animation Pioneer Charles Thorson*. Winnipeg: Great Plains Publications, 1998.

Warren, Jean-Phillipe. *Hourra pour Santa Claus! La commercialisation de la saison des fêtes au Québec, 1885–1915*. Montreal: Boréal, 2006.

Wittenberg, David. "Going Out in Public: Visibility and Anonymity in Michael Warner's 'Publics and Counterpublics.'" *Quarterly Journal of Speech* 88, no. 4 (November 2002): 426–33.

Wright, Cynthia. "Rewriting the Modern: Reflections on Race, Nation, and the Death of a Department Store." *Histoire Sociale – Social History* 35 (May 2000): 153–68.

Zipes, Jack. *When Dreams Came True: Classical Fairy Tales and Their Tradition.* New York: Routledge, 1989.

– *Fairy Tales and the Art of Subversion.* New York: Routledge, 2006.

Index

www.ingramcontent.com/pod-product-compliance
Ingram Content Group UK Ltd.
Pitfield, Milton Keynes, MK11 3LW, UK
UKHW032121310125
454513UK00004B/169